Counselling Children with Psychological Problems

Counselling Children with Psychological Problems

Malavika Kapur

Associate Acquisitions Editor: Qudsiya Ahmed
Assistant Development Editor: Jaydeep Paul
Production Editor: Vamanan Namboodiri

The copyright for the Appendix entitled, Developmental Psychopathology Check List (DPCL) vests in the author.

Copyright © 2011 Dorling Kindersley (India) Pvt. Ltd.

This book is sold subject to the condition that it shall not, by way of trade or otherwise, be lent, resold, hired out, or otherwise circulated without the publisher's prior written consent in any form of binding or cover other than that in which it is published and without a similar condition including this condition being imposed on the subsequent purchaser and without limiting the rights under copyright reserved above, no part of this publication may be reproduced, stored in or introduced into a retrieval system, or transmitted in any form or by any means (electronic, mechanical, photocopying, recording or otherwise), without the prior written permission of both the copyright owner and the above-mentioned publisher of this book.

Although the author and publisher have made every effort to ensure that the information in this book was correct at the time of editing and printing, the author and publisher do not assume and hereby disclaim any liability to any party for any loss or damage arising out of the use of this book caused by errors or omissions, whether such errors or omissions result from negligence, accident or any other cause. Further, names, pictures, images, characters, businesses, places, events and incidents are either the products of the author's imagination or used in a fictitious manner. Any resemblance to actual persons, living or dead or actual events is purely coincidental and do not intend to hurt sentiments of any individual, community, sect or religion.

In case of binding mistake, misprints or missing pages etc., the publisher's entire liability and your exclusive remedy is replacement of this book within reasonable time of purchase by similar edition/ reprint of the book.

ISBN 978-81-317-3044-7

First Impression, 2011
Ninth Impression, 2024
Current Impression, 2026

This edition is manufactured in India and is authorized for sale only in India, Bangladesh, Bhutan, Pakistan, Nepal, Sri Lanka and the Maldives. Circulation of this edition outside of these territories is UNAUTHORIZED.

Published by Pearson India Education Services Pvt. Ltd, CIN: U72200TN2005PTC057128.

Head Office: 1st Floor, Berger Tower, Plot No. C-001A/2, Sector 16B, Noida - 201 301, Uttar Pradesh, India.

Registered Office: 6th Floor, Tower A, Unit A and B, International Tech Park, CapitaLand Chennai, 200 Feet Radial Road,Zamin Pallavaram, Old Pallavaram Chennai – 600117, Tamil Nadu, India

Website: in.pearson.com; Email: companysecretary.india@pearson.com

Digitally printed in India by Trinity Academy for Corporate Training Ltd, New Delhi in the year of 2026.

About the Author

Malavika Kapur is Visiting Professor, School of Humanities, National Institute of Advanced Studies (NIAS), Bangalore. She retired as the Head of the Department of Clinical Psychology at the National Institute of Mental Health and Neurosciences (NIMHANS) and has been an honorary professor for NIAS from 2003 to 2010. Besides being a fellow of the British Psychological Society and the Indian Association of Clinical Psychologists, Professor Kapur is also an honorary fellow and recipient of the Lifetime Achievement Award of the Indian Association of Child and Adolescent Mental Health and the National Academy of Psychology. She is also a consultant for organizations like WHO, UGC, ICSSR and has been twice awarded Scholar in Residency at the Rockefeller Foundation Study and Conference Center at Bellagio in Italy. Her research interests include developmental psychology, community mental health programmes for children and adolescents in urban and rural schools, primary health care and Anganawadi workers under the Integrated Child Development Services of the Government of India, and development of assessment tools and intervention packages for children and adolescents in the Indian context. Her main contribution is her work in developing integrated models of mental health service delivery for children and adolescents. Her work is deeply embedded in the Indian cultural context, as revealed in her study of child care in ancient India based on Ayurveda. She has authored four volumes dealing with the subject of Indian children, has edited and contributed to a number of books in collaboration with other scholars, and has over 100 academic publications. Professor Kapur has also published two books of children's fiction, *Adventures at Kudremukh* (Bangalore: Hitha Publications, 2003), and *Doogoo the Baby Elephant and Other Stories* (Bangalore: Unisun, 2005). One of her most recent volumes, *Learning from Children What to Teach Them*, was published in 2007. In a similar vein, this volume also focuses on children, delving further into their psychology with characteristic sympathy and care.

Contents

Preface

This book is an ambitious yet necessary effort. It is a product of the experience and thought that has gone into training professional mental health workers, teachers, lay volunteers and postgraduates in clinical psychology at the National Institute of Mental Health and Neuro Sciences in Bangalore, India, since 1976.

In most of Africa and South Asia, children are a neglected population with regard to education and health, including mental health. While teachers focus on education and paediatricians and physicians deal with physical problems, the child as a whole is neglected. In a typical Indian scenario, graduates with or without a degree in psychology start counselling children after attending workshops of a few hours to a few days. This happens especially because none of the developing countries have a statutory body to regulate the practice of counselling. In addition, these practitioners often have no access to libraries, books and even the Internet. To enable counsellors to have easy access to knowledge and information related to the methodological and practical aspects of their work, I have tried to create a single sourcebook for counsellors who work with children.

To state simply, this book provides the rudiments of the nature, assessment, causes and treatments for psychological problems in children. The idea that all these aspects, necessary for counselling, can be assessed in a similar way led to the development of a tool called the Developmental Psychopathology Check List (DPCL). In the past six years, this tool has been used for noting down the basic history of children at a child guidance centre in Bengaluru, where my colleagues, Akila and Geetha, and I have supervised the work. The DPCL requires some training but not a great deal.

Counselling children is a joyful experience. But it requires some training, some supervision and a great deal of practical experience, leading to self-learning. In this book I hope to provide the background material for counsellors to work with children. But it is good to have some expert supervision, or in the absence of it some peer consultation, so that one gets some feedback when someone goes wrong. Keeping detailed case notes and reviewing them as the counselling progresses is one of the best methods of self-learning.

The book covers four themes. Part I introduces the themes of classification of developmental psychology, psychopathology, assessment and therapies. Part II deals with commonly seen psychological disorders such as developmental problems, conduct, emotion and learning disorders. Psychosomatic disorders and psychoses are also dealt with, albeit briefly. Part III discusses methods of counselling using art, psychodynamic, behavioural and supportive approaches and deals with working in different settings such as families, groups and schools. Part IV combines the disorders and techniques to produce the best fit and provides case illustrations. The book includes summaries and self-evaluations in all the parts. It also contains a brief manual of the Developmental Psychopathology Check List (DPCL) for the use of the reader.

I hope that this sourcebook will reach all groups of adults who professionally deal with children in developing countries, including psychologists, counsellors, teachers, NGOs and others who work with children. The paucity of Asian literature in this context is a shortfall and I welcome contributions that can be incorporated in future revisions of this book.

ACKNOWLEDGEMENTS

I thank children in clinics, schools and orphanages from urban and rural areas and tribal belts for enriching my life by teaching me what I know. My students, colleagues and schoolteachers have also contributed to my education, and I am grateful to them. I especially thank the volunteers at the Child Guidance Centre of Prasanna Counselling Centre for giving me the courage to write this book based on our experience of running a free counselling centre for children.

I owe my husband Ravi Kapur, who is no more, for being a driving force in my work in community settings, in schools, primary care settings and the social welfare sectors. My children Svapna and Sharad and their spouses Samir and Stella have always been supportive and loving, and my grandchildren Nishant, Rahul, Elina and Keira have been the greatest joy in my life—I owe a lot to all of them. I wish to thank Girija for her enormous help while writing the book and Rama Krishna for his timely inputs. My special thanks to Poornima Bhola , Akila Keshav and Shalini Shetty for their careful proofing of the manuscript. I thank Praveen Dev, formerly of Pearson Education, for the help rendered initially, and Amarjyoti Dutta, Debbie Dhar and Jaydeep Paul for their excellent and coordinated effort in providing me with highly interactive editing for which I am truly grateful.

Malavika Kapur

PART

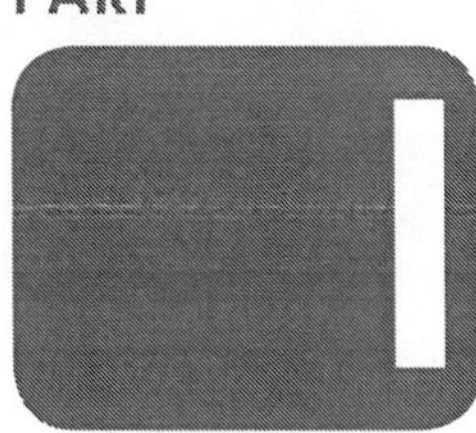

General Background

CHAPTER

Introduction

Most Western textbooks deal with children in a compartmentalized manner. The textbooks concentrate exclusively on child development, abnormal child psychology, psychological assessment of children and psychological counselling or therapies, with children as independent and unrelated subjects. Superspecializations also exist within these areas. For example, within child development there can be specializations such as cognitive, emotion, social, language, moral or sexual development. In the area of normal child psychology, there may be books on attention deficit hyperkinetic disorders, emotion or conduct disorders. This is not to say that there should be no such specializations, as it is in the very nature of scientific study to pursue such inquiries. However, in the present book the author takes a different route in view of Asian realities in the delivery of psychological services to children. Childhood psychological problems receive scant attention in developing nations and psychological services are hard to come by. Training of personnel and infrastructural demands are mostly unmet. If a teacher or someone with a basic degree in psychology wants to help children, it is almost impossible to access a trainer or books.

This book has been written keeping this reality in mind. It is the author's ambitious plan to combine normal and abnormal development, psychological assessment, counselling, and therapies and present these as a single sourcebook. This courage of conviction to go against the tide of academic textbook trends stems from 30 years' experience in training teachers, lay volunteers and postgraduates in clinical psychology and from the psychological management of children in India.

International classificatory systems come under fire and also fall woefully short of fulfilling needs in the Asian context, being essentially Eurocentric in their approach. These systems classify disorders based on the phenomenology in a cross-sectional manner. They pay scant attention to the overlap in symptoms and focus essentially on clearly defined syndromes that do not always reflect the ground reality of clinical conditions. They also fail to incorporate the most important aspect—the developmental perspective—except in a notional manner. Normal child development occurs in phases across age, gender and psychological and social contexts. The main domains are: physical, cognitive, language, emotional, social, moral and sexual development. Developmental psychology adopts a longitudinal, life-span or life-cycle approach from the time of conception to death.

Contexts assume greater importance, as socio-cultural aspects in the Asian and African countries magnify the differences between developed and developing nations. It is crucial for counsellors in developing countries to understand the influence of one's own culture in normal and pathological child development and alleviate distress through culturally appropriate methods.

A study of normal development across infancy, childhood and adolescence is crucial to the understanding of abnormal behaviour in childhood. Abnormality is not independent of normal development. The interruption of normal processes by internal or external forces, psychological or otherwise, can lead to the manifestation of behavioural abnormalities. Understanding the causes enables us to plan appropriate strategies for treatment. Thus, the developmental diagnosis leads to an aetiological diagnosis. This, in turn, facilitates the planning of effective therapeutic strategies.

Development occurs across age and gender in the biological, psychological and social realms, which interact in a dynamic manner. Family, society and culture influence child-rearing practices, maturation and learning, and contribute at critical stages to the complex process of development. The development of an infant is not independent of the family and culture in the Asian context. In the West, the various theories of child development are viewed separately as applicable to different domains. There is a need to view them in a holistic manner to offer a better understanding of normal as well as abnormal child development.

This book deals with abnormal child development as presented in the various disorders of childhood, namely, pervasive developmental disorders, internalizing and externalizing disorders, learning disorders, and somatization disorders along with some serious childhood disorders such as psychoses.

Children with psychological problems and those at risk require psychological help. In the Asian context, services offering psychological therapies are almost non-existent except for a few well-established centres. There are large numbers of people—teachers, psychologists, counsellors—and NGOs who work with children. These workers stand to benefit greatly with knowledge of some basic skills in the identification and management of psychological problems amongst the children with whom they work. Learning some child-friendly therapeutic techniques and ways of dealing with the families would go a long way to alleviate the distress of these children and their families. The crucial steps in this regard are: identification, referral when required, and management of childhood disorders.

This book describes some basic techniques for dealing with children such as interviewing and assessment of a case, individual, group and family therapies, and among a host of other innovative approaches, specific techniques such as play, art, behaviour therapies, supportive techniques, remediation, and psycho-education. A holistic and eclectic approach will be adopted and therapies will be individually tailored to the needs of the children. Although most Western books on therapy describe these techniques, information on the linkages between therapeutic techniques and specific disorders is hard to come by. In the present book, the strategies most appropriate for specific disorders will be described and studies in the Indian context will be highlighted. The book also aims to sensitize readers to those conditions which require referral to the experts.

This book focuses on the need for therapy for children as embedded in the family context and on the requirement to treat the child and family as a single unit. In addition, a brief description of strategies to be used in community settings such as schools and other institutions will be covered. The main thrust is developmental, eclectic yet holistic.

In brief, Part I introduces common themes of psycho-social development, normal or otherwise, assessment of the child, and counselling techniques. Part II deals with some common psychological disorders of childhood such as specific developmental disorders and delays, learning disorders, externalizing and internalizing disorders, as well as disorders with physical symptoms of psychological origin, and chronic physical disorders and associated psychological problems. Some of the serious psychological problems of childhood are also described. Finally, the nature, causes and patterns of disorders in the Asian countries are discussed. Part III focuses on specific techniques of counselling such as play, artwork, and psycho-dynamic, behavioural and supportive approaches with an individual child. In addition, methods of working with families in groups and in the school setting have been described, keeping in mind their utmost relevance in the Asian context. Part IV attempts to match the disorders with suitable techniques, mostly through case descriptions.

Each part is supplemented by figures, a summary and self-evaluation.

CHAPTER

2 International Classifications of Psychiatric Disorders

A great deal of effort and international collaboration of experts has gone into the making of the international classificatory systems of medical as well as psychiatric disorders. However, despite the efforts of pioneering minds, there is an obvious Eurocentricity of approach in these systems, such as various versions/revisions of the International Classification of Diseases (ICD–10 and the upcoming and controversial ICD–11), and the *Diagnostic and Statistical Manual of Mental Disorders* (DSM–I to V) of the American Psychological Association. There has been scathing criticism of the classification of disorders in adults and this problem is further accentuated while dealing with childhood psychiatric disorders. This chapter focuses entirely on the issues pertaining to children.

The two most used international classificatory systems will be examined in brief. Both systems use codes for the various diagnostic categories. The ICD uses an alphabet code of F and number codes with the digits 1–9 for sub-categories. On the other hand, the DSM uses three digits with two-digit number codes for the sub-categories under it. In addition, the disorders are listed under number codes mentioned or arranged alphabetically for each disorder. However, as completely revised versions of the ICD and the DSM will be published in the next few years, a critique of the two systems is not considered necessary.

The creators of the two systems have sought to address criticism, especially from developing countries. Over the decades, it has been noted that only 10 per cent of the world's population can use the two systems because of their complexity.

A simple way of looking at psychological problems of children is as follows:

Disorders of learning, emotion, conduct (behaviour), hyperkinesis, and pervasive and developmental problems occur only in childhood. Children can also have adult forms of disorders such as psychoses or the old-fashioned term neuroses consisting of anxiety, phobia, obsessive compulsive disorder (OCD) or hysteria (conversion/dissociative disorders).

The formats of these systems raise some basic questions. Taxonomy based on common features that cluster together, along spectrums of disorders running parallel or crisscrossing each other, would make more sense than using alphabetical or numerical orders.

These classifications could be based on clinical experience of pioneers like Freud, who gave the best and aetiologically-based treatment anchored to a diagnosis of hysteria with primary gains and secondary gains in focus. There are also other classifications that are empirically and phenomenologically based, such as the classification of externalization and internalization (Achenbach and Edelbrock, 1983).

The diagnostic categories should permit the clinician to conceptualize disorders and lead to better understanding. Number codes and alphabetical order are of least relevance. It would be more relevant to categorize symptoms by clusters and proximity to other syndromes. Code numbers in consecutive order do not imply that the syndromes are similar. So why use them? While these codes can facilitate sound research practice, without empirical validation they can mislead research.

Several specific questions reflecting the general concerns of practising clinicians dealing with children may be posed:

i. Is psychiatric diagnosis a means to an end, that is treatment, or an end in itself? Despite claims to the contrary, psychiatric diagnosis tends to become the end in itself.

ii. Can psychiatric diagnosis focus *only* on psychopathology and *not* on aetiology, treatment, context and even prognosis? Lip service has been paid to multi-axial diagnosis—both under the ICD and DSM systems, with the best example being Rutter's multi-axial classification in 1975. While this remains useful, it overlooks important contributors such as temperament and culture-specific contexts.

   In contrast to the Western medical classifications, in Ayurveda—the ancient Indian medical system, context is in the foreground. For example, treatment is the pivot—while other factors are relevant only in the context of management or treatment.

   The Ayurvedic physician may diagnose the problems of children on the basis of the patient's *prakriti*—physical and psychological (constitution), *vyadhi* (disease) and the *desha* (site or place) before deciding upon treatment. Concepts of multiple causation, with internal and external factors being influenced by the bio-psycho-social contexts, are essential for the management of these disorders. Diagnosis, thus, is only a means to an end.

iii. Are developmental domains that emerge throughout childhood paid sufficient attention in the modern diagnostic system? Evidently not, as seen by the sketchiness of the syndrome description. Developmental context in the bio-psycho-social realms needs to be incorporated into the system of diagnosis in order to lead to effective treatments. Developmental psychology implicitly holds the view that the life trajectory in all the domains of development such as physical, cognitive, language, emotional, social, moral and sexual development is more important than the cross-sectional manifestation of symptoms.

iv. Do interactions between factors such as heredity and environment, maturation, learning, and motivation play similar roles in the development of normal as well as abnormal behaviours? The answer is, yes, they do.

v. Do the psycho-therapeutic approaches have blind spots depending on their theoretical stance? This may in turn lead to an emphasis on one or the other of the factors discussed earlier. The diagnostic classifications and treatments should, thus, be empirical, theoretical and holistic.

vi. Should the outcome (positive or negative) be considered and lead to a revision of the diagnosis, consequently leading to a better outcome?

Fallibility of diagnosis should be a rule rather than an exception in the clinician's conceptual realm. Diagnosis is meant to be *discarded*, *revised* and *accommodated*—not to be held as sacrosanct and infallible. For example, there is a case report where an autistic child recovers totally in the foster home with good maternal care. The diagnosis of autism has an aura of a prognostic doom. Labelling condemns the child to a certain kind of treatment, as the cause is not part of the diagnostic process. In childhood, many manifested symptoms are caused by significant stressors in the environment. Discovering the cause is the route to treatment and not the diagnosis.

vii. Do poor caretaking practices such as over-indulging, neglecting, and a punitive approach produce symptoms severe enough to fall under the conventional diagnostic syndromes? For example, a severely battered child who is fearful of all adults cannot rightly be labelled as emotionally disordered.

In short, the present international diagnostic classificatory systems have the following problems from the viewpoint of a practitioner:

i. Focus should be equally on phenomenology (and not on aetiology), developmental context and treatment.
ii. Focus should be on commonalities as well as on differences that enable us to examine culture-specific features. For example, hysteria or dissociative disorder—which is a very common syndrome in developing countries—is often relegated to a minor section as it is uncommon in the West.
iii. Overlapping of symptoms is more common than clear-cut diagnosis and is very common in clinical practice.
iv. There is a tendency to discard psycho-social contexts in favour of rigid yet dubious biological aetiology. Biological aetiology may effectively exclude possible interventions in terms of counselling, psychotherapy, family therapy, etc., resulting in drug management becoming the first choice.

There are definite lobbies and pressures from the pharmaceutical and insurance industries for the medicalization of diagnostic practice even in the treatment of childhood disorders. One classic example is the long-term use of stimulants for children with hyperkinesis. There should be clear distinctions among specific developmental problems as a function of delayed maturation, poor school systems or developmentally inappropriate school systems and other long-standing problems like pervasive developmental disorders.

In India, the study of child psychopathology from a developmental context should ideally take into account the specific Indian context for age and gender differences, developmental history and temperament along with psycho-social correlates such as family interaction, stressors and social supports. In clinical settings in India, there is a need to develop a screening tool to assess psychopathology in children; this must be brief, comprehensive, developmental in perspective and should be usable after relatively little training. Such a tool can also form the basis for developing strategies to treat a child. In addition, it should be designed to bridge clinical practice and research. One such assessment tool has been developed by Kapur, Barnabas, Reddy and Uma (1994).

DESCRIPTION OF THE DEVELOPMENTAL PSYCHOPATHOLOGY CHECKLIST (DPCL)

Developmental History (items 1–10)

This consists of pre-, peri- and postnatal problems, possible brain injury, sensorimotor handicaps and delays in motor, language, cognitive, emotional, and social development.

Developmental Problems (items 11–28)

This section elicits responses on developmental problems such as clumsiness, breath-holding spells, habits, speech and language problems, feeding, elimination, sleeping and sexual problems.

Psychopathology (items 29–78)

This section assesses externalizing problems of hyperactivity and conduct disturbance, scholastic problems and internalizing problems of emotion, somatic, neurotic kinds, and psychoses.

Psycho-social Factors (items 79–101)

In this section, the family history of illnesses, interactions within the family, child-rearing practices, child's relationships with parents and siblings and relationships in the school setting are explored.

Temperamental Profile (items 102–118)

This is a simple version with the three major categories of *satva*, *rajas* and *tamas*, and a special focus on the 'resilient' or 'competent' child. The dimensions measured are: manageability, trust, dependence, sleep, appetite, activity level, emotionality, sociability and aggression. The dimensions go beyond the Western conceptualization of temperament and comprise the ancient Indian model of *trigunas*.

Social Supports and Assets of the Child (items 119–124)

In this section, details regarding the presence of helpful people within and outside the family, friends, and special interests, talents and hobbies of the child are checked.

A cluster analysis of 221 child psychiatric cases using DPCL yielded seven clusters. These were emotional disorder, hyperkinesis, childhood psychoses, learning disorder, hysterical syndrome, conduct disorder and autism. A high inter-rater reliability coefficient of 0.968 was found between two independent raters. Validation against the Child Behaviour Checklist (Achenbach and Edelbrock, 1983) revealed significant correlation at 0.05 level of internalizing disorder with emotion disorder, and at 0.01 level of externalizing disorder with conduct disorder and hyperkinesis.

While the current international classificatory systems are certainly useful in making a diagnosis, linkages to psychological counselling require much more information. DPCL on the other hand provides information on other parameters such as temperament and other important psycho-social factors, thus enabling the planning of therapeutic strategies in the Asian context.

CHAPTER 3

Child Psychology and Psychopathology from a Developmental Perspective

Developmental psychopathology is an emerging discipline. It attempts to bring about a liaison between disciplines such as abnormal psychology and developmental psychology. The approach is essentially holistic in nature despite the current ethos of extreme specialization.

Developmental psychopathology is a discipline within developmental psychology, with special emphasis on pathology. It also has an equal interaction with child psychology and clinical child psychology. The latter two specialties are primarily interested in differential diagnosis, interventions and prognosis. Developmental psychopathology is described by Sroufe and Rutter (1984: 18) as 'the study of origins and course of individual patterns of behavioral maladaptation, whatever the age of onset, whatever the causes, whatever the transformations in behavioral manifestation, and however complex the course of developmental pattern may be'.

This particular area of research has several applications that are of interest to practising clinicians in terms of primary, secondary and tertiary interventions. From the developmental perspective, one can unravel the multiple aetiological contributors, and effective intervention strategies can be planned in terms of remedial work, family therapy or various forms of psychological therapies. While the developmental psychologist offers normative studies of development, the clinical psychologist could try the framework which best fits the individual child and plan effective intervention strategies.

Widely used classificatory systems such as various versions of ICD or DSM provide guidelines for differential diagnosis, but only developmental psychopathology offers possible ways of setting up hypotheses about the evolution of specific disorders, which enable the clinician to plan out effective intervention in the context of a particular child and his family, and also to test the developmental hypotheses in a systematic fashion.

KEY RESEARCH ISSUES IN DEVELOPMENTAL PSYCHOPATHOLOGY

The complex area of interface between developmental psychology and psychopathology can be teased out into several strands. State-of-the-art developmental psychopathology can be best understood if its various segments are looked at first and are subsequently viewed in a holistic fashion. We now look at the various aspects involved in research in the area of developmental psychopathology.

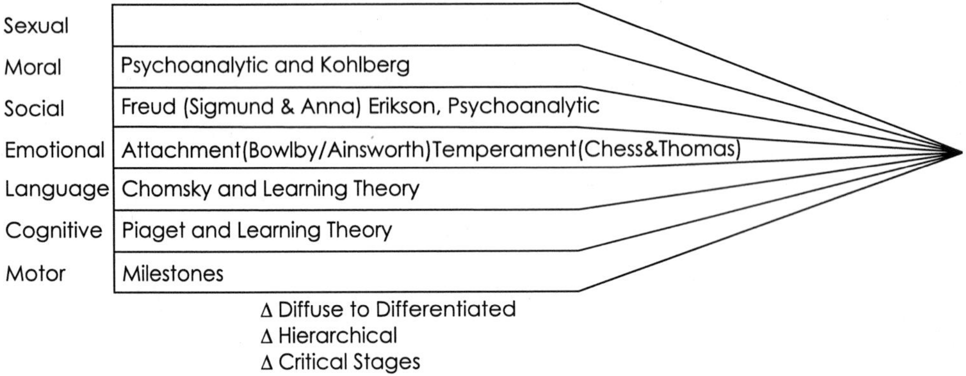

Figure 3.1 Some theoretical models of normal development

1. Models of biological, psychological and social development with reference to motor, cognitive, language, emotional, moral and sexual development are already available. The pioneers of these models have been Freud, Piaget, Erikson, Chomsky, Skinner, Bowlby, Ainsworth, Kohlberg and others. The various aspects of development, though described segment-wise, are essentially interactive in nature, i.e., having to do with the child herself and the child and her/his family. These models also refer to biological as well as psycho-social factors and seem to emphasize the theme that development proceeds in a systematic fashion from a diffuse state to differentiated states, in a hierarchical fashion, with critical stages in development, and in a complex interaction between the organism and the environment. This theme appears to be common to embryology as well as developmental psychology. Figure 3.1 depicts some of the theoretical models of normal development mentioned here.
2. The currently available classificatory systems for childhood disorders are versions of the ICD and the DSM. The multi-axial classification system of Rutter, Shaffer and Shepherd (1975) attempts to incorporate the developmental context into classification. In the multi-axial classification, the first axis refers to psychiatric diagnosis as per the ICD. The second axis refers to developmental delays of multiple types, such as speech delay, learning disabilities, etc. The third axis refers to the level of intellectual functioning. The fourth axis refers to organic underpinnings; and the fifth axis focuses on psycho-social stressors coded along 16 points such as mental disturbance in the family, discordant relationships, anomalous family situations, etc. But this is only the beginning of rapprochement between the developmentalists and the clinicians. These schemes do not take into account normal stages of development with reference to age and developmental context. The diagnosis remains cross-sectional. A developmental diagnosis which traces the evolution of the disorder would perhaps be more effectively utilized by a psychopathologist or a clinician.
3. One of the themes currently in the foreground in the area of developmental psychopathology is continuity of psychopathology. Essentially, it consists of the pathways to study disorders from infancy to adulthood. The methods used are: prospective study of high-risk groups, follow-back and follow-up studies. The issue of continuity has three important implications for classification of childhood psychopathology as highlighted by Garber (1984).

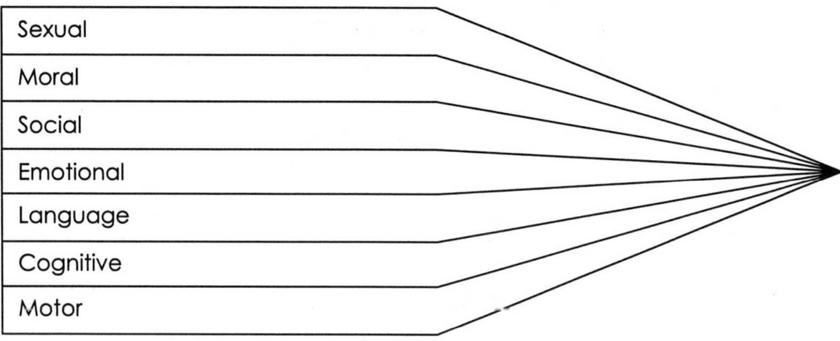

Figure 3.2 Areas of development from infancy to adolescence

4. A system for classifying children's disorders should not simply be based on the classification of adult psychopathology without first validating it. Childhood disorders may have their unique symptomatology, aetiology, course and prognosis independent of the adult form of the disorder (if at all one exists). Figure 3.2 illustrates the areas of development from infancy to adolescence.
   - The validity of a psychopathological disorder during childhood is not necessarily dependent on there being future disorders over the course of development into adulthood.
   - Classification should have a way of capturing the process of change and development that children undergo. Classification should not be limited to static and isolated behaviours but to the coherence of the individual in terms of his or her manner of organizing and integrating information and experiences.
   - Thus, the definition of health and pathology is a crucial issue. The developmental perspective suggests several important dimensions and parameters by which normalcy and deviance may be defined and classified. The classification system should be comprehensive enough to make judgment about poor or good adaptation with respect to:
     a. What is expected of the child given her/his age, sex, developmental phase and level of functioning. Figure 3.2 illustrates the areas of development from infancy to adolescence.
     b. The particular context of behaviour in terms of the developmental tasks and crises and the possible environmental, familial and cultural influences.
     c. On the background of the above variables there are other important parameters such as intensity, frequency, duration, number and combination of symptoms.

THEORETICAL MODELS IN DEVELOPMENTAL PSYCHOPATHOLOGY

A classification system that juxtaposes the stages of normal development with various kinds of dysfunction will contribute to the understanding of developmental psychopathology by allowing one to:

- identify what types of psychopathological disorders are associated with impairment or distortions in which area of functioning,

- discover the nature of these deviations with respect to their quality, timing or reversibility,
- disentangle the direction of causality of those deficits in terms of either effects of psychopathology upon normal developmental functioning or, conversely, the role that disruption in normal functioning plays in the aetiology of psychopathology, and
- examine the transaction between development in two or more domains of functioning (Garber, 1984).

The challenging task for developmental psychopathology is to incorporate a classificatory system into the fluid concept of developmental progress. An early attempt at conceptualization was made by Anthony (1970). He juxtaposed age, stages of psycho-sexual, psycho-social, psycho-cognitive and psycho-affective development with various types of psychopathology hypothesized to be associated with these stages. However, little empirical research has been carried out to investigate its validity. A recent classificatory system of Greenspan, Lourie, and Nover (1979) postulates early developmental stages that focus on levels of processing, organizing and differentiating experiences. This framework attempts an integration of symptom configuration, aetiology, as well as 'developmental structural diagnoses'. Ciccetti and Hesse (1983) cross-map Piagetian stages of cognitive development on emotional development. It is suggested that a classificatory system should similarly cross-map major areas of functioning. Garber's classificatory framework (1984) cross maps developmental tasks and disorders. For example, object permanence, attachment and dependency are the developmental tasks that correspond to the disorder of separation anxiety. Deficient differentiation of self, self esteem and social comparison may manifest as depression, and concept of death and time perspective (future) may emerge as suicide. Conduct disorder on the other hand may be a product of failure in the developmental tasks of moral development, characterized by perspective taking, empathy, delay in gratification and so on.

Achenbach's framework, which focuses on psychopathological disorders in the developmental context of age and sex, is based on extensive empirical research and statistical analysis and is a benchmark (Achenbach and Edelbrock, 1978). Achenbach's notion of broad-band factors of externalization and internalization is a very significant contribution in the area of developmental psychopathology. The Child Behaviour Check List (CBCL) has 113 items. Profiles are provided separately for boys and girls, for 4–5 year-olds, 6–11 year-olds and 12–16 year-olds. The source of information may be parents, teachers or self. The scales consist of description of symptoms such as anxious, socially withdrawn, depressed, unpopular, self-destructive, inattentive, nervous, overactive and aggressive. Obsessive compulsive symptoms are added to the scales of older children.

Apart from the Achenbach model, other models have limited application. For example, the Attachment Theory is used to explain a disorder that may not be commonly encountered, like separation anxiety. The focus is on a small number of disorders which are less frequently encountered in clinics, such as autism, feeding disorders and separation anxiety, which appear to fit best. Thus, a framework which encompasses all aspects of development as well as common disorders would be of equal interest to developmentalists and clinicians alike. According to Rutter and Garmezy (1983) the database as it exists is too inadequate for global theories.

An attempt is made in the next section to conceptualize developmental psychopathology in terms of superimposing templates of development and psychopathology, and in the context of some specific disorders. The psychoanalytical, learning and attachment theories, and Piagetian, Chomskian and

Kohlbergian models of cognitive, language, emotional, social, moral and sex-role development focus on development in a systematic fashion. Growth and development occurs from diffuse to differentiated, simple to complex hierarchical models with critical sensitive periods through infancy to adolescence. Though these are excellent models segment-wise, the interaction between the various domains of development is yet to be understood in a detailed fashion. A beginning has been made in understanding this. For example, the relationship between the sensorimotor stage (Piaget) and the stage of bonding and attachment has been studied. The relationship between the development of cognition and language has been explored. The development of abstraction, superego and moral codes could be linked up. Freudian and Eriksonian systems, despite the differences in their emphasis on sexual and social contributors, do overlap in the descrition of the early stages of the child's psychological development. Cognitive and language development, as well as emotional and social development can be explained equally well through learning theory models. What we need is a perspective that has a healthy respect for all models, as they all contribute a good deal to the understanding of development. Figure 3.3 gives such a perspective on psychopathology in the context of development.

Following this, yet another template, that of psychopathological disorders, and how they develop through childhood to adolescence, needs to be superimposed on the interactional model. These may be seen as developmental trends in psychopathology:

- With separation anxiety, speech and language problems, hyperkinesis, problems of feeding, sleeping and bowel and bladder regulation of preschool children
- Internalizing and externalizing problems of childhood
- Typical problems of adolescence

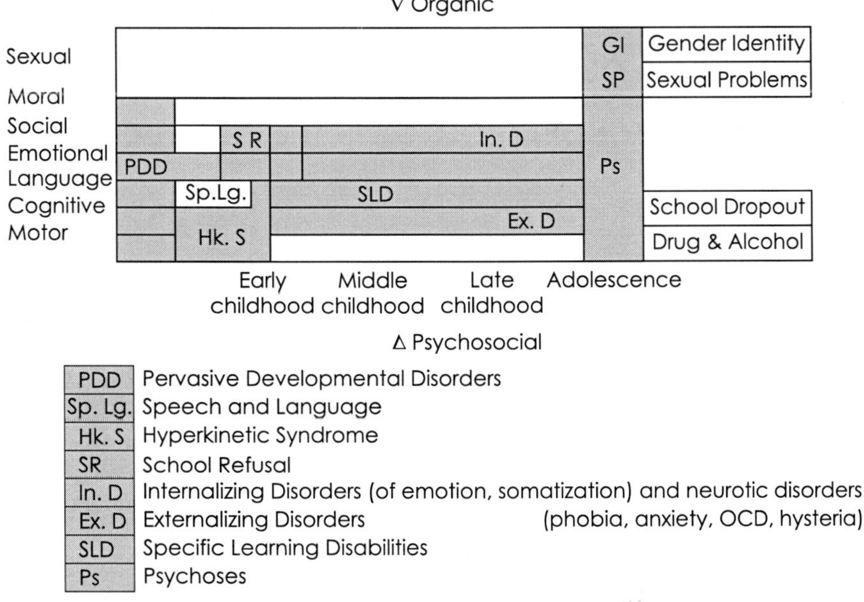

Figure 3.3 Psychopathology in the context of development

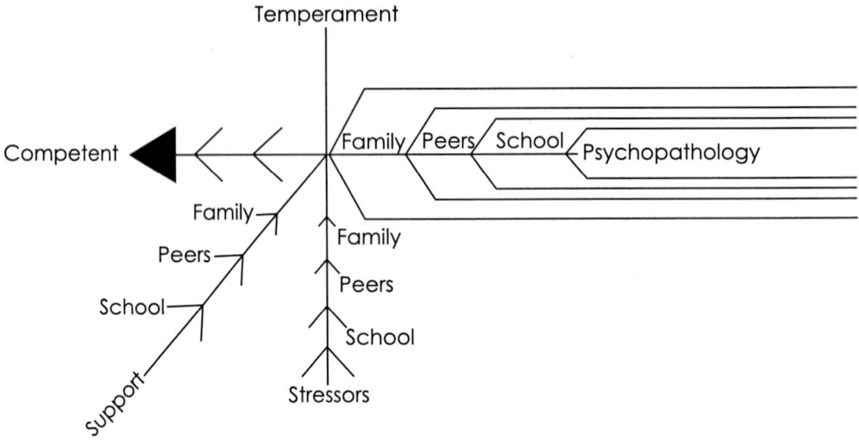

Figure 3.4 Psychopathology and psychosocial factors

All these need to be viewed against the background of various developmental theories. Aetiological contributors from the bio-psycho-social spectrum have to be integrated into the schema. Figure 3.4 illustrates the relationship between psychopathology and psychosocial factors.

In the absence of holistic theories of child development, one is compelled to view various theories developed in the West segment-wise. Ideally, the 'whole' should be studied before the segmental aspects. It has to be noted that in the Indian context an interface between psychopathology and development is yet to emerge. Hence the linkage between the present chapter and those to follow may at best appear minimal. The interface calls for multidisciplinary efforts by mental health professionals and developmentalists in order to develop strong linkages.

DEVELOPMENTAL PSYCHOPATHOLOGY IN THE INDIAN CONTEXT

India is undergoing rapid socio-cultural transformation. The developmental psychopathology of the West may be different from that of the East. There are factors which are culturally determined and may influence development. These could be aspects of temperament, child-rearing practices, nature of developmental and other stressors which are culture-specific, as well as symptoms which might be considered pathological in a particular family, sub-culture or society as a whole.

In the Indian context, child-rearing practices, family interactions, peer and school influences, nature of temperament, protective factors and social supports in the environment, social and cultural values, etc., are important areas of research. At-risk populations, such as those below the poverty line, working children, and neglected and under-stimulated children need to be studied in relation to developmental psychopathology and resilience. This would enable us to plan universal intervention at the community level.

The nature of cognitive, language, emotional, social, moral and sex-role development in some core groups—such as those who are dependent or insecurely attached, those with attention deficits, those with internalizing or externalizing problems, and those who are mentally healthy or resilient—needs to be studied on a longitudinal basis. In a high-risk population of children, this would be of great value in terms of intervention planning.

This holistic approach would enable one to derive testable hypotheses as to what makes a child competent or disturbed, what maintains the behaviour and what is, eventually, the final outcome in adulthood. Longitudinal studies in the area of developmental psychopathology fulfil the needs of the developmentalist in terms of scientific curiosity, of policy-makers in terms of database, and of health-care providers in terms of intervention programmes based on sound empirical data. The outcome may contribute immensely to improve the quality of life of children.

The author has developed a 'Developmental Psychopathology Check List' (See the Appendix at the end of the book) to study some of the important aspects of development and psychopathology. These are:

1. Developmental history
2. Developmental problems
3. Psychopathology (hyperkinesis, conduct disorders, learning problems, emotion disorders, obsessive compulsive disorder, neurosis, somatic problems including hysteria and psychoses)
4. Psychosocial stressors
5. Temperamental profile
6. Supportive factors

The check list may be used across age groups and gender, both cross-sectionally and longitudinally, and is specially simplified to suit the Indian population. Unlike the other tests used with child population, the DPCL is holistic in approach.

CHAPTER

Abnormal Child Psychology from a Developmental Perspective

THE EXAMINATION OF THE CHILD

The examination of the child includes the examination of the child as well as her/his family. This differs significantly from the examination of an adult as the child does not seek help by himself and is brought for consultation by an adult. A child's understanding of what troubles her/him may be at variance with the reports of his parents and teachers. Thus, it is necessary to collect information about the child from multiple sources. In addition, many behaviour problems are situation-specific. For example, a child may have severe temper tantrums only when with her/his parents, or a child who is obedient at home may be disruptive in the classroom. Sometimes, the problem may be seen only in one setting and not in others. Enuresis may be reported at home, but not at school; scholastic difficulties may be reported by the teacher in the school. To understand the dynamics and aetiology of the problem, the child and the family have to be explored as a single unit.

DEVELOPMENTAL CONTEXT

Children's problems as presented by their parents often tend to vary according to different age groups. For example, in younger children, the problems may be related to development, such as over-activity, or problems with language, sleeping or feeding, which are developmental problems. In older children, the symptoms may be related to emotional, behavioural or scholastic problems which occur in the context of the child's interaction with the environment.

TECHNIQUES

Techniques of exploration adopted by the clinician have to be tailored to the needs of the child. With a younger child, a clinician's acumen in observing the child in his natural setting and an ability to engage the child in play in order to establish a rapport are required. With an older child, although the medium of communication may be verbal, the child may have to be involved in tasks of drawing, colouring or story-telling, as the clinician can rarely conduct a formal interview.

It is recommended that the child should first be seen alone, and then the family or parents separately, and then all of them together. However, if the child is anxious and clinging, it may not be possible to see the child alone. The child, especially an older one, must also be assured that what has been revealed during the session will not be divulged to family members without her/his permission. On occasion it may be necessary to acquire information from the relatives, brothers, sisters, teachers (or teacher's report) and friends at school, in order to get a complete picture of the child's problem.

The present chapter attempts to provide a simple yet comprehensive framework for examining the child and the family. This framework is drawn from several sources, including Barker (1976) and Cooper and Wannerman (1977). It provides a brief outline so that professionals other than those concerned with mental health, such as teachers, can make use of it. The framework aims to include components to be used for diagnosis as well as interventions.

It is important to remember that the presence of a symptom may not always mean that the child is ill. Whether a symptom is pathological or not is to be considered in terms of the following:

1. Multiplicity of symptoms: The higher the number of symptoms, the more severe the pathology.
2. Severity of the symptom: Occasional restlessness in certain situations is acceptable, while pervasive restlessness is pathological, and even one or two episodes of violence or aggression require attention.
3. Frequency and duration: Persistent and frequent complaints are to be viewed with caution.

The Kannerian preamble of meaning of symptoms should always be kept in mind as it is of great value in understanding psychopathology. The symptom and its meaning in child psychiatric practice are paraphrased from the classic description of Kanner (1957).

THE SYMPTOM

The complaint or the symptom which the patient presents indicates the existence of a cause of which it is the effect. The parents bring a child for examination because they are bothered about her/his behaviour; they begin by naming the symptom that bothers them and request the clinician to remove the symptom. Experience shows that such limited attention is an ineffective shortcut as it disregards the causes of which the behaviour item is the effect. The symptom, in addition, also serves a number of important and closely related functions.

The Symptom as an Admission Ticket

The symptom may be looked upon as an admission ticket to the clinician's curiosity. An admission ticket to a playhouse arouses one's curiosity about the play but does not tell one about its contents. A fever may mean several underlying conditions. A physician who treats the fever without looking for its cause falls short of his goal. The fever is not the illness; it merely indicates that there is an illness to be investigated. The symptom, thus, is not the problem; it merely indicates that there is a problem to be studied.

The Symptom as a Signal

A policeman on the beat notices there is a riot. As he cannot cope with the situation alone, he blows his whistle to summon help. The whistle plays the role of a signal which calls attention to the real problem. But the whistle itself is not the problem. Similarly, behaviour problems indicate that there is something wrong with the child. Exclusive attention to the whistle or the symptom alone will not serve any purpose. The policeman who blew the whistle knew exactly what his act meant; while the misbehaving child seldom knows what her/his behaviour means, what this signal means, or even that she/he is signalling anything. It is left to the clinician to search for the source of the trouble.

The Symptom as a Safety Valve

Sometimes behaviour such as stealing or lying is considered 'bad' behaviour for which the child is punished and scolded. Often, such behaviour is the outcome of severe family pathology. The 'bad' behaviour, thus, is a safety valve which allows the child to survive instead of 'drowning'. It is an aggressive defence against powerful forces, with which the child could not possibly cope in a socially acceptable manner. It keeps the child's inner resources intact.

The Symptom as a Means of Solving Problems

Sometimes the symptom solves the problem. A child with difficulties in a new school, which is some distance away, may develop conversion (e.g. paralysis of the lower limbs) or dissociative symptoms (e.g. fainting spells), and the symptoms keep the child away from school, thus offering a solution to his/her problems. The clinician's task is to find an alternative and a better solution than the one opted for by the child.

The Symptom as a Nuisance

Many symptoms are of nuisance value, such as restlessness and fighting. But generally children with symptoms of nuisance value are brought for treatment by parents and teachers earlier than those children who suffer inwardly. These symptoms may be mismanaged by parents who themselves have a low threshold for tolerating annoyances. For example, sloppiness in a child may not bother one mother at all, while another mother might be driven to punitive behaviour due to her low tolerance or her perfectionism.

In addition to these factors, there is a strong cultural element in the evaluation of a symptom. In the Indian context being quiet and obedient is considered to be 'model' behaviour and 'talking back' to elders is seen as bad behaviour. Thumb-sucking is considered bad behaviour, while over-activity in a youngster may be considered an indicator of high intelligence when the child grows older. What is considered normal or abnormal in a particular culture or subculture is of crucial importance, and a clinician must be familiar with the cultural context in which the symptom is reported. A child may use different symptoms as means of communication in varying settings.

THE FORMAT OF THE EXAMINATION OF THE CHILD AND THE FAMILY

Identifying Data

1. Age of the child, parents, siblings and others in the household.
2. Description of family circumstances, such as housing, economics, school, health, family structure (nuclear, joint, etc.).

Presenting Complaints

1. Nature and history of the child's difficulties presented in chronological order, with the specific duration of each of the symptoms.
2. Who referred the child and why, according to the child and the adult informants.

Description of the Parents

1. A family genealogical tree and general description of the parents and rest of the family, including family structure, nature of interactions among members, and of members with the child; child's adjustment at school and with peers and teachers; and child's participation in school, sports and other activities.
2. Attitude of family members towards the problems of the child, and their own ideas about aetiology.

Relevant Family History

1. History of psychiatric illnesses, psychosomatic disorders, epilepsy, mental retardation, reading difficulties, stammering, drug or alcohol dependence, or problems identical to those presented by the child.
2. Significant life events and stressors in the lives of the parents, particularly in the year during which the child's problems began (e.g. illnesses, change of homes, jobs or other stressors).
3. Selective enquiry about parents' own experience as children, especially in relation to their parents: Parents' own upbringing as children has a marked influence on how they bring up their children, either by repeating the same pattern or by completely compensating for it. For example, punitive upbringing of the parents themselves either leads to over-indulgence with total lack of discipline or to strong punitive treatment of the child.

Developmental History

1. A sequential account of the child's development, complications during pregnancy, birth, prenatal/neonatal and subsequent progress, illnesses and injuries.

2. The child's acquisition of skills such as motor skills, speech, toilet training, along with school adjustment, peer relationships and preferences. These must be studied meticulously from birth onwards, noting specific milestones.
3. Past history of problems related to the following should be explored:

- Digestive system: Overeating, food refusal, faddism, pica (eating non-edibles), nausea, vomiting, abdominal pains, constipation, diarrhoea and faecal soiling
- Urinary system: Bedwetting, wetting by day, and frequent micturition (passing urine)
- Sleep: Problems in going to bed, sleeping, nightmares, night terrors, bruxism or grinding of teeth, and sleepwalking (the last two are not considered strong indicators of psychiatric disturbance)
- Circulatory and respiratory systems: Breathlessness, cough, and palpitation
- Habitual manipulation of the body: Nail-biting, thumb-sucking, nose-picking, head-banging, rocking or similar habits, and masturbation
- Speech: Over talkativeness, mutism, faulty speech (including speech delay and stammering), and poor comprehension of spoken language
- Thought processes: Poor communication, distractibility, disordered thought and day-dreaming
- Cognitive processes: Attentional processes
- Vision and hearing: Any defects, and evidence of hallucinations
- Personality traits and behaviour: Happy or unhappy, submissive or aggressive, shy or bold, calm or excitable, anxiety-prone, prone to sulking, irritability or temper tantrums, follower or leader, and relationship with siblings, parents, teachers and friends

Apart from the impressionistic observations described above, one could also use the Thomas and Chess dimensions of temperament, particularly of early childhood. They broadly saw a child as a: *difficult child, easy child* or *slow-to-warm child.* The major dimensions detailed by Thomas and Chess (1977) are:

1. Rhythmicity of biological functions
2. Activity level
3. Approach to or withdrawal from new stimuli (people/situations)
4. Adaptability
5. Sensory threshold
6. Predominant quality of mood
7. Intensity of mood expression
8. Distractibility
9. Persistence/attention span

If the child presents problems in any areas such as sleeping, speech, toileting or attention, efforts should be made to determine the environmental context in which they occur. There are often situations or patterns of child-rearing which initiate and maintain the symptoms. For example, many of the feeding problems of the infant are associated with maternal anxiety and behaviour.

EXAMINATION OF THE CHILD

Establishing a rapport with the child is of crucial importance. The examiner should use a judicious mixture of techniques of play, drawing, painting, story-telling, and talk on topics that interest the child, without necessarily focusing on the presenting symptoms. Verbal, non-verbal, gestural and behavioural cues should be picked up by the examiner.

1. General appearance: Large or small build, well- or poorly-nourished, cuts and bruises, appearance (dress, etc.). The examiner should be alert to a happy, unhappy, tearful, or worried attitude towards the examiner.
2. Motor function: Overactive/underactive, slow, quick, clumsy, whether the child is/was left handed, and whether she/he can draw, paint and write.
3. Speech: Articulation, vocabulary, talks freely, does not talk, repeats what is asked, disjointed speech, stammering or stuttering, understands what is being said but cannot express what he wants to say; and whether or not she/he has the ability to read, write and work with numbers.
4. Content of talk and thought (subjects can be introduced or avoided by the examiner): Abnormal use of words and expressions.
5. Perception: Behaves as if, or reports seeing and hearing things that do not exist (this does not include 'pretend play' that is common in children).
6. Intellectual functions: Knowledge of date/day, knowledge of people's identity, knowledge of events, for example sports or TV shows appropriate to the age of the child, and knowledge of plants, animals, festivals or details of what parents do, etc.
7. Moods and emotional state: Happy/elated, depressed or crying, anxious, hostile, suspicious, suicidal threats or attempts, attitude towards school, teachers and classmates, and whether the child daydreams (if so, about what?).
8. Inquiry about fantasy life: For example, three wishes the child would make if a fairy (or God) appears and asks what she/he would like. What are the child's dreams? What does she/he like or dislike the most? What does she/he want to be when grown up?
9. Indications of social adjustment: Friends, hobbies, interests, games played, social activities involving friends in school (drama, etc.). Is she/he a follower or leader and the bully or the bullied?

Always observe the behavioural cues and end the interview by asking the child if there is anything else she/he would like to add. This question may often elicit matters of concern to the child.

EXAMINATION OF THE FAMILY

The history of specific psychiatric or physical illnesses (if any) in the parents must be investigated. The examiner should try to explore details of recurrent problems, financial, occupational, problems of a chronic nature, migration, changes in family structure, illnesses, alcoholism, poverty, marital conflicts, and neglect and abuse of children in the context of parents and other significant people in the child's life. One should also explore early separation and who the caretakers have been during the entire life of the child till date. Often one may focus on the current family living arrangements but might need to ask about any recent changes. The examiner must always attempt to locate significant family events alongside the chronology of complaints. This helps in building up a developmental psychopathology of a particular child. Other aspects to be examined are:

1. Interaction between parents
2. Attitude of parents towards the child (accepting, rejecting, anxious, consistent, protective, disinterested, tolerant, overprotective, etc.)
3. Who the main caretaker is and with whom the child spends long hours
4. Who supervises the child's daily activities such as waking up, washing, bathing, meals, and who disciplines the child
5. Who the child confides in
6. Whose company the child enjoys and prefers
7. Role of other members, such as grandparents (for example, the parents' attempt at disciplining the child may be undermined by an indulgent grandfather)
8. Presence of other relatives or domestic helpers who may play a key role in the child's life: The family systems described in Western countries do not cover the complex interaction amongst the multiple caretakers in the Indian context. Generally, the father may have very little involvement in the care of the child in joint or extended families, where mothers are housewives. In nuclear families, where the mothers work outside, the fathers, relatives and domestic helpers may handle much of the caretaking, especially of young children. To get a complete picture of the family dynamics in relation to the child, an attempt should be made to interview all significant family members first separately and then together, in order to get a coherent picture. One might be astounded by the nature of discrepancies in the feedback about the child given by the mother and father separately. In addition, combined interviews also act as a corrective force in reducing distortions in the perception of parents. A good interview with the child and the family together often becomes a therapeutic interview and not merely a fact-finding one.

Having gathered such information, it is useful to code it along the multi-axial system developed by Rutter, Shaffer, and Shepherd et al. (1975).

First axis	:	Diagnostic category (or categories on ICD-10 classificatory system)
Second axis	:	Developmental delays (such as speech delay, specific learning disabilities)
Third axis	:	Level of intellectual functioning
Fourth axis	:	Medical conditions likely to have influenced the symptoms
Fifth axis	:	Psycho-social stressors

A holistic approach to an understanding from the developmental context helps in planning effective intervention strategies as described in the chapter on developmental psychopathology. Thus, pathological/normal development in physical, emotional, cognitive, language and social competencies and the pattern of child-rearing and school influences have to be seen from a holistic perspective. It necessarily means that the examination of the child and the family is to be carried out keeping in mind the cultural context. Deciding whether or not the child suffers from some pathology must be guided by the cultural contexts of her/his behaviour, rather than a list of symptoms from a standard textbook of psychiatry from the West.

CHAPTER 5

Psychological Assessment of the Child

Doubts about the adequacy of tests and their relevance to clinical and educational problems (Haney, 1981; Kaufman, 1979; Sattler, 1982) have contributed to a decline in the use of psychological testing in Western clinical practice. This discontent stems from two sources: (*a*) the absence of a well-articulated framework for the use of tests in clinical practice; and (*b*) the failure to understand the nature of psychological measurement. As Berger (1985) points out, administration and scoring of tests are essentially technical skills. The interpretation and integration of test results in clinical practice, however, demands more than the skills of a technician. It requires an understanding of the theories, principles and techniques of psychological measurement, the knowledge associated with theories of psychological functioning, and familiarity with developmental psychology, childhood disorders and research literature related to the procedures used.

It is important to distinguish between the 'process of assessment' and 'psychological testing'. An assessment is a set of statements about an individual and his circumstances in relation to some problem. Assessment is also a process of bringing together relevant information from a variety of sources, that is, the systematic collection, organization and interpretation of information about a person and her/his situations, which may be used to predict her/his behaviour (Sundberg and Tyler, 1962).

Thus, psychological assessment is a term which goes beyond psychological testing. The term implies that there are many ways of evaluating individual differences. According to Goldstein and Hersen (1987), testing is one way, but there is also the interview, along with observation of behaviour in a natural or selected environment. A textbook on psychological testing views it from an experimental psychologist's perspective, with the resultant reliance on norms, reliability and validity components. A clinician, in addition, seeks information on the test performance affected by the abnormal conditions in an individual child with a psychiatric disorder. Obviously, testing is not carried out under standard conditions as expected. The only common ground is rigorous adherence to the administration and scoring. A psychometrician and a clinician would, thus, differ vastly in their approach to test interpretation.

In the field of child mental health, there is no recognizable tradition of evaluation and assessment in India (Prabhu, 1987). The few tools which have emerged are not based on planned action or users' demands. In spite of these disadvantages, there has been some work on tests in the area of research as well as clinical practice. This chapter focuses on some of the tests available in India and how they can be used effectively in clinical practice. The focus, hence, is more on the philosophy of psychological assessment which is of relevance to developing countries, than on the sophistry of test technology.

TESTS OF COGNITION

Developmental Schedules for Young Children

Gesell's Developmental Schedule. The schedule provides norms for children aged between four weeks and 36 months. The norms are based on longitudinal data. The items are largely observational and classified under four types of development, namely motor, adaptive, language and personal-social (Gesell and Amatruda, 1947). The Indian adaptation, which is fairly extensive, was developed by Muralidharan (1983) as well as Bhakkoo, Kaur, Narang, and Verma (1977).

Bailey Scale of Infant Development. This is based on longitudinal data on a relatively large number of tests for children below one year of age. The items are sensori-motor in nature. The tests show little or low correlation with intelligence at later ages. The Bailey Scale of Infant Development was studied on a longitudinal basis in Baroda from 1963 onwards for children up to the age of 30 months (Phatak, 1989). Out of 230 items, 163 items assess mental abilities and the remaining 67 items assess motor abilities.

The Vineland Social Maturity Scale. The Vineland Social Maturity Scale (Doll, 1965) is a developmental schedule concerned with an individual's ability to look after and take responsibility for his practical needs. It covers age ranges from birth to adulthood. The scale consists of eight categories: general self-help, self-help in eating, self-help in dressing, self-direction, occupation, communication, locomotion and socialization. A social age as a social quotient (SQ) can be obtained. The highest level that can be achieved extends to 25 years. The Indian adaptation was carried out by Malin (1970) based on data obtained after 10 years of use in the Nagpur Child Guidance Centre. Malin's adaptation removed several original items and replaced them with culturally appropriate ones. In the Indian adaptation, the highest level to be achieved is 15 years.

The Vineland profile is used for baseline assessment of self-help skills and to plan strategies based on deficit skills. It enables the clinician to identify deficit skills due to poor training. However, uneven spread of items may produce a misleading profile and suggest skill deficits. In some areas, items cover a very narrow range, while others have a wider spread. The tool is particularly sensitive to highlighting parental mismanagement in terms of overprotection and poor training in children with inadequate social skills. More recent adaptations of the scale are yet to gain wide usage in India.

Seguin Form Board (cf. Cattel 1936). Developed by Seguin, the Seguin Form Board is the most extensively used test in India. Ten pieces of wood in simple to complex shapes are to be fitted into a form board. The time taken and accuracy of performance determine intellectual endowment in the young, and speed of motor performance and visuo-motor coordination in older children. Bharath Raj (1977) tried out the Seguin Form Board on a population of 1,068 normal children up to the age of 16 years. In comparison to Western norms, the Indian children were marginally slower, and sex differences, though present, were uniform across ages in the sample.

The Binet Scales. This earliest test of intelligence has undergone several revisions, the most prominent being the Stanford Binet Revision (Terman and Merril, 1937) with extensive standardization. The scale contains 129 items, grouped into 20 age levels, ranging from two years to the Superior Adult level. The test proceeds by six-month intervals up to five years, and from five to 14 years the age levels correspond to yearly intervals. The 15-year level is equivalent to the adult level. Kamat (1940) modified the test in Kannada and Marathi. This established the Binet-Kamat test as the foremost test of intelligence in India.

The Raven's Progressive Matrices (Coloured). This is another widely used test of intellectual functioning, especially of abstraction and reasoning. It is based on Spearman's 'g' factor theory (Raven, 1965), and is for use with children in the age range of five years to 11 years. The test has three subsets, consisting of a total of 36 items with coloured designs that have to be matched in a series of increasing complexity. The test is considered a culture-free test with very high reliability and validity indices. Its main advantage is that it is a non-verbal test. It has been extensively used in India. However, those below eight years and children from illiterate and deprived homes appear to have a distinct disadvantage in comprehending instructions about the tasks to be performed.

Wechsler's Intelligence Scale for Children (WISC). WISC (Wechsler, 1949) and its variants are the most widely used tests of intelligence in Western countries. The test gives verbal, performance and full-scale IQ. The sub-tests of the verbal scale are: Information, Comprehension, Arithmetic, Similarities and Vocabulary; and the subtests of the performance scale are: Digit Span, Picture Completion, Block Design, Picture Arrangement, Object Assembly and Coding. The WISC was standardized for the Indian population by Malin (1971) and was named the intelligence scale for Indian children.

There are three tests specifically for use with Indian children. These are: the Developmental Psychopathology Check List (Kapur, Barnabas, Reddy, Rozario and Uma, 1994); the NIMHANS Index of Specific Learning Disabilities (Kapur, John, Rozario, and Oommen, in Hirisave, Oommen and Kapur, 2002); and the NIMHANS Tests of Memory for Children (Barnabas, Subbakrishna, Kapur, and Sinha, in Hirisave, Oommen and Kapur, 2002). Details of the psychological assessment of nine children in a clinical setting are available in Hirisave, Oommen, and Kapur (2006).

Following the assessment, a profile of strengths and weaknesses is drawn for the individual child and a remediation programme is prepared, tailored to suit the needs of the child. The battery is a brief yet helpful tool for planning remediation in a clinic or a school setting. However, it requires further work in order to be used for research.

TESTS OF MEMORY FUNCTIONS FOR CHILDREN

These were developed by Hirisave, Oommen, and Kapur (2006). Barnabas has established norms for the battery of tests to assess memory functions in children in the age range of seven to 11 years, on a sample of 500 normal boys and girls, with 100 children in each of the five age groups. The battery used to test memory functions consists of personal information, mental control, sentence repetition, story recall (immediate and delayed), word recall (meaningful words), word recall (non-meaningful words), digit span test, delayed response learning, Cattel's retentivity test, picture recall, BVRT (Benton visual retention test), and paired associate learning.

TESTS OF PERSONALITY AND TEMPERAMENT

Assessment of the personality of children consists of objective measures of questionnaires, rating scales, check lists, reports by others and self, as well as projective tests. The assessment is beset with many problems as the developmental perspective does not favour the approach of using on children diluted versions of tests used on adults. Of the tests described in this section, some have been used on adults and the children's version has been subsequently developed (as in Cattell's tests of personality), while some have been developed on the child population. The Children's Personality Questionnaire represents the first group, while Temperament Schedules and Achenbach Scales represent the second group. The approach of the second group is undoubtedly superior as it accommodates the developmental perspective.

OBJECTIVE TESTS

Children's Personality Questionnaire (CPQ). The CPQ (Porter and Cattell, 1963) gives 14 factors (consisting of narrower and broader factors) and aims to assess children in the age range of eight to 12 years. Each of the factors carries 10 items. The test has four parallel forms, and has satisfactory reliability and validity in the Western context. The High School Personality Questionnaire (HSPQ) is the version meant for older adolescents and young adults.

Temperament. Temperament is a concept specifically meant to describe a child's personality as constitutionally endowed. The concept has emerged out of the pioneering efforts of Thomas and Chess (1977) from their New York Longitudinal Study (NYLS) of 136 children. In India, Malhotra and Malhotra (1988) have modified the Thomas and Chess scale to suit Indian children. In their sample of 100 parents each of disturbed and normal children, four factors were isolated. These were Sociability, Emotionality, Energy and Attentivity. Rhythmicity was set aside as the fifth factor. Kapur's temperament profile as seen in DPCL focuses on *Satvik*, *Rajasik* and *Tamasik* temperamental variants.

The Pre-school Behaviour Check List. The Pre-school Behaviour Check List (PBCL) of Richman and Graham (1971), comprising 19 behaviour items—each graded on a three-point scale—is a check list for behaviour problems of young children.

Conners' Abbreviated Rating Scale. Conners' Abbreviated Rating Scale (Conners, 1973) consists of 10 overlapping parent and teacher items from the 39-item Teacher Rating Scale to identify hyperactivity in children. The 10 items are rated on a four-point scale, ranging from 0 to 3 points. The cut-off score lies at 15 out of the possible 30 points. The test has satisfactory reliability and validity.

Rutter Pro Formas. The Children's Behaviour Questionnaire was developed by Rutter (1967) and is filled by the teacher. Pro forma A of the Questionnaire has nine items which assess school performance in terms of consistency of performance, attendance, extracurricular activities, specific problems in reading and writing, physical ailments of a child, etc. Pro forma B has 22 items, including presence or absence of several behaviour problems along with conduct and neurotic problems.

The test is a quick screening device in a school setting, particularly suited to large-scale epidemiological surveys. Studies across the world report exceptionally high reliability and validation. In India, the scale has been used in several epidemiological studies.

Achenbach Check Lists. Achenbach and Edelbrock (1983) have brought out forms of the Child Behavioural Check List test suited for the child population, with provision for teachers, parents and self as informants. The parents' form of the Child Behaviour Check List (CBCL) measures behavioural problems and competencies of children aged four to 16 (Achenbach and Edelbrock, 1981). The CBCL is a 113-item check list. Profiles are offered separately for each sex, from ages four to five years, six to 11 years and 12–16 years. The scales consist of a description of symptoms such as anxiety, social withdrawal, depression, lack of popularity, self-destructive behaviour, inattention, nervousness, overactivity and aggressive behaviour. Obsessive-compulsive features are added on to the profiles of the older children. Two major dimensions—factorially derived—are Externalizing Disorders and Internalizing Disorders, apart from the provision for clinical profiles with individual cut-off points. The variations of the scale are, Teacher Report Form and Youth Self Report for the older children. Standardization, validation and reliability have been reported to be satisfactory.

The Achenbach check lists have been used across cultures and have been found to be satisfactory, especially in epidemiological studies.

PSYCHOLOGICAL ASSESSMENT FROM A CLINICIAN'S PERSPECTIVE

For a clinician, questions regarding a child may be framed as:

- Why does the child perform poorly? What are the reasons for it?
- What can be done about it?

- How should one intervene to reduce the problem?
- What kind of changes can be brought about by interventions?
- Can the performance be understood in the light of the child's sex, age, temperament, illness, and the home and school situation?

In order to answer such questions, psychological tests need to be viewed from different vantage points. The test performance needs to be seen on the background of information provided by the case history, interview and observation of the child's behaviour. The clinician derives answers only by integrating information from these different sources.

A brief description of the relevant aspects of information from the case history and the behavioural observation includes the following:

1. Details about the pre-, peri-, and postnatal history which may be suggestive of brain damage in infancy.
2. Delays in the developmental milestones either of a global or of a specific nature, such as poor speech or motor coordination.
3. Sensorimotor handicaps which may be present at birth or acquired later. For example, visual or hearing disabilities which may be partial or complete. Developmental dysphasias or stammering also need to be considered.
4. Central nervous system damage that is present at birth or acquired later. History of contributory maternal illnesses or epilepsy, encephalitis, AIDS/HIV-positive status or head injury must be noted. For example, epilepsy is a prevalent condition in India. One must look into whether or not epilepsy has been controlled. Children with epilepsy are likely to be vulnerable to learning difficulties.
5. Psychiatric condition of the child: Children with infantile autism, psychoses or hyperkinesis are likely to have behaviour problems which interfere with testing procedures, leading to poor or erratic performance. In disorders of conduct and emotion or hysterical syndromes, performance may also be affected by poor motivation, fear or anxiety, and manipulative behaviour. Knowledge about clinical symptoms along with observation of the child's behaviour during the testing session would enable the clinician to understand how factors not associated with intelligence or personality can interfere with the child's performance.
6. Interaction between a child's temperament and examiner's characteristics: Temperamental characteristics described by Thomas and Chess (1977), such as 'slow-to-warm', 'easy' and 'difficult' children, have their impact on the performance of children in relation to the examiner's characteristics, such as being aloof, friendly or strict. A 'slow-to-warm' child may react adversely to a strict examiner while a 'difficult' child may perform well with such an examiner.
7. Socio-economic and educational factors: Factors such as illiteracy in the parents and familial poverty, rural or urban background, and quality of schooling all influence a child's performance on tests. For example, an 8-year-old child from a rural home with no schooling may perform in a manner similar to that of a 4-year-old urban child from upper socio-economic strata on tests assessing academic skills.
8. Presence of psychosocial stressors: The presence of pathological child-rearing practices and psychosocial stressors is important as children are very responsive to their immediate environ-

ment. Events such as sickness in the parents or separation from parents, chronic stressors like marital disharmony in parents or punitive behaviour towards the child could also result in lowered test performance.

9. Developmental issues: Developmental context of age, sex and continuity and discontinuity in maturation are some of the variables which influence performance on tests.
10. Temporary states: The child's temporary or general states of fatigue, poor motivation and lack of interest also impact performance. In such cases, reassessment or exploration into reasons for poor performance is necessary.

The variables mentioned here may act singly or in complex interaction with several other variables to affect the performance of the child. Each of these influencing variables has to be isolated and its impact on performance has to be understood in the framework of multiple causation.

It is, thus, clear that success in the performance, or performance in accordance with the norms, is not essential for a clinician's interpretation. Even failures give equally helpful information as the clinician is primarily interested in carrying out effective interventions.

Test performance is a function of a child's age, sex, home and school background, stressors of bio-psycho-social origin, temperament, clinical condition, child's interest and motivation in the testing session as well as skills of the examiner. The interplay of all these factors makes the interpretation of results a complex process of unravelling the series of aetiological factors, leading to the current performance of the child. Interpretation of results is, thus, a dynamic process to be carried out at any cross-sectional point of time. This can only be done in a holistic manner where the interpretation is based on information from the clinical history, behaviour observation and test results.

USES OF PSYCHOLOGICAL ASSESSMENT IN CLINICAL PRACTICE

There are many functions of psychological assessment in clinical practice. Some of these are enumerated here:

1. It provides the clinician with a clear picture of current phenomenology, a profile of assets and liabilities of cognitive functions, and intra-psychic, interpersonal and psycho-social problems.
2. It provides a basis for the clinician to build an aetiological hypothesis regarding what may have led to the current disturbance.
3. The performance of the child provides the clinician with clues for estimating the real potential of the child.
4. A profile of assets and liabilities—rather than a simple index of performance—provides the clinician with a better framework for intervention strategies.
5. Identification of a single or multiple possible aetiological factors help the clinician in planning effective intervention strategies.
6. Reassessment after the strategies have been implemented enables the clinician to evaluate the efficacy of the strategies; in addition, this can be used to change strategies which have not been effective.

In order to gain optimal information, the following aspects need to be looked into.

1. A note should be made of relevant aspects of family and developmental history which are likely to affect the child's performance.
2. Detailed observation of the behaviour of the child which can be understood as being caused by the illness process, for example, autistic preoccupation, hyperkinesis, conduct problems, dissociative spells, genuine inability to perform because of mental retardation, brain damage, temperamental characteristics of easy distractibility, tendency to get bored easily, being shy, timid or fearful, temporary state of fatigue, hunger or boredom, and lack of motivation. There could also be variability caused by disability due to the disorder itself, such as difficulties of a learning-disabled child or the slow reaction time of an epileptic child.
3. Consistency or variability in performance: Consistency of performance within the subtests measuring the same function is expected. However, to describe the discrepancy in performance which does not conform to normal expectation, the term 'scatter' is used. 'Scatter' is an indicator of intra-test or inter-test variability. It is of crucial importance in a clinical population, as it sheds light on the factors contributing to poor performance.

   Thus, analysis of scatter forms the core of the building-up of aetiological hypotheses about the nature of the dysfunction. An example is that of unreliable performance on Raven's Progressive Matrices (Coloured) where discrepancy scores are beyond the expected frequencies, in set A and set B respectively, with expected performance in set AB. This performance reveals that a child who performs poorly on easy items and better on difficult items is likely to be bright and easily bored and works better under challenging circumstances. Variability in the performance profile can lead to several hypotheses about the causes. These can be confirmed or disproved through further testing or interventions.

   Scatter or variability may be seen even on the tests which are not traditionally believed to measure the same function. For example, a child who obtains an IQ of 70 on Binet-Kamat test may give innovative Children's Apperception Test stories steeped in fantasy or give a Rorschach protocol rich in determinants, particularly Human Movement (M) responses. This would suggest that the Binet-Kamat has given a dubious measure of the intellectual endowment of the child. If a child with an IQ of 120 gives no Human Movement response on Rorschach, it may indicate extreme constriction of personality or even depression.
4. In addition, at times clues may emerge out of test results which may not have been reported in the case history or during examination of the child. One may further explore and find important missing links by following up on such clues.
5. Testing of hypotheses through reassessment: On the basis of intra-test and inter-test scatter, a hypothesis can be set up about the causes of dysfunction. In the case of a child who found set A of Raven's Progressive Matrices (Coloured) too easy, it is simply because he is a bright child who made careless mistakes. He should be made to do the test once again with greater care. In the case of a child with a high intelligence quotient and poor Rorschach performance, further exploration for emotional disturbance and accurate diagnosis would lead to a sound basis of treatment. When the child recovers, the Rorschach could be re-administered. The protocol is likely to be enlivened by rich determinants in keeping with the potential of the child. In the case of a child with rich Children's Apperception Test (CAT) scores and low IQ, the poor per-

formance may be due to fear of tasks resembling school work, caused by treatment at home and school, rather than poor intellectual potential. The rich fantasy is, thus, used by the child to escape from unpleasant reality at home and school.

These explanations are simplistic, but are offered to make a point. Practice of psychological assessment, with information gleaned out of case history, behaviour observation and psychological test results, is a complex process which can yield rich dividends. It is essential that a clinician does not rely on the results of a single test but looks for consistency among several tests, and when discrepancy or scatter is evident, follows it through—detective-like—with persistence and acumen.

CHAPTER

Psychological Therapies, or Counselling with Children

THE HISTORY OF PSYCHOLOGICAL THERAPIES IN INDIA

The first child guidance clinic in India came into existence at the Tata Institute of Social Sciences in 1937. Yet today, after seven decades, there are less than 200 child guidance clinics in the country. The first well-documented therapies with children can be found in the pioneering work of Erna M. Hoch (an existential therapist) in her book *Indian Children in a Psychiatrist's Playground* (1967). Work on psychological therapies with children flourished at the B.M. Institute in Ahmedabad in the 1970s under the stewardship of B.K. Ramanujam, only to fade a decade later. The All India Institute of Mental Health, Bangalore started a Child Guidance Clinic at its inception in 1954. A full-fledged child psychiatry unit came into being in 1975 under the leadership of Illana Cariapa, a child psychiatrist trained in the UK. The All India Institute of Mental Health, presently known as the National Institute of Mental Health and Neurosciences, runs the largest in-patient and out-patient services for children in the country and has been training psychiatrists, psychiatric social workers and clinical psychologists at the post-graduate level besides offering several short-term courses for those working with children.

However, at present the basic data on services offered to children in India in terms of manpower resources or infrastructure remains relatively unknown. Thus, the status of psychological therapies with children as practised across the nation remains largely unexplored due to limited published work except occasional case studies and limited outcome evaluation studies.

PSYCHOLOGICAL THERAPIES WITH CHILDREN

The child as a miniature adult, understood by adult considerations, has been the perspective embedded in the ancient and contemporary ethos in India. In recent years, there has been growing insight about the nature of working with children among practitioners of psychological therapies in the West. These are:

1. The child is a social being. Behaviour occurs in the context of the family, friends and the school. Most of the problems are situation-specific. Therapeutic gains made in one setting (e.g. the clinic) may not generalize into other settings (home or school).

2. The child is an active agent, a thinking person and has a distinct emotional make up (temperament).
3. The child is a developing organism. Fostering normal development is seen as essential.

In the light of the above considerations, the goals of therapy thus become symptom-reduction, promotion of normal development, fostering autonomy and behavioural gains, maintaining improvement and bringing about changes in the environment.

Child mental health is a neglected area in India despite there being excellent policy documents on the subject. People working with children at risk strongly demand psychotherapy/counselling in school and NGO settings. Several problems are encountered in this respect in the Indian setting. These are:

1. Indian literature grounded in the professional practice of psychological therapies is nearly non-existent.
2. Techniques transported from the West that have been used with adults are indiscriminately adopted for use with children without suitable modifications. Often, a single technique in which the counsellor is trained is used indiscriminately with all children.
3. Techniques used in the West for children are directly transplanted without suitable modifications. These turn out to be ineffective in Indian family or school contexts.
4. The need for detailed psychological assessment as a background for planning therapies including psychological tests is often overlooked.
5. Important child variables such as age, gender, temperament and cognitive potential which have a bearing on the therapeutic outcome are frequently overlooked.
6. The developmental context of normal and abnormal behaviour needs to be understood to enable planning of appropriate strategies. For example, in a younger child, the symptom of overactivity may be normal in the absence of attentional difficulties. But if attention deficit and pervasive overactivity are present, the child may be suffering from hyperkinesis disorder. In an older child, the manifestation may be that of conduct disorder. The therapy needs to be calibrated to meet the child's needs and the family context.
7. The importance of bio-psycho-social contexts is often overlooked. The match or mismatch between the child and the environment needs to be considered.
8. The need for a special relationship that develops between the therapist and the patient, which is a replacement of the parent-child relationship. 'Transference' is an essential ingredient of an effective therapeutic relationship with adults. Anna Freud (1946) has examined whether the term can be used for children. To paraphrase her, 'How can you use it? Transference refers to the transposing of your early experience on to later adult life. If the competing figures are here and present now in the child's environment, like the father and the mother with their young child, you cannot really technically call it transference'.
   Sigmund Freud had recommended that therapists must adopt a 'neutral' stance with adults. According to Anna Freud, this is not very useful in children. To paraphrase her, if therapists want to work with children, they have to relate to them, so that children come to like them. Children should like being in the company of the therapists. She says that therapists need to adopt all possible ways to garner the affection of the child. They need to be allies of the child. They can-

not be 'neutral' with children, but have to very actively interact with children and possibly, love children. If they cannot love children, they cannot do therapy with them. While psychotherapy is possible with adult patients even if the therapist does not much care for them, with children this is impossible. If therapists cannot show affection, they will be seen as being aligned with the parents, and therapy will be ineffective. The relationship between the therapist and the child has to be cultivated and strengthened.

9. Theoretical stance of the therapist: Theoretical stances of therapists vary greatly. Some are very directive and others are non-directive. Some are analytically or behaviourally oriented while others are eclectic. However, different disorders require different strategies to be used in combination or alone, which may even represent conflicting theoretical viewpoints. For example, take a common psychiatric condition in India such as dissociative disorder, one of these being 'functional fits'. We may use an eclectic framework appropriate to the case, combining techniques from more than one theoretical model. It is common practice to use a psychoanalytical model to understand the aetiology, behavioural techniques for symptom removal along with supportive techniques like environmental manipulation and parental counselling. With a hyperkinetic child, much of the work is behavioural along with parental counselling and training.

WORKING WITH THE FAMILIES

All families require different kinds of interventions at individual and family levels. The detailed assessment of the child, the family and the context in which the disorder occurs and is maintained becomes very important. To quote Professor Narayana Chirovolu Surya, a pioneering psychiatrist (personal communication , 1978), 'Treat the situation and the child will take care of himself.' Many difficulties that arise in the children are linked to the situation or context in which the child is placed, rather than the child really having a disorder or disturbance. Recently, I came across a child with school refusal at the age of five. She said, 'I will not go to school. The teachers beat me, I don't want to go to school'. I asked the mother, who is also a teacher in the same school, who said, 'I am also a teacher there and all the children get beaten. What's wrong with my daughter? Why can't she be beaten?' We were surprised that the mother felt this way. We tried to explain that the temperament of each child differs: some are very soft and fragile and cannot tolerate any aggression. Any particular boy or girl or quite a number of children do not mind being beaten up and they survive. But for this girl, the aggression from the teacher caused a great deal of distress. We recommended a change of school where children were treated better.

PSYCHOLOGICAL MANAGEMENT OF CHILDHOOD PROBLEMS

In recent years, the efficacy of psychological interventions has earned them a marked preference as compared to the traditional medical model of therapy, with the exception of the treatment of psychoses and some forms of severe behaviour disturbances. Drug management of child psychiatric problems is still of great importance and can be practised only by qualified child psychiatrists, with adequate hospital and laboratory facilities. The focus of the present chapter is essentially on the psychological management of child mental health problems, with or without drug management as an adjunct.

Psychological management of child psychiatric disorders is often viewed—by mental health professionals uninitiated in state-of-the-art child psychiatric practice—as a diluted version of psychological management used with adults. This is essentially because mental health professionals lack a perspective on developmental psychopathology which highlights the major differences between children and adults in phenomenology and in aetiology. This has additional implications for evolving effective intervention strategies, not only for disorders of a psycho-social nature but also for those disturbances that are caused for biological reasons.

Western models of psychological therapies have emerged in the context of the philosophical approach of body–mind and subject–object dualism. It is only in recent years, with better understanding of psychosomatic disorders and with the advent of health psychology that a holistic approach to human problems has met with some approval. Despite the increase in awareness of the need for a holistic and developmental perspective, practitioners in the West have preferred therapy of one kind or the other and have not been adept in the use of a combination of techniques.

In the Indian setting, multiple approaches—which are apparently contradictory in Western eyes (especially in the English-speaking world)—have been used in a complementary fashion and found effective. The combination of therapies, though eclectic, is not arbitrary. It is a planned strategy based on a developmental and holistic perspective.

The main prerequisites for such a holistic and eclectic approach are:

1. The interventions should be based on data from multiple sources—namely, case history, interview and psychological assessment of the child and the family.
2. The psychopathology must be understood from a developmental perspective in order to establish an aetiological hypothesis that subscribes to multiple causative factors of bio-psycho-social origins.
3. Intervention strategies, thus, would involve the child, family and school.
4. Known therapeutic techniques should be suitably tailored in a flexible fashion to help the child and the family, and if need be, multiple techniques must be used.
5. The techniques used would be anchored in the theoretical framework from which they are derived, yet tempered by common sense and must be suitable for the cultural milieu in question.

In the West, the psychological treatment of disorders has changed a great deal over time. The two major approaches of the 1920s and 1930s were behavioural and psychoanalytical. Play therapy emerged as an important technique of therapy in almost all the schools of thought. In the 1960s, the role of parents in therapy was seen as crucial. In most cases, individual work with the child is only part of a larger treatment programme. Parent guidance, family therapy, remediation, school consultation and/or group therapy occur concurrently with individual psychotherapy. Koocher and Broskowski (1977) point out that many types of interventions are necessary for the optimal treatment of multi-problem families. Thus, in many cases, it is actually a disservice to treat only the child.

In Western countries, even if the holistically oriented 'systems' approach is used, working with the child, the family and the school is often taken care of by different professionals forming a network.

However, in India, due to the paucity of trained professionals and financial resources, a single therapist should be prepared to carry out whatever interventions are necessary in a much less elaborate fashion. At times, a single therapist has the added advantage of coming to grips with a very complex situation and finding a simple solution because of the very nature of the holistic approach adopted. This helps to maintain the effectiveness of the therapy, since there are fewer instances of delays and inefficiency in holding together and streamlining elaborate networks.

TECHNIQUES OF THERAPY

The kind of therapy to be used is determined by the age and competencies of the child. In general, more work has to be with the caretakers of a younger child. Work with the child involves psychotherapy using verbal communication or play, adopting psycho-dynamic, behavioural or other supportive approaches. When the child's competencies are poor due to developmental delays or maturational lags, the intervention could consist of sensorimotor training, attention-enhancing training or remediation. Work with the parents could be dynamic or behavioural counselling, family therapy, structuring of the child's daily schedule, environmental manipulation at school and so on. The use of parents as co-therapists for the work to be carried on outside the clinic setting, for example, is a very efficient strategy in in-patient as well as out-patient settings in India.

Establishing a warm, therapeutic relationship with the child is a prerequisite for any kind of individual psychotherapy. There should be a good rapport between the child and the therapist. One should not talk down to the child. The therapist should be interested in the child and the child should find the relationship trustworthy and interesting. The therapist should have the ability to put himself in the child's shoes. Knowledge of development from a lifespan perspective often enables the therapist to explore developmental stressors in an intuitive fashion. What the child says or communicates through behavioural clues, reveals in play, drawing or other creative pursuits should all be seen as forms of communication and considered as important as explicit verbal communication.

Play Therapy

Though play is a universal activity of childhood, Indian parents and teachers view it as a purposeless and useless activity. However, it is one of the firmly established principles of psychology that play is very essential for the child's development process. Through play, children develop their intellectual, emotional, perceptual, motor and social skills (Schaefer and Conner, 1983). If one looks at any of the games played by children in India, one would be astounded by the abilities required in playing marbles or hopscotch, or the sensori-motor skills required to execute the traditional art of drawing *rangoli* (decorative line drawings) in front of the house in South India.

Psychologists and educators now take play very seriously and are engaged in extensive research to uncover its full potential in normal child development. Apart from promoting growth, play is also of therapeutic value to children with emotional and behavioural problems. Erikson (1963) considered playing the most natural healing process in childhood.

The therapeutic usefulness of play lies in the fact that it is a natural mode of child's self-expression. It also helps in the establishment of rapport and contact with peers since it is interesting, enjoyable and provides for a natural relationship. All this is particularly important in view of the largely passive–receptive nature of present-day so-called 'recreation', particularly TV and video.

Play has been used by many therapeutic approaches. Some of these approaches are psychoanalysis, structured therapy, relationship therapy, group therapy and behaviour therapy. Extensive use of play has been made by Klein (1937) and Anna Freud (1946) in the psychoanalytic framework. Axline's book, *Play Therapy* (1947) highlights the important steps of play therapy. With her model, it is particularly easy to initiate a novice therapist into the world of play therapy. It is also well-suited to the Indian setting. Even non-professionals can use this approach. Play can also be used in therapeutic groups.

Though not absolutely essential, it is good to have a play-therapy room. Even a play corner in an office or materials packed in a briefcase will do. For therapeutic play, selection of play material is critical. Some toys elicit self-expression, while others elicit cooperative social play (cards, checkers) and still others tend to result in isolated play (jigsaw puzzles). In general, the toys should be simple, durable (not mechanical) and capable of being adapted for different purposes. They should also be familiar and within the child's cognitive and manipulative skills. The toys generally recommended are:

1. Toys representing the child's family and physical environment: Doll house, doll family, puppets, animals, cars, trees, costumes, etc.
2. Art materials: Paints, crayons, etc.
3. Material toys or those that can be manipulated: Blocks, modelling clay, clay, water, sand, etc.
4. Special-purpose toys: Feeding bottles, kitchen sets, doctor sets, etc.

The Handbook of Play Therapy (1983) by Schaefer and Connor is an excellent sourcebook on play therapy for children with different types of disturbances.

Psychoanalysis and Psycho-dynamically Oriented Therapies

Psychoanalysis as a treatment for emotional disturbances of children can be said to have started in 1909, with the now famous case of Little Hans published by Sigmund Freud. But the real impetus for psychoanalysis with children came with the pioneering work of Anna Freud (1946) and Melanie Klein (1937). Although the basic psychoanalytic tenets are adhered to in child psychoanalysis, the special characteristics of the functioning of the mind of children at different stages of development have led to the use of special techniques. For example, free association is substituted by play. Lack of motivation to seek therapy—as the child is brought for treatment by an adult—results in the need for an introductory preparatory period, as elaborated by Anna Freud in a fascinating manner in her book, *The Psychoanalytic Study of the Child* (1946).

The age of the child is seen as an important variable, and the two necessary preconditions for therapy are that the child must have the minimum capacity for comprehension of language and that the child should be capable of verbalization. This is usually possible around children who are above two and a half years of age. The young child may at times refuse to separate from the mother.

This creates an alliance where a trusting relationship with the parent can be transferred to the therapist if necessary. The frequency and timing of the sessions is also determined by the convenience of adults. What happens in the environment, the family or the school may undermine the analysis. At such times, one may have to go out and deal with the situation directly—always, of course, with the permission of the child and the parents.

While Melanie Klein claimed psychoanalysis was useful in dealing with all conditions, Anna Freud believed that it was particularly effective in the cases of infantile neuroses. Theoretically, they differed in their approaches to certain key constructs such as transference and the way to handle it. Anna Freud accommodated the needs of children much more realistically in analysis while Klein rigidly followed the Freudian approach to interpretation of these constructs.

For example, a top of the class eight-year-old boy had suddenly stopped going to school. Exploration revealed the father whom the child hero-worshipped had sent the mother away to her parental home after a quarrel. He told the son, 'We don't need this woman any more. We men can manage.' The boy could not express his distress openly. It was suggested that perhaps the mother's return would help and she was asked to come back. Promptly, with no other treatment, the child went back to school.

As has been noted in recent years, the child's problem is linked to his temperament, family and psycho-social stressors. Dealing with the child alone in analysis often provides only partial solutions. Working directly with the child is important. In the Indian setting it is not only expedient, but also effective to practice brief dynamically oriented therapy using psychoanalytic constructs—not classical psychoanalysis—along with working with the family and school to alleviate the child's distress. In India, for the majority of families, more than 10 sessions are beyond their economic means and the manpower resources of the community.

Behaviour Modification

Behaviour modification with children dates back to John B. Watson and Rosalie Rayner's (1920) experiments with Little Albert in 1920. Yet, child behaviour therapy as a specialty has emerged only in the past four decades. Behaviour modification techniques in use with adults are anchored firmly in laboratory settings and in learning theories. Work with normal and disturbed children, however, reveals that their behaviour seems to be governed largely by the environmental settings where they are observed. Establishing a relationship between complex events in the environment and the child's specific behaviour is too complicated a process and often yields simplistic equations. There are at least three other reasons for modification of existing techniques being used with children.

These are:

1. The analysis of current behaviour, of antecedent behaviour and of consequences has to be done in the context of behaviour in natural settings. Some behaviours can be observed easily and a chain of events can be established, like in the case of temper tantrums. In other cases, such as stealing or setting fire to objects, it is hard to establish such a link.
2. Symptoms often occur in clusters, with each symptom having its own chain of events.

3. Symptoms undergo changes as the child goes through his/her lifespan, and some innocuous ones such as thumb-sucking, sleep disturbances and bed-wetting remit naturally over a period of time.

Behaviour modification techniques need to be carried out by those around the child in her/his natural setting, such as the parents and siblings at home, or teachers and peers at school. These must happen with the child's concurrence and acceptance. Thus, training significant others in the child's environment is essential, particularly in the 'here-and-now' context of what initiates and maintains a problem behaviour.

One practical suggestion is that the younger or the more severely disturbed the child (as in autistic or psychotic children), the more behavioural control has to be managed with the help of caretakers and by actual environmental manipulation. With older (those over six years of age) and more cooperative children, techniques of self-control and self-monitoring can be used effectively. In fact, by not involving the child in planning the strategy or in deciding upon reinforcements and the rationale, an older child might become resistant to the programme and fight against the suggested regimen.

Thus, the caregiver, the child and the therapist have equal roles to play. One of the crucial issues affecting the outcome of behaviour modification in childhood disorders is generalization of the learned behaviour. This is too complex a process to yield simple quantifiable results, though attempts to measure it should be made.

SOME CONCEPTS UNDERLYING BEHAVIOUR MODIFICATION

Positive reinforcement is central to solving children's behaviour problems. It is viewed in conjunction with extinction through the following logic: The parent or teacher should provide social (a smile or praise) and material (a chocolate or TV viewing time) reinforcements so that only the child's desirable behaviours are reinforced. This implies that for dealing with undesirable behaviours such as temper tantrums or aggressive behaviours, punishment (because of ethical issues) is considered only under certain conditions. Only certain forms of punishment, for example 'time-out', is used to suppress problem behaviours. These are used as temporary loss of reinforcement, contingent on the occurrence of the problem behaviour.

For example, in 'time-out', every time the child throws a temper tantrum, he is removed from the company where he throws his tantrum and sent into a room to be isolated for a brief period of 5–10 minutes, the rule of thumb being one minute per year of the child's age (a four-year-old gets four minutes). When an aggressive child hits at people, he loses the privileges (such as chocolates) he has earned through good behaviour. But it is important that these techniques should be used consistently.

Both forms of punishment should be covered by a contract drawn up by the therapist, the child and the parents at the beginning of the therapy. But punishment, when used, should be seen as a temporary measure in situations where extinction is not possible with time-out or response-cost, as one cannot ignore injurious behaviour to self (head-banging) or others (hitting or biting). Positive reinforcement always represents a stable, long-term ingredient of a successful treatment programme. Hoch's observation (1970) that Indian parents prefer methods of immediate control of children's behaviour, not taking into account the long-range objectives, must be noted in planning strategies in the Indian setting.

Behaviour modification techniques have been used very successfully for minor problems such as temper tantrums and the severe disturbances of autistic children. Whether one believes in orthodox learning principles or not, behaviour modification techniques have contributed a great deal to the effective management of behaviour problems, particularly externalizing disorders when the behaviours are disruptive. Symptom removal is carried out efficiently in many of the conditions. However, if one views the symptom as a manifestation of distress in the child in the context of his family, a dynamic understanding of symptom formation is essential. In fact, dealing with dynamic issues in symptom formation may in fact enhance the effectiveness of behaviour modification techniques in the symptom removal.

The experience in India reveals that the actual demonstration of techniques, without technical jargon, can be practised very effectively by parents belonging to lower socio-economic strata. In our experience, a combination of behavioural techniques with dynamically oriented individual and family therapy gives the best results. These can be carried out by parents from an impoverished background, be it at the clinic or at home. But the techniques have to be demonstrated and explained in simple language.

FAMILY THERAPY

Family therapy does not owe its beginnings to any single person. John Bowlby (1949) noted that problems presented by the child often reflect the tension between members of the family. The shift in theory from the individual child to the parent–child relationship and to the whole family unit is a relatively recent phenomenon in the Western context. Several workers dealing independently with the child, parents and the family and other agencies are gradually becoming disenchanted with the slow progress in finding solutions. However, in India, due to the presence of strong family ties, the family is the main unit the therapist has to work with, not by choice, but by necessity. The closely linked family system offers ideal opportunities for family therapy. For example, in the in-patient admission unit at NIMHANS, a child is always admitted together with a significant adult member, and often other relatives are also involved in therapy if it is deemed necessary by the therapist. Indian families do not require anintroduction to the idea of family therapy as the Indian psyche automatically accepts the family as a primary unit and the child as embedded in it. Family therapy is a natural and indigenous mode of intervention, making it a preferred mode of treatment in Indian society.

The majority of theories developed on the adult population apply equally to the child population. Boszormenyi-Nagy and Spat (1973) developed a conceptual framework to bridge individual psychodynamic and family therapy. It is a complex model of family dynamics, and focuses on the need for autonomy and relatedness. Many problems in the West, particularly of an inter-generational nature, may also be found at the heart of family conflicts in India. Minuchin, Baker, Rosman, et al. (1975) focused on changing the structure of the family in terms of 'enmeshment' and 'disengagement', which again are very relevant to the Indian family subsystems. Most traditional Indians are 'normally enmeshed' in their relationships. Even when the families are physically separated they could still be psychologically enmeshed. In our setting, family therapy is a preferred mode of therapy along with individual therapy with the child.

On the other hand, in the West, there are endless arguments about reconciling individual dynamic therapy with family therapy. The latter offers a briefer, more cost-effective option. It becomes imperative to effectively combine individual therapy with family therapy and also carry out marital therapy separately with the parents. This holistic approach offers the opportunity for environmental manipulation at home, in school and in the neighbourhood with the help of the family members.

Family therapy consists of the following:

1. Understanding the meaning of the presenting symptoms of the child in the family homeostasis (some kind of stability): For example, a family with multiple problems would rally round the child with problems and her symptoms to maintain an apparently stable relationship. A child who used to have fainting spells whenever her parents quarrelled, on recovery said, 'Even if I am well, when I go home they will fight,' pointing to the fact that they don't quarrel when she is ill.
2. Assessing the family schedule (daily schedules of all family members in the important interactions): This includes examples of who does what with the child.
3. Assessing the flexibility of the family structure and acceptability of alternative patterns.
4. Uncovering the family's developmental stage: Young couple with toddlers to middle-aged parents with teenaged children.
5. Analysing internal conflicts in the family and the degree of cohesion or dissociation in the family.
6. Recognizing sources of external stress and support.

Thus, family therapy is a process of understanding why the child has a symptom in a particular family context, what triggers off and maintains the symptom in that system, and how to change it by engaging the whole family.

SUPPORTIVE TECHNIQUES

Supportive techniques are the principal form of therapy in children, as their problems are yet to be crystallized. These techniques are particularly suitable for children whose symptoms interfere with treatment, who lack motivation and who are developmentally delayed, or where the environment is grossly disturbing. In terms of economy of time and resources, supportive measures do top the list of techniques. The specific techniques in use with children are: Guidance, environmental manipulation (at home and school), externalization of interests, reassurance, pressure or coercion, emotional catharsis and desensitization, psycho-education, remediation and direct suggestion or hypnosis. Even activities like helping the child with school work and going out for a walk with the child are supportive techniques. Structuring the daily schedule of the child is one of the important ways of supporting a child who is emotionally immature or has weak ego boundaries. This is particularly helpful with brain-damaged, severely disruptive, autistic or psychotic children.

Supportive techniques are best used with vulnerable and fragile children when the environment is not congenial. Supportive measures are often adjuncts to other therapies. But due to a paucity of time and personnel resources, they remain the technique of choice and are used with many of the children in out-patient therapy in India.

GROUP THERAPY

Group therapy, though essentially described as American, has its roots in religious movements, ancient Greek theatre, and group work with parents and children. Group therapy represents a broad range of psychological therapies where group processes are an essential component. Groups can comprise different diagnostic categories and can be either homogenous or heterogeneous. They may be open or closed, educational (or strongly insight-oriented) or therapeutic. The therapeutic effects may be stronger than those in individual therapy, and help can come from multiple sources. This provides a practice-ground for 'generalization' of new modes of behaviour acquired in individual therapy. One of the major advantages is that it is economical, requiring less time and fewer manpower resources. In the Indian setting, it is particularly advantageous as people are more receptive and comfortable in a group encounter. People in India are used to a community approach to healing, as seen in religious settings, in traditional healing, and even in the out-patient medical facilities.

Often, it is helpful to have a few sessions with parents in 'open' group settings, where they discuss the problems faced by them and their ways of coping with them. Such open group settings are the only possible form of group work with the majority of the parents of children who come as out-patients. On the other hand, closed groups can work effectively in an in-patient facility where the parents form a captive audience. At NIMHANS, short-term group work (of 4 to 5 sessions) in an out-patient setting has been conducted with moderate efficacy for parents of the mentally retarded, autistic, conduct-disordered children as well as for parents of children with specific learning disabilities. This generally consists of educating the parents about the nature of their children's problems, and uses the parents' own experience in effectively coping with the problems. Group work can also be carried out with adolescent patients, though the experience with this in a clinical setting is rather limited.

SCHOOL COUNSELLING

Working in the school setting is a crucial area, especially in developing countries due to the paucity of child guidance centres. The schools remain a safety net for all school-going children. Provision of child mental health, disabilities counselling and promotion of normal development is both feasible and possible as revealed in work in India by the author (Kapur, 2007).

HOLISTIC APPROACH

In India, we need to work with the child, the family and also in the school setting using multiple techniques. Aetiological speculations about the case in question need to be examined in the light of bio-psycho-social aetiologies. The strategies of management need to be tailored to suit the needs of the child in order to be effective. In India, historically, the body and mind as well as the child and the family are seen as a single unit. This makes it possible for the therapist to combine the techniques and use them effectively at different levels. Figure 6.1 gives an overview of the various disorders caused in the different developmental phases by aetiological factors.

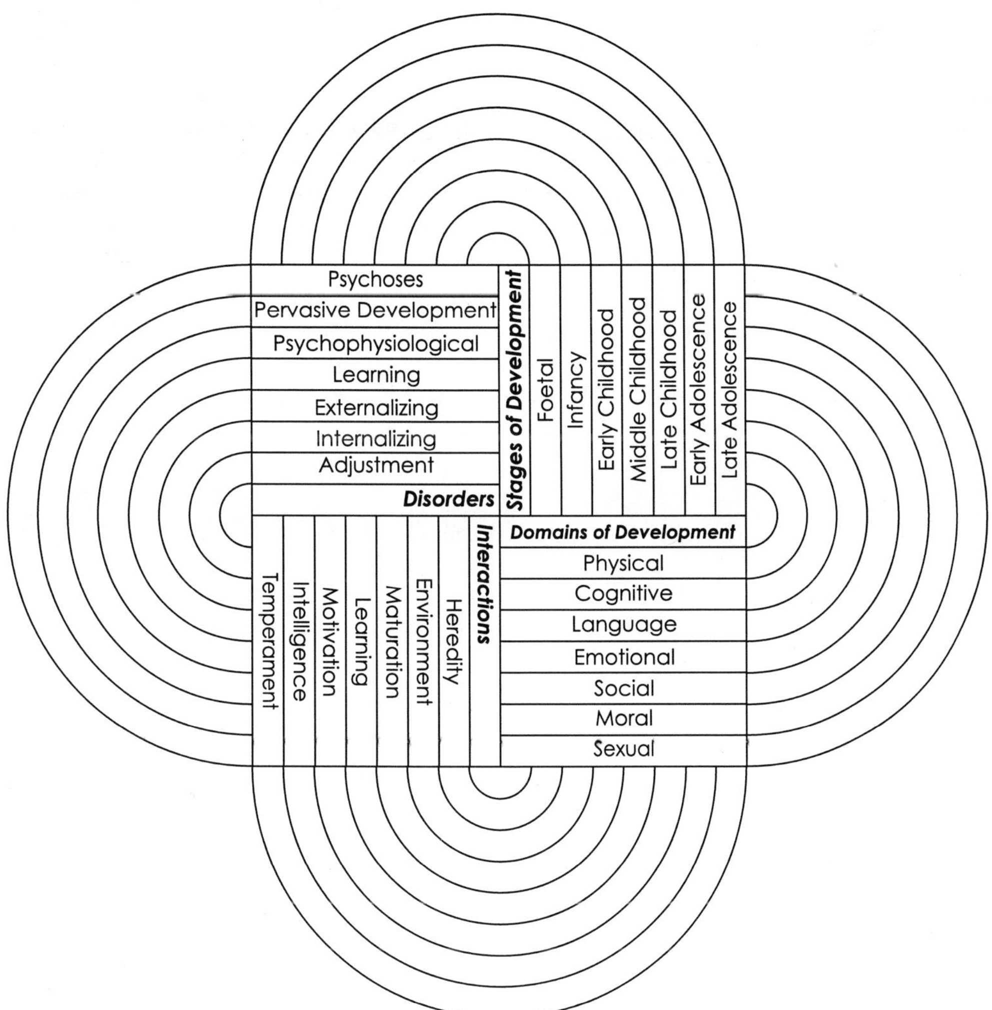

Figure 6.1 A complex interaction: disorders caused by aetiological factors in different developmental phases

ECLECTIC APPROACH

The above approaches seem to indicate that you should be an expert in a specific technique. Children are creative in their thinking and sometimes, they suggest the technique. One of my children would take up a toy telephone and call me up to say a lot of things. He would never talk to me directly, always using the toy telephone to speak to me. This was his medium of communication. Another child would simply write things in a big diary.

Different children adopt play, mutual story-telling, and/or games of radio stations, storybooks and telephones for their communication with the therapist. The child decides the technique and the therapist should follow. You put paper, colours, and a lot of toys in front of the child. The child takes the decision as to how she/he wants to communicate with the therapist. Verbal techniques hardly ever work with younger children. Older children may choose to talk about a problem but not younger children. The therapist's personal style is also very important. She/he has to be affectionate and able to relate to the child. This means that you sit on the ground with the child, spread things around and play with them. Thus, a developmental, holistic and eclectic approach holds the key to effective psychological therapy with children.

Psychological therapies in India are primarily guided by the needs of the family, the child's preferred mode of communication, the therapist's personality, the developmental context and the nature of intrinsic variables in the child like psychopathology, cognitive potential and temperament. Thus, the selected techniques need to be developmental, holistic and eclectic in order to be effective.

PART

Psychological Disorders

CHAPTER

7

Specific Developmental Delays and Disorders

Before beginning with sections on various disorders, it is perhaps worthwhile to examine some of the problems that occur during the course of the child's development. Children may normally present the parents with problems that are typically present in different phases and in different domains of development—for example, in toilet training, eating, sleeping, etc. Some achieve these tasks easily with little help from parents while others may be resistant and take a much longer time, causing much friction between the parents and the child. Or, if the child is not up to the mark as compared to other children of the same age, these may be termed *developmental delays*.

There are some other problems that present typically at different developmental phases but are considered disorders as they do not normally occur in all children but only in some of them. These include tics, mannerisms, odd habits and breath-holding spells which also have their onset in childhood. Although these difficulties may wane as the child grows up, they can be exceedingly distressing to the child and parents if they persist. These are termed *developmental disorders*.

DEVELOPMENTAL DELAYS

The first group of problems is specific delays in development. Childhood development is characterized by individual differences. Children differ a great deal in achieving age-appropriate skills in motor coordination, speech and language development. In addition, socio-cultural differences too play a major role. Girls and boys differ in attaining these skills. There may be an overlap between developmental problems and delays in development. For example, prolonged bed-wetting or daytime wetting may be associated with delayed bladder control. The important aspect to note is that children eventually outgrow these problems. Prompt treatment helps the child and the family to cope with the problem effectively and prevent the emergence of future problems stemming from the deficits.

PROBLEMS OF EATING/FEEDING

The more severe kinds of eating disorders such as failure to thrive, anorexia and bulimia have been dealt with in Chapter 11. The present section focuses on day-to-day eating problems in children which may or may not be encountered in psychiatric clinics as a presenting complaint. A counsellor needs to know about the normal development of feeding skills, physical and developmental causes of deviations and the management of these problems.

Prevalence of Feeding Problems

Estimates based on reports from a variety of settings suggest that 25–35 per cent of children have recognizable or reportable eating or feeding problems. These have been classified under several schemes. Linschid (1983), for example, gives a simple yet extensive system of classification:

1. Meal-time problems
2. Bizarre food habits
3. Multiple food dislikes
4. Prolonged subsistence on puréed or finely mashed food
5. Difficulty or delay in sucking or swallowing
6. Delay in self-feeding
7. Pica (eating non-edibles such as mud, dirt, plaster from the walls)
8. Overeating (bulimia)[1]
9. Undereating (anorexia)[1]
10. Rumination

The major causes for these problems could be behavioural mismanagement at home, neuromotor dysfunction, mechanical obstruction, and medical and genetic abnormalities. Behavioural mismanagement alone could be the main cause in all of them except for delay in sucking or chewing. For example, difficulty in chewing or sucking may lead to a demand for puréed food. Delay in self-feeding may be due to parental over-indulgence or poor motor coordination in early childhood. Genetic or medical abnormalities could cause bizarre food habits, pica, over-eating, under-eating and rumination. Contributions from the child in terms of difficult temperament, or biological reasons for the problem or even parental mismanagement needs to be examined in each individual child.

A study in India by Uma and Kapur (1990) screened 50 urban and 100 rural preschool children for behaviour disorders. They reported no significant differences between boys and girls, poor appetite being present in 2 per cent of the urban and 7 per cent of the rural children, and food fads in 20 per cent of the urban and 23 per cent of rural children. This study indicates a lower prevalence than suggested by Western studies, particularly in the rural settings.

The normal feeding pattern in infancy and childhood is often culturally determined. In the Western setting, infants are weaned from a liquid diet between the ages of four to six months, while in a traditional Indian home, the weaning is done at 10–12 months of age. Weaning from the breast in the rural areas and from the bottle in the urban areas is delayed, leading to resistance to giving up breast or bottle in children of two to five years of age. Self-feeding is often discouraged in the middle and upper class, and in a poor home the child learns to feed himself. Often feeding difficulties are

1. Overeating and undereating appear later, around puberty, and not in early childhood.

not considered as problems and are accepted more easily in Indian homes, though these may be very distressing to the mother.

In the psychoanalytic framework, the 'oral phase' is an important stage of development, and problems at this stage are linked to problems in adult life. Anna Freud (1946) suggested different levels of conflicts involved in feeding problems. At the first level, the problem could be due to organic changes or defects. At the second level, poor intake could be related to emotional factors when eating is seen as a chore rather than a pleasurable activity (this is mainly due to unhealthy interaction between the mother and the child). At the third level, difficulties with food become internalized and are present even in the absence of the mother. In addition, when one describes behavioural lines, the focus is again on the interaction between the child and the caretaker. For example, the child who is capable of feeding himself is fed by the mother, or she expects the child to eat more than what she/he can cope with, or she gives in to her/his unreasonable demands, or the mother pays too much attention to problem behaviour in the child. Often, the mother's behaviour is associated with her anxiety about the child's food intake. The more she insists, the more likely it is that the child becomes fussy. The child might also imitate the fussy behaviour of those around him.

Children between the age of four and six months are generally more amenable to the introduction of new foods and solids, and the period between seven and 10 months is critical for learning to eat different types of food, self-feeding and regular schedules of eating. If carried out without much anxiety and over-expectation, the child is likely to develop into a normal feeder. Initial refusal does not mean that the child will always refuse a new type of food. Generally, it is possible to strike a balance between a nutritionally balanced diet and what the child likes to eat. At the end of the first year, the child's appetite normally declines and starts to improve again around the time the child goes to school. Inexperienced mothers may expect continuity of the pattern of increasing food intake which occurs in the first year.

The assessment of feeding problems consists of checking on medical and nutritional problems, learning about the child's food preferences, her/his current intake of food, and an analysis of eating-related behaviours. Children can often say what food they like and what they do not. Food intake is to be checked only if there is weight loss; otherwise, consistency or minimal gain in weight is expected in the growth chart. Finally, all the aspects of difficult feeding behaviours—including how long it has lasted, and how the mother responds to it—have to be noted down before planning the treatment.

PROBLEMS OF SLEEP

A commonly used expression is 'sleeping like a baby'. Yet many a harried parent would contest it, having been kept awake night after night by their infants. Sleep disturbance in children is fairly common and has to be viewed from different perspectives.

1. The physiology of sleep is different in children as compared to adults.
2. The parents may have a mistaken notion as to how the child should sleep or may themselves be poor sleepers. They may in fact awaken the child or believe that the child is awake, or they may be inexperienced about the sleep needs of the child.

3. The parents may create an environment where the child cannot sleep properly, such as giving caffeinated drinks, having the TV and other sources of noise on, keeping the lights on and playing or talking to the child whenever he wakes up and similar other disruptive activities.

Infants spend approximately half of their sleep time in rapid eye movement (REM) and their non-rapid eye movement (NREM) cycles are much shorter than the 90-minute cycle seen in adults. In the first few days of life, an infant sleeps 16–17 hours a day, and by the sixth month, the average sleeping hours are between 13 and 14. By the first year, 90 per cent of infants settle for sleeping five hours at a stretch. At times they tend to sleep through the night. Younger children need one daytime nap apart from the usual sleep, and this need gradually disappears by the time the child goes to school.

Different kinds of sleep disorders may occur in children. Some of the common ones are sleep-walking, sleep terrors, nightmares, sleep-talking, sleep-rocking, head-banging and sleep bruxism (teeth grinding). These are generally believed to be related to the maturation of the nervous system and tend to disappear as the child grows older. Often, several of these problems may occur together, and there may be a family history of similar problems. It is necessary to alleviate parental anxiety and to check if the episodes are associated with distressing events in the child's life. In night terrors, the child does not remember what frightened her/him, while in nightmares she may recall the dream. Recurrent nightmares may be associated with emotional problems. At times, bed-wetting may be associated with sleep disturbances. Head-banging and teeth grinding are often self-limiting and tend to disappear as the child grows older. Sometimes excessive sleep may occur, particularly in adolescence. Sleep-related breathing disorders could be due to mechanical obstruction of air passageways or certain medical conditions such as asthma. A fatal condition, namely, the sudden infant death syndrome (SIDS), is thought to be related to sudden cessation of breathing. Such short episodes occur in young infants but infants generally recover from them.

In a study of a sample of 150 normal preschoolers in India, 14 per cent of the urban and 6 per cent of the rural children had difficulty in settling in the evening (Uma and Kapur, 1990). Waking up at night was significantly higher in 34 per cent of the rural children when compared to 12 per cent of the urban children. In 20 per cent of the urban and 14 per cent of the rural sample, children slept along with their parents. Rural mothers also soothed the children who were awakened during the night.

Thus, it is necessary to look into the effect of the sleep disturbance on the daily schedule of the child and the effect of daily events on the sleep pattern of the child. For example, merely re-enacting the exciting events of the day through sleep-talking and walking has no pathological significance, while the same symptom in relation to severe punishment by a teacher can be significant. Thus, it is necessary to know the background factors which cause sleep problems, whether they are related to child–parent interaction or environment. Further, it is important to remember that the pattern of sleep may change, particularly during adolescence.

Though many of the sleep-related problems disappear in time, some methods can help a child who is a poor sleeper:

1. Pre-bed routine with some bedtime rituals, such as telling stories, saying a prayer, etc., may help the child feel less anxious and help her/him to settle down to sleep.

2. Bedtime demands such as 'go to sleep', may make the child more anxious than when a parent gives a picture or story book and allows the child to relax and go to sleep.
3. Regular bedtime is helpful, preferably going to bed early and having a full quota of sleep by the morning. Indian parents generally allow children to stay up very late and sleep when they themselves go to sleep.
4. A light snack and milk, but not chocolates or caffeinated drinks, is helpful.
5. Daytime naps induce decreased sleep in the night and need to be discouraged in an older child.
6. Environmental factors such as TV, bright lights, or a crowded room are also not helpful in inducing sleep for a child with sleep problems.

PROBLEMS OF TOILET TRAINING

The mastery of bowel and bladder control is a major milestone in the physical and social development of children. Approximately 25 per cent of all four-year-olds are enuretics (wetting in clothes) (Cohen, 1975) and 3 per cent are encopretic (soiling in clothes) (Levine, 1975), while some are constipated (withholding stool). By the age of 36 months, most children achieve bowel and bladder control, although occasional accidents occur till five years of age (Simonds, 1977).

Uma and Kapur (1990), in a sample of 150 preschoolers in India, reported 24 per cent frequency of wetting in the night in urban children and 26 per cent in rural children, while daytime wetting was 2 per cent and 5 per cent for the urban and rural children, respectively. This is suggestive of early daytime continence in Indian children in the age range of two years and ten months to three years and eight months. In India, some children may be considered toilet-trained by the mothers even when the bladder control is simply a habit training by the mother rather than the child understanding the concept.

Brazelton (1962) has implicated coercive toilet training in the development of encopresis and enuresis. Quite often, inexperienced parents have unrealistic expectations about toilet training. Occasional wetting up to the age of six to eight years need not be considered as a problem. Central to the task of toilet training is the concept of readiness. Brazelton has suggested several physiological and psychological criteria.

Physiological readiness criteria include:

- Reflex sphincter control
- Myelinization of pyramidal tracts, which is completed between 12 and 18 months

More important and obvious ones are the psychological criteria, which include:

- Established motor milestones of sitting and walking
- Understanding of verbal communication
- Desire to please the adults whom the child loves
- Imitation of the behaviour of important persons in the child's life
- Wish to be independent and control primitive impulses: This readiness appears to be at the peak in most children between 18 and 30 months.

Some behavioural packages, such as those by Azrin and Foxx (1974), have been suggested for rapid and effective training, while Brazelton (1962) suggested a package which takes much longer. These methods consisted of personally training the child and training the mothers to train the children. But these methods assume that bladder training occurs automatically, along with bowel training. This section focuses more on helping older children with problems of bladder and bowel control than young children who tend to respond normally to gentle persuasion of the parents when they are physiologically and psychologically ready.

Enuresis

Wetting may occur during the day or night , and it can be persistent or may occur in the absence of urological, neurological and psychological causes beyond the age when most children are dry (McKendry and Stewart, 1974). Approximately 40 per cent of children wet the bed at three years of age, 22 per cent at 5 years, 10 per cent at 10 years and 3 per cent at 15 years of age (Binderglas, 1975). When a child has been enuretic from an early age, such enuresis is considered 'primary', while if the child starts wetting after being continent over a period of time, such enuresis is called secondary.

A positive family history of enuresis among family members of enuretic children has been frequently noted. Enuresis is generally self-limiting with a spontaneous cure rate of 12–15 per cent per year on each subsequent year (Binderglas, 1975). A number of factors have been reported as causes, including food allergies, deep sleep, small bladder capacity, developmental delays and faulty training (Cohen, 1975; McKendry and Stewart, 1974; Simonds, 1977). There is a general agreement that enuresis is not primarily a psychopathological disorder. However, secondary emotional and behaviour disorders may develop as a result of being enuretic.

In India, Kishore (1988) compared 30 primary enuretics to normal controls in the age range of five to 16 years. He found a significant family history of enuresis, presence of soft neurological signs and reduced functional bladder control in these children. Pathological child-rearing practices, characterized by over protectiveness and dominance, were found to be significantly high in the families of enuretic children. In another Indian study by Agarwal, Saksena, and Singh (1978) of enuretics in the age range of four to six years, primary enuresis was reported in 60 per cent of children, with 88.8 per cent being nocturnal. Forty per cent of the sample had a family history of enuresis. There were significant developmental delays and stress in early childhood, such as parental ill-health, conflicts and sibling rivalry. The enuretics also had higher frequency of temper tantrums when compared to the normal controls.

It can be seen that in primary and secondary enuretics, certain measures used for management are common, while secondary enuretics require more intensive individual and family counselling. These methods combine behavioural, psychodynamic and family-oriented approaches.

The management of enuresis consists of the following steps:

1. In primary and secondary enuresis, medical problems must first be ruled out, especially if there is dribbling or burning while passing urine.
2. Family history of enuresis should be checked. The period when bladder control was achieved by the family members should be established and the information should be used to reassure the child and the family.

3. It should be checked whether the parents or siblings ridicule or get angry with the child. In case they do, they should be dissuaded from doing so.
4. Advise the family to give the child the last meal of the day late in the evening rather than at night (as most Indian families have late dinners), give non-spicy food to withhold fluid intake after dinner and get the child to void at least twice before he goes to bed. In addition, the child should be awakened a little before he usually wets the bed in the night. You can also set up an alarm for an older child.
5. Advise several bladder training exercises for the child especially during the day, such as checking the time gap between voiding and gradually increasing the intervals slowly over a few weeks. Also encourage the child to control the urine midstream to gain better bladder control.

If wetting is secondary, exploration into various psychosocial stressors at home, school or with peers should be carried out. Events which frighten the child or stress during the day may lead to bed-wetting at night. Some children may react to the parents' compulsion for cleanliness with wetting. Counsel the parents, reassure them and explain how ridicule or punitive measures worsen the problems instead of curing them. With younger as well as older children, rewards for dry nights play an important role, for example maintaining a daily chart, where a 'star' is given for dry nights and a certain number of stars entitles the child to a reinforcement of his/her choice (a chocolate, an outing or even a smile and praise for an older child or an adolescent). However, as a rule, accidental wetting should be ignored by parents. The approach should be that of encouragement, which helps the child to regain his/her self-esteem. Pharmacological treatment is recommended in resistant cases, particularly in adolescents. In Western countries, several gadgets, such as a bell and pad are used, but in the Indian setting, the above-described eclectic approach works effectively.

Constipation and Encopresis (Soiling)

Chronic constipation and soiling in children from an early age is related to (*a*) insufficient roughage or bulk in the diet; (*b*) insufficient water intake in diet; and (*c*) excess intake of milk and milk products. These lead to constipation and the situation grows worse when defecation becomes painful and the child tends to withhold. Change of diet and increased physical activity in terms of games and exercises instead of reading and watching TV are also helpful. Ridiculing when accidental soiling occurs should be avoided, but the child may be requested to clean his/her clothes. With the majority of children, a better diet consisting of green leafy vegetables, fruits and honey (which have natural laxative effects), butter and oil (which have lubricating effect) and intake of about 10 glasses of fluid (other than milk) often help in reducing constipation. If these measures fail to reduce the problem, medical advice should be sought regarding the use of laxatives, enema or suppositories. The child should be praised when successful voiding of the bowels occurs in the toilet. The school-going child should get up an hour before he is ready to leave the house and be asked to sit in the toilet for five minutes and then again after breakfast so that a routine schedule is set up for voiding the bowels. In addition, at the approximate time when encopresis usually occurs, the child should be asked to sit in the toilet.

When encopresis is secondary, i.e., it occurs in a child who was toilet-trained earlier, it is often associated with emotional disturbance, particularly of passive–aggressive nature towards the adults in the child's life. Young children when severely disturbed, such as a child who is sent to an orphanage where there is no emotional support, might start passing stools indiscriminately anywhere. This may also happen in an older child, where parents or teachers are punitive and over-expecting and the child is too docile to retaliate. But these conflicts are at an unconscious level and are not deliberate, though the parents may believe them to be so. In these cases, dynamically oriented individual and family therapy should supplement the methods described earlier for chronic problems of constipation or incontinence.

SEXUAL PROBLEMS

Children display a variety of sexual interests as they grow into adulthood. Yet, what is normal in a child may be perceived by the adults around him as socially undesirable and even repugnant. This section is aimed at dispelling some misconceptions that Indian parents harbour about a child's interest in sexual activities.

Masturbation

This is a normal developmental phase which involves playing with the genitalia in a habitual fashion. When it occurs in young children, parents and teachers may view it as a predictor of promiscuity in adulthood. Reassurance that it is normal and not indicative of pathology needs to be communicated in the Indian setting. It is also necessary to educate the mothers about hygiene of the genitalia, as irritation due to infection or poor hygiene can also lead to manipulation of genitalia. The advice to ignore the problem generally seems to enable parents to cope better. However, on occasions, pathological or excessive masturbation may occur in a child who is under-stimulated, or at times isolated in a very uncongenial environment fraught with strife. In general, whether in a normal child or in an under-stimulated child, masturbation should be dealt with by enrichment of the environment. If the child can indulge in interesting activities, preferably with other children, the tendency to self-stimulate, to relax through thumb-sucking or masturbation, is automatically reduced. During adolescence, masturbation is a rule rather than an exception. Parents and teachers need to be educated regarding normal processes of masturbation in boys and girls and night emission in boys. In Indian society, masturbation is associated with several misconceptions, for example that it produces weakness of the body and the brain, impotence, madness, poor concentration and memory.

Homosexuality

Interest in a partner of the same sex can also be viewed as a passing phase. In some youngsters, this happens in hostels and residential institutions. Some adolescents may 'seduce' to gain control over the others. Indulging in homosexual activity is perceived as a very offensive activity, particularly in residential homes and hostels, and may lead to very unpleasant consequences when handled by punitive adults. The staff of the institutions, teachers and parents need education as well as reassurance about the innocuousness of the problem and the need to deal with it in a caring and compassionate manner.

Heterosexual Activities

Heterosexual activities in youngsters are frowned upon by society in India, be it in the home or at school. In fact, it is a ticklish issue for a mental health professional as the parents are correct in their need to protect their children who are financially and emotionally dependent on them. Whether Indian adolescents are mature enough to handle the problems which arise out of heterosexual relations is a major concern. An unwed mother or an adolescent who wants to live in with her/his companion, does not have the institutional support available nowadays to their Western counterparts. Being dependent on the parents makes the adolescent answerable to them in various matters. From an authoritarian, orthodox perspective, where as a rule marriages are arranged by the family, the issue is too complex to lend itself to simplistic solutions.

There are several, other, known psychopathological disorders in the adult classificatory systems but these are not part of psychological development and have to be considered independently as sexual disorders. In addition, sexual abuse of children and incest are some of the social issues which need to be looked at in the context of the Indian society, provided there are remedial measures to counter them.

TICS, HABITS AND MANNERISMS

There are transient developmental problems which disappear in adulthood. These are tics, La Tourette's disorder, movement disorders such as voluntary banging of head, rocking, repetitive movement of hands or arms, and habits such as breath-holding, nail-biting, thumb-sucking, hair-pulling, teeth-grinding and so on. Tics are sudden, brisk, non-purposeful but recurrent muscle spasms such as blinking, nodding, grimacing, clearing the throat, shrugging, etc. They are often automatic and are not consciously carried out, though they can be consciously controlled for short durations. Azrin and Nunn (1977) indicated the prevalence of tics in children as being between one and five per cent. They are common in children between the ages of eight and 10 years and occur more in males than in females (a ratio of 3:1). Spontaneous recovery occurs in 50 per cent of the population. The causes for tics include increased attention from others for certain movements and increased stress. Genetic or familial factors also play an important role, for example, in children with special status in the family. At times, tics may start when a child imitates others who have tics. The treatment consists of behavioural techniques such as operant conditioning, negative practice and habit reversal, and also psychodynamic therapy. In some cases, pharmacological therapy is recommended.

La Tourette's Disorder

Although the prevalence of this is extremely low, this disorder is one of the widely publicized disorders in the West because of its unusual presentation. It is a chronic tic on the face and body, accompanied by shouting obscenities or making strange noises such as barking. It occurs mostly in males, with the male to female ratio being 5.6:1. Though Tourette's disorder has generally been considered a neurotic disorder, it is now believed to be caused by abnormal catecholamine metabolism and genetic factors, although stress, emotional disturbance or fatigue can precipitate as well as exacerbate the symptoms. Yet, it must be pointed out that extreme bizarreness, the symbolic nature and variations in the symptomatology are suggestive of a combination of tic and conversion disorders of psychogenic origin. Behavioural, psychodynamic and pharmacological treatments for this disorder have been suggested.

Stereotyped Movement Disorders

Breath-holding, head-banging, rocking, repetitive hand movements as self-stimulatory or self-injurious behaviour can occur in psychotic and retarded children. These occur in 15–20 per cent of the very young children and usually disappear by 30–36 months of age. They are 3.5 times more common in boys. The symptoms persist when there is under-stimulation, emotional deprivation and aggression directed against the infant. Brain damage and developmental delays are contributory factors in many of the cases. Environmental manipulation and provision of a congenial and stimulating environment and operant conditioning techniques are effective in treating these problems.

Breath-holding Spells

Breath-holding spells can occur in very young children and consist of holding the breath for approximately 30 seconds. They may last longer, and on occasions result in twitches and unconsciousness. They can be very frightening for the parents, especially if the child turns blue or becomes stiff. This is a common, though not a dangerous condition. It occurs between the age of six months and four years, and disappears by the time the child is six when the period of violent crying generally ends. It occurs equally in boys and girls who are tense and active (Simmons, 1977). Such spells are a learned response, generally preceded by violent crying so as to manipulate the parents to yield to the child's demands. It often indicates an overwhelming rage when something is denied. Because of the alarming nature of the symptoms, parents generally yield to the demands of the child, thus, reinforcing the behaviour. There is generally a family history of breath-holding. In a newborn, breath-holding occurs due to constitutional factors.

Srinath, Vinutha, and Indiramma (1992), in a study of 20 breath-holders in the Indian setting, found 75 per cent of the episodes in one–two-year-olds; 90 per cent of the children had normal development. Eight-five per cent of children were last in the order of birth. On routine follow-up after six months, 70 per cent had recovered fully and 25 per cent were better than before.

The treatment for breath-holding consists of teaching the parents to ignore the symptom and help the child to develop greater frustration tolerance. Parents need reassurance about the non-fatal nature of this behaviour, which has few, if any, long-term consequences. With young children, distracting their attention by introducing something interesting may also prevent an attack from occurring.

Thumb-sucking and Nail-biting

These are the most common problems in children, present equally in boys and girls. Thumb-sucking has its onset between three to four months of age. Forty-five per cent of all two-year-olds indulge in thumb-sucking, and gradually it reduces to about 21 per cent in six-year-olds, and to 5 per cent in 11-year-olds. There is a consensus among researchers that it is an innocuous habit, and contrary to the general belief, it is not harmful psychologically or otherwise. It can be stopped by behavioural techniques and by providing a stimulating environment. The positive role of thumb-sucking in soothing the child before going to sleep or when disturbed should not be overlooked.

Nail-biting occurs around the age of four, and the highest incidence of nail-biting is around adolescence. It is generally considered a tension-reducing activity with no special association with any psychopathological disorder. The most commonly used behavioural treatment is shaping.

Hair-pulling

It is a rare condition but can be distressing to the child and others. Its prevalence is less than 1 per cent in the psychiatric population. It may start between one and five years of age and may persist till adolescence. Eighty to 85 per cent of patients are females. The behaviour is episodic, occurring only during periods of stress (Bakwin and Bakwin, 1972). Severe hair loss due to hair-pulling is considered pathological and is seen as aggression against oneself and others. Behavioural and psychodynamic therapies are often used effectively in this condition. It may also present as a symptom in an obsessive–compulsive spectrum disorder.

SPECIFIC DEVELOPMENTAL DELAYS IN SPEECH AND LANGUAGE

A developmental language disorder exists when there is a deficiency in *expressing* or *understanding* verbal communication which is not primarily due to mental retardation, hearing loss or defects in peripheral oral mechanism (such as the cleft palate). Language is a symbolic system used for communication, while speech is the product of oral movement resulting in articulation of sounds to express words to communicate thoughts. Speech and language may both be impaired or just language or just speech may be impaired. Development of speech and language occurs at specific stages of development.

- Six months: Cries and babbles
- Eight to nine months: Speaks a word or two
- One-and-a-half years: A few words and short sentences
- Two to three years: Achieves fairly normal speech

In some children, who may otherwise be normal, only speech delay may be present. Some may start speaking only at four years of age, yet grow up to have normal fluency. Thus, it is important to establish whether *comprehension* of spoken language is age appropriate. If the child can understand simple as well as complex instructions, the delay in the expression of language may not lead to severe problems later.

Speech Disorders

Speech disorders include articulation difficulties and stuttering or stammering. These can occur in normal young children as a part of the developmental process. Yet, persistence of these beyond the age of six to seven years needs to be seen as a problem. Both of these problems respond effectively to speech retraining. Stammering can occur in brief spells when the child starts to speak and usually disappears if ignored but can become a persistent pattern if the adults respond to it with anxiety. However, stammering which starts suddenly in an older child under stressful conditions or after imitating someone can become persistent and create psychological problems secondary to it.

Stammering occurs in 1 per cent of the population and mostly in boys. Speech and language problems are known to occur particularly in children who are left-handed and are forced to become right-handed. Stuttering is related to faulty learning, anxiety and neurological dysfunction. A late onset of stammering may be indicative of deeper conflicts. Referral to a speech therapist is helpful in removing the symptoms and helps the child to return to normal social interaction. Unlike many of the other habit disorders, stammering may not remit in the course of time. Hence, it is imperative that the child should undergo speech retraining if the problem persists.

Language Disorders

Language disorders include specific delay in language development (both expressive and receptive), echolalia (repetition of the words and phrases spoken by others), autistic communication and elective mutism. Aetiological speculations on language disorders range from high familial incidence (Fennuci, 1978) to atypical cerebral lateralization (Kinsbourne and Hiscock, 1978), specifically impairment of left-hemisphere functions, as suggested by Heilman (1978). Language disorders are reported in approximately 8 per cent of white middle-class children and a higher incidence is reported in the lower socio-economic strata (Ludlow, 1980).

Echolalia occurs in retarded and autistic children, but transient occurrence of echolalia when children begin to speak is considered normal. Persistent echolalia is a manifestation of language disorder.

A close association has been reported between language disorders and hyperkinesis, specific learning disabilities and some disorders of neurological origin such as epilepsy. Detailed speech and language assessment and remediation may help these children. In a younger child, developmental language assessment may not be as complex as in a school-going child, where reading and writing skills become part of the linguistic system.

In India, 30 language-delayed and 30 normal children from ages three to nine years and matched for sex and age were studied in-depth by Prabha Chandra (1987). In the clinic group, there was a higher incidence of inadequate stimulation and communication and special ordinal position, with 43.3 per cent being the 'only' child. The language-delayed group had significantly more peri-natal problems and associated problems of hyperactivity, clumsiness and poor school achievement. All the 30 children of the clinic group had receptive and expressive language defects (76.6 per cent had both, while 23.3 per cent had only expressive disorder). Delay in motor development (clumsiness), and reading and writing problems were found in 56.6 per cent.

SPECIFIC DELAY IN MOTOR DEVELOPMENT

In children with language delay, hyperactivity and specific learning disabilities, minimal brain dysfunction or a certain degree of maturational lag have been hypothesized as causes. These may be manifested in neurological soft signs, electroencephalogram (EEG) abnormalities and so on. These children may be clumsy, with poor fine-motor coordination and gait disturbance. Presence of signs of immaturity of the nervous system has implications for intervention, which consists essentially of remediation to strengthen the deficit areas by training in those skills. Principles of remediation are common to all the spheres of specific developmental delays, whether they overlap or not.

Developmental problems and developmental delays are unique to childhood and adolescence and may be transient in many cases. However, mismanagement by the families may lead to long-lasting consequences while appropriate care may facilitate normal development. For example, a young child with minimal delays in motor coordination and speech and language development may not be able to achieve normal development if parents are over-protective or impatient and do all the chores themselves around the child, such as feeding, bathing and even carrying the child. In India and perhaps in other Asian countries, as one-child families are becoming common, over-protectiveness is considered an acceptable sort of parenting. This difficulty delays or compromises the skill acquisition of the child.

De Souza, Kapoor, Jagtap, and Sen (2007) studied the prevalence of enuresis amongst 1,473 primary school children in Mumbai, India. The overall prevalence was 7.61 per cent and it was more in boys. About 28.57 per cent had a family history of enuresis. Causes are seen as many. The interplay of psychological and physical factors was seen and it was suggested that interventions should be multi-pronged.

SUMMARY

Delays or disorders may occur during different phases in the development of children in various domains. The delays that occur in normal development may not persist and become disorders. But there may also be disorders that occur at different phases of development. These, too, may or may not persist but can be very distressing to the child and the family alike. The important aspect to remember is that children vary enormously in their rate of development as these problems are linked to the maturity of the nervous system. When there is a delay that persists and the child does not catch up with his/her age mates, there is a need for intervention as in the case of a disorder.

CHAPTER

Learning Disorders

INTRODUCTION

Child mental health problems or psychological disorders in children have received scant attention in Asian countries, despite the concern parents and teachers have expressed for their wards. This poses an even greater challenge as children form half the population. As the developing nations strive towards universal primary education, the task of promoting healthy psycho-social development of children remains a daunting one. Teachers have become a focal point on whom much of the hopes for the future generation are pinned, especially by parents from disadvantaged backgrounds who can hardly fulfil these expectations themselves. It is obvious that they need to understand the normal and abnormal development of the children, but this has not been recognized by professionals in the fields of education and mental health.

The school system and the parents appear to be content in dealing solely with the educational achievement of their wards. Scholastic backwardness is a major preoccupation of the teachers, the parents and the children alike but no professional help is offered to the school children, except the gruelling and unhealthy long hours put into what are termed as 'tuitions', especially in the urban schools.

The ignorance of what in the long run promotes or hampers the child's growth and development is appalling. Scholastic backwardness or learning disorders are simply viewed as the children's deliberate neglect, lack of motivation and poor discipline. Learning disorders have been least understood by the teachers, the parents and the clinicians alike.

Whether learning disorders reflect the basic lack of intellectual potential of the child needs to be examined carefully. Low intelligence or intellectual disability (mental retardation), which is present at birth is the cause only in a very small percentage of the population, whereas learning disorders have a much greater prevalence. The terms 'learning disorders' and 'intellectual disability' are often used interchangeably in countries like the United Kingdom, leading to further confusion. Measurement of the intelligence quotient through psychological tests to label a child has been a contentious issue in the Western world, leading to legal, ethical, economic and educational problems.

The term 'learning disability' has emerged from the need to identify and serve the children who continuously fail at school, yet are not mentally retarded. In 1905, Witmer's case of a child with learning problems in fact heralded the specialized discipline of Clinical Psychology. Since then,

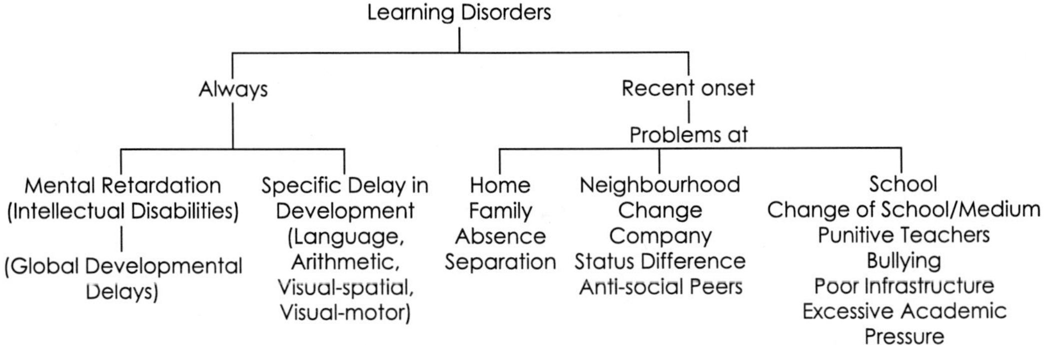

Figure 8.1 Factors that lead to learning disorders

the concept has undergone distinct phases of development. In the early 1940s, these children were described as 'brain injured' as they shared defects similar to those seen in adult brain-injured war veterans. In the 1960s, the term Minimal Brain Dysfunction (MBD) was introduced as the brain lesions that were implicated earlier were in fact found to be absent. Figure 8.1 explains the factors that lead to learning disorders.

BROAD AND NARROW DEFINITIONS

Learning disorders have been identified by Grossman (1978) as anything that interferes with the students' learning. This could be mental retardation, perceptual handicaps, neurological dysfunction or immaturity, behavioural difficulties, socio-cultural disadvantages and a host of other problems. This definition highlights the complex factors which play a role in causing scholastic backwardness. Other definitions are narrower in scope. For example, the National Advisory Committee on Handicapped Children USA (1968) defines it as follows:

> Children with special learning disabilities exhibit a disorder in one or more basic psychological processes in understanding or using spoken words and written languages. These may be manifested in disorders of listening, thinking, talking, reading, writing, spelling or mathematics. These include conditions referred to as perceptual handicaps, brain injury, minimal brain dysfunction, dyslexia, developmental aphasia, etc. They do not include learning problems which are primarily due to visual, hearing or motor handicaps, mental retardation, emotional disturbances or environmental disadvantage.

Young and Tyre (1983) describe it as a disorder in children who, despite conventional classroom experience, fail to attain the language skills of reading, writing and spelling commensurate with their intellectual abilities. In the International Classificatory System (ICD-10), the classification of learning disorder has the following codes and categories:

F.81	Specific developmental disorders of scholastic skills
F.81.0	Specific reading disorder

F.81.1	Specific spelling disorder
F.81.2	Specific disorder of arithmetical skills
F.81.3	Mixed disorder of scholastic skills
F.81.8	Other developmental disorders of scholastic skills

In the American diagnostic classificatory system under the DSM-IV, unlike the ICD-10, the category codes for childhood disorders are mixed with adult disorders. This can be confusing as the childhood disorders do not merit their own diagnostic classificatory system. For example, writing disorder is 315.2, learning disorder is 315.9, mathematics disorder 315.1 and reading disorder is 315. In fact, the specific mathematics disorder falls under learning disorder. The codes in general do not help us to understand the relationship among these different categories.

The DSM-IV classifications rely on the assumption that the children have been exposed to normal schooling. Obviously, the assumption cannot be applied to the majority of the school-going population in developing countries. In contrast, in the developing countries, all the contributory factors need to be examined and assessed, and remediation strategies have to be planned accordingly.

PREVALENCE OF LEARNING DISORDERS

Most Western studies suggest a prevalence rate of learning disorders at around 10 per cent. In India, the studies mostly reflect the urban reality. A study by Rozario (1988) of 1,374 adolescents in the age group 12–16 years found 32 per cent to be scholastically backward, of whom 46 per cent had psychological disturbance. Sarkar (1990) in her study of 408 middle-class children between the ages of 8–12 years found 33 per cent to be scholastically backward with additional psychological problems and psycho-social stressors. Rozario (1991) reported that from 110 children in the age range of 9–10 years from a lower socio-economic background, one-third had scholastic backwardness and most of them had specific learning disabilities. Shenoy (1992) studied a population of 1,549 children in the age-group 5–8 years from a middle socio-economic status and reported scholastic backwardness in 11 per cent of the boys and 8 per cent of the girls. She observed an age trend of decline in the percentages of scholastic backwardness in girls and an increase in the boys. A study by the author (Kapur, 1993) of 481 primary school children from low socio-economic status reported that 14 per cent had scholastic backwardness and 41 per cent suffered some psychological disturbance. Venugopal and Raju (1988), in a study of learning disabilities in students of Class V and VI, reported 20.61 per cent prevalence.

In a study of 2,064 children aged 4–16 years, Srinath, Girimaji, Gururaj, et al. (2005) reported the prevalence of learning problems in 9.4 per cent, with 11.7 per cent in the rural areas, 9 per cent in the urban slums and 6.6 per cent in the other urban children of the sample.

Reports from rural areas are often harder to interpret as on assessment these children do exceedingly poorly yet do not get reported for scholastic backwardness due to low expectations from the teachers and parents. It may be suggested that reported scholastic backwardness ranges from 10–33 per cent but appears to increase with age as the children move to higher classes. Prevalence rates also appeared to be higher for boys. However these conclusions are confounded by the nature of tests used for assessment, type of schools, mother tongue of the child, language and medium of instruction, age, gender, and socio-economic divides as suggested by a vast number of studies in India (Bapna and Ramanujam, 1976; Gopala Rao, 1970; Kakar, 1970, Mukherjee, Uma, Kapur, and Subbakrishna, 1995; Sachdeva, 1974; Wig and Nagpal, 1972; and others).

The above research data appears to indicate that learning disorders have to be assessed and understood from multiple perspectives. The next section offers a brief overview of some common theoretical perspectives on learning disorders.

THEORETICAL PERSPECTIVES

In the West, cases of children with learning problems were reported in the last quarter of the previous century. A clearer understanding of the nature of learning disabilities came much later. Such understanding emerged out of the pioneering efforts of several workers. The term used for learning disabilities is 'dyslexia'. Earlier it referred to problems only in reading. But there has been a gradual widening of the scope of the term and it now includes problems of reading, comprehension, spelling, writing, arithmetic and visuo-spatial skills—in short, everything that is essential for academic work. There have also been attempts to define these problems by excluding several seemingly obvious reasons for underachievement. These are sensory motor deficits, mental retardation, severe psycho-social deprivation in infancy and faulty educational practices.

In the following section, the aim is not only to focus on specific learning disabilities as a syndrome, but also to view the disabled child from a holistic perspective, taking into account all the variables which are likely to come in the way of her/his academic performance. As Lahey, Vosk, and Habif (1981) emphasize, learning disabilities should be seen on a continuum from least disabling to the most disabling problem. Parallel to this continuum runs yet another continuum of emotional and school-related problems which interacts with and compounds the effects of learning disabilities.

Several aetiological theories have been proposed to explain specific learning disabilities. But each of these describes some facet of the problem and none of them wholly explains specific learning disabilities. Each theoretical perspective claims to be the only one that is right—reminding us of the proverbial four blind men and the elephant as illustrated in Figure 8.2.

Biological Approaches

Medically oriented theories view learning difficulties as overt symptoms of underlying biological pathology. The inferred pathology has been conceptualized by different theorists as affecting, for example, perceptual systems, perceptual-motor functioning, neurological organization and occulo-motor functioning (Mann, 1979).

Biophysical factors which are considered as the cause for learning problems include genetic, brain injury, missing biochemicals, allergens and toxic substances such as lead. Biological factors are most frequently suggested for problems related to hyperactivity and learning disabilities. No convincing evidence, however, links hyperactivity or learning disabilities to specific biological factors (Hallahan, Kauffman, and Lloyd, 1985).

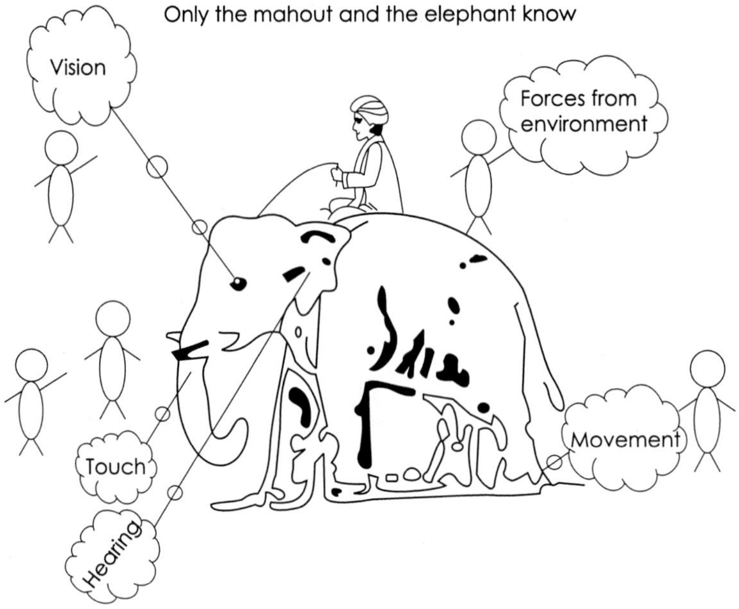

Figure 8.2 Blind men and the elephant

A child's genetic endowment and physical status obviously have a profound effect on her/his learning pattern (Cravioto and DeLicardie, 1973). Birth trauma, oxygen deprivation, infectious disease, drug intoxication, malnutrition, environmental pollutants and congenital defects are only a few of the biological events that may predispose a child towards learning and behaviour problems.

Delacato (1969) and Kephart (1971) suggested developmental theories consisting of stages of perceptual development parallel to Piagetian theory. If early perceptual development is deficient, normal intellectual development fails to occur. Training for spatial perception of letters and spatial-body orientation exercises were used. Getman (1962), a development optometrist, hypothesized that uncoordinated eye muscles caused dyslexia, and that the problem could be remedied by exercises to strengthen eye muscles. Frostig and Horne (1964) used copying exercises and geometrical figures to improve visual perception. Fernald (1943) used techniques involving the integration of visual, auditory, kinesthetic and tactile sensory modalities.

Attempts to pinpoint specific biological correlates of individual learning problems by researchers in the early 1960s have not often been productive. However, biological factors can contribute to the development of learning problems which may result in scholastic backwardness.

Neuropsychological Approaches

In the earlier decades, symptoms such as dyslexia were viewed as being similar to those manifested by adults who were brain injured, particularly during World War II, and hence the term 'brain damaged' was initially used. Later, in the absence of evidence of gross brain damage, the term was replaced with 'minimal brain damage', which was then used to describe hyperactive and learning-disabled children. The fact that dyslexia in adults was 'acquired' and not 'developmental' was overlooked at that time. Subsequently, the term 'minimal brain damage' was replaced by the term 'minimal brain dysfunction' as there was no clear evidence of brain damage in the young poor readers. However, in recent years, there is a move away from simplistic notions of brain dysfunction to more complex neuropsychological explanations. Taylor (1988), for example, describes the following dysfunctions in specific learning disabilities:

- Somato-sensory and motor skills
- Language and auditory processing
- Visuo-spatial, constructional skills
- Memory and learning abilities
- Attention and psychomotor efficiency
- Abstract reasoning and problem-solving

Psycho-educational Approaches

Proponents of the psycho-educational model of learning disabilities interpret academic deficits as reflecting aberrations in the ability to perceive, integrate and remember auditory and visual information associated with listening, speaking, reading and writing tasks (Johnson and Myklebust, 1967). Assessment procedures are used to identify specific strengths and weaknesses in auditory and visual processes related to academic functioning. In contrast to the medical model, the psycho-educational approaches advocate teaching academic skills by taking into account the student's modality preferences or areas of processing strength (visual, auditory or kinesthetic), the nature of the content (verbal or non-verbal) and the response requirements (oral or written). The emphasis on remediation of the underlying process deficiency is secondary. Unfortunately, it is difficult, if not impossible, to find any evidence beyond testimonials and anecdotal reports that support the assumptions, treatment methods and stated outcomes associated with medical and psycho-educational models (Lyon, 1985). No data exists that indicates that underlying processes can be strengthened and that such improvements are generalized to academic skills development (Wong, 1986).

Psycho-linguistic Approaches

In this model of learning disabilities, children are viewed as deficient in a variety of language functions. Linguistic deficits are associated with reading, writing and spelling disorders (e.g. dyslexia). More specifically, deficiencies in phonological coding and short-term memory for linguistic material have been causally linked to poor spelling, word retrieval and comprehension difficulties (Mann and Liberman, 1984). According to these theories, the major deficiency associated with poor reading skills is not auditory, visual or kinesthetic but involves a higher linguistic deficit which interferes with the ability to grasp the concept that words have parts—phonemes, syllables and morphemes—and that these are represented by alphabetical codes. The remediation is obviously phonetically-oriented.

Educational Approaches

Kauffman (1985) suggested six ways in which educational factors may contribute to scholastic problems.

- Insensitivity to the student as an individual
- Expectations that are too high or too low
- Uncertain classroom situations
- Uninteresting instructional tasks
- Reinforcement of undesirable behaviours
- Undesirable models of behaviours in the class, crowded classroom and poor study habits

In India, studies by Mistry and Mohite (1984) indicate that a large number of children, even after two years of schooling know neither how to read letters, nor know how to write simple sentences using common words. Bernstern (1990) found that 50 per cent of Class III students in Maharashtra had not mastered the basic skill of reading in Marathi.

Psycho-developmental Approaches

Learning problems are often said to stem from an underlying psychological disturbance or developmental delays. Family problems may interfere with learning. Spreen (1989) has speculated that emotional disorders may precede or follow learning difficulties, or even occur at the same time, if both learning difficulties and emotional difficulties have a common biological aetiology. The speculation is simplistic, yet it highlights the strong association that exists between learning difficulties and emotional problems in terms of aetiology.

Behavioural Approaches

In contrast to medical, psycho-educational and neuropsychological models and theories, behavioural approaches conceptualize learning disabilities as resulting from characteristics of academic tasks (Treiber and Lahey, 1983). There is no assumption of underlying pathology or process deficiency. Assessment and instructional activities are directed towards identifying academic skill deficits and modifying them with techniques derived from learning theory. The major assumption guiding this approach to instruction is that academic behaviours such as reading, writing and mathematics are dependent on adequate development of prerequisite, enabling academic behaviours. Recent reviews of the effectiveness of behavioural interventions with learning-disabled individuals have generally indicated favourable results with respect to increasing attentional and academic skills (Gadow, Torgesen, and Dahlem, 1985).

ASSESSMENT OF LEARNING DISORDERS

The term 'learning disabilities' has emerged out of a need to identify and serve students who continually fail at school yet are not mentally retarded. In assessment, the following features may emerge:

- A discrepancy between the child's ability and academic performance across one or several skills
- Academic problems exist in reading, writing, spelling and mathematics, individually or together
- Perceptual difficulties characterized by the inability to recognize, discriminate and interpret sensations: This may occur in either auditory or visual or both modalities
- Meta-cognitive ability consisting of self-regulatory mechanisms such as planning and executing moves, evaluating their effectiveness and correcting them if required
- Memory problems which may be due to learning and language difficulties
- Lack of fine motor skills which may lead to poor and slow handwriting

In view of the complex nature of learning disorders, when children with learning difficulties need to be assessed the process has to be viewed from the perspective of multiple causal factors for the condition. The assessment must consist of:

- Detailed case history, including the educational history of the child
- Behaviour observation and interview of the child regarding the nature of difficulties faced by her/him
- Psychological/educational evaluation of the child, which needs to cover multiple domains including cognitive domains and actual skill profiles of reading, writing, spelling, comprehension and mathematics

The above assessment may appear too elaborate and cumbersome but is essential if one wishes to go beyond diagnosis into actual remediation. Actual and effective remediation often needs to be tailored to suit the individual needs of the child. The Check List for Learning Disorders included in this chapter is one of the methods of assessment of the child.

In the West, the assessment of children with learning disabilities has been determined by the theoretical stance of the examiner, for example, from an angle of neuropsychology (Taylor, 1988). The dysfunctions identified are in the areas of somato-sensory and motor skills, language and auditory processing, visual, spatial and constructional skills, memory and learning abilities, attention and psychomotor efficiency and abstract reasoning and problem solving. A psycho-linguistic approach (Mann and Liberman, 1984) would examine the linguistic material in terms of deficiencies in phonological coding and short-term memory. Educational approaches on the other hand would focus on several environment-related problems. It needs to be emphasized that all the viewpoints are valid only when viewed in a holistic fashion. The segmental approach adopted by an individual rigidly following one approach will not benefit the child, nor will the remediation be optimally effective.

Check List for Learning Disorders

Name: Date:

Address:

Age: Gender:

Mother Tongue: Class:

Medium of Instruction: School:

Informant:

Actual Complaints:

Duration of each:

A. Recent onset:

Stressors at home: If yes, what?

Stressors at school: If yes, what?

Change in school ________

Medium _______ Teachers ______

Classes _______ Peer group _____

Punitive Teachers _____ Examination _____

B. Always:

History of delays in developmental milestones:

- Motor
- Intellectual
- Language

Delay in speech and language:

- Poor attention, over-activity and impulsivity
- Illnesses such as epilepsy, encephalitis or head injury
- Sensory-motor handicaps, poor hearing, vision/speech problems and poor motor coordination
- Parents/siblings having similar learning problems
- Other emotion or conduct disorders (see Chapter 3, where the Developmental Psychopathology Check List has been described)
- Parental problems (marital, social, economic, etc.). There may be neglect, indifference, punitiveness, over-expectation or over-involvement by the family.
- Temperament of the child (described in earlier chapters)
- Impression of intelligence (tested or otherwise based on milestones of development.)
- Structure of Asian languages

The following assessment includes psychological tests available in the market with appropriate agencies in India and the West. Where they are not available (where neither tests nor psychologists exist), some suggestions based on the author's experience will be given later in the section.

In addition to the matters discussed above, it has to be recognized that Asian languages that are phonetic or pictorial may have their own inbuilt problems. These need to be examined through empirical research in the context of learning problems. This has been observed in India where there are several phonetic languages and dialects (Bernstern 1990; Mistry and Mohite, 1984).

Assessment of learning disorders is further confounded by the coexistence of other childhood psychological disorders such as hyperkinesis and disorders of emotion and conduct which cannot be excluded from assessment. The association between learning disorders and childhood psychological disorders is strong. But what came first is unclear as one may have preceded, followed or both may have a common root. What role the other disorders play in initiating, maintaining, or aggravating learning difficulties can only be understood by a detailed study of the child covering bio-psycho-social domains. Research in India by Bhola, Hirisave, and Kapur (1997) found that children with learning problems had low general, academic, social and parallel self-esteem as compared to normal achievers. Mukherjee, Uma, Kapur, and Subbakrishna (1995) found low self-esteem and high-state anxiety in children with learning difficulties. Lall et al. (1997) found children with learning difficulties reporting cordial relations with peers and parents—but the teachers and peers did not view them favourably.

The section that follows will describe some of the tests used or developed to suit Indian conditions, especially for schools catering to upper- and middle-class children. The next section will outline some innovative ways of evolving and evaluating programmes for enhancing the learning environment in schools in rural and backward areas. The programmes are described, albeit briefly, so that the inapplicability of Western educational technologies can be circumvented effectively.

Assessment of children in the different classes may be carried out in three separate groups for the sake of convenience. These are:

- Level I: Pre-academic, for children in the nursery section who are below the age of six years
- Level II: For primary school children in Classes I to VII
- Level III: For high school children in Classes VIII to X

Of the tests that can be used, those which are copyrighted can be purchased from reputable agencies and the rest that are described in detail (Uma, Oommen and Kapur, 2002) are available with the NIMHANS Publication Division at Bangalore. In this section, only Level I and II will be described as these skills form the foundation for adequate learning skills. The high-school group at Level III can be helped through better learning strategies only if they have attained the seventh grade performance of Level II. The following tests are used in the NIMHANS SLD Index (Kapur, Barnabas, Reddy, Rozario, and Uma, 1994).

Level I: Pre-academic Skill Profile

Attention. Measured through colour cancellation test series of coloured dots, wherein a specific colour (single colour cancellation) or two specific colours (double colour cancellation) will be cancelled out by the child. The time limit is two minutes. Errors of omission and commission are noted. The difficulty levels are based on using one or two colours (Kapur, 1984).

Intelligence. The Seguin Form Board is an easy test to use with young children.

Pre-academic skills as measured by Brigance (1977). This tests their visual motor skills of copying simple designs, repeating the English alphabet, writing the alphabet in capital and small letters, knowing the preceding alphabet or alphabets that follow a particular letter (e.g. what comes before D or after K?), repeating numbers 1–20, what comes before a number or after a number, discrimination of simple shapes and sounds, auditory memory and noting speech and language difficulties if present.

Level II: Specific Learning Disabilities at Primary School Level (for Children in Classes I to VII)

Attention. Number and letter cancellation test (Kapoor, 1972): This involves a record sheet with a series of numbers/letters where a particular number or letter has to be cancelled by the child within two minutes. To examine complex attention, two numbers or letters have to be cancelled within two minutes. Errors of omission or commission are noted.

Adequate attention is a prerequisite for all the activities, whether for taking a test or class work. If attention is poor, performance on any assigned task is inevitably poor. Thus, remediation for enhancing attention is essential.

Language Difficulties. Language difficulties consist of reading, comprehension, spelling and writing when assessed in the medium of instruction, which mostly was English. The language tests were developed from the standard language text books used in the government schools, in Kannada, Tamil and English from Classes I to VII. Three paragraphs from the beginning, middle and last chapters of each class were taken. Reading and comprehension check lists were assessed based on these. The child was expected to read, answer questions, copy, and write dictation. Detailed analysis of the errors would then be carried out. Language difficulties often consist of letter by letter reading, slow reading, missing out letters, wrong reading, not paying attention to punctuation and not understanding what is being read or copied.

Writing difficulties consist of slow and illegible writing, writing letters in a haphazard manner without appropriate spaces between the words, missing out letters, not knowing when to use capitals and small letters and not using punctuation.

In general, learning disabled children were two years below their expected reading level as defined by their class at school.

Arithmetic Test. The arithmetic test is a modified and shorter version of Sheonell's diagnostic arithmetic test and consists of:

- Addition (simple and graded)

- Subtraction (simple and graded)
- Division (simple and long)
- Multiplication (simple and long)
- Fraction (simple and graded)

Visual-Motor Coordination. The tests include the Bender-Gestalt test (Koppitz, 1975) and a developmental test of visual motor integration (Beery and Buktenica, 1967).

Visual-Motor Memory. The Benton visual retention test (Benton, 1955). This requires the child to copy 10 designs after short exposure.

Auditory Memory. This tests the child's memory for paired associates, both familiar and unfamiliar, from lists of words. The assessment often revealed that each child had her/his own profile of deficits and strengths. A child may have reading, writing and mathematics problems or have problems in only one of these areas. Even within an area like mathematics, the problem may only be multiplication. Thus, obtaining the actual profile of deficits is essential for planning remediation.

SUMMARY

Learning Disorders (LD)

- LD from a narrow perspective is skill-deficits in reading, writing and mathematics. A broad perspective is scholastic backwardness and a disabilities perspective is intellectual disability in the presence of delayed milestones.
- The theories are biological and psycho-social: The biological theories attribute the LD to brain damage, brain dysfunction, neuropsychological, biochemical, genetic, allergens/toxins, perceptual motor and visual-spatial reasons. The psycho-social theories are psycho-educational, educational, psycho-linguistic, psycho-developmental or psychological/psycho-analytical and behavioural.
- LD may be associated with Attention Deficit Hyperactivity Disorder (ADHD), Conduct Disorder (CD) and Emotion Disorder (ED).

CHAPTER

Externalizing Disorders: Hyperkinesis and Other Disruptive Behaviours

Anxiety plays a normal adaptive role through development. To label anxiety as abnormal is not an easy task. As pointed out by Freud for adult neurotic disorders, anxiety lies at the core of childhood disorders. These may include externalizing or internalizing disorders, or disorders with a physical manifestation of symptoms, as in psychosomatic (psycho-physiological) or psychological disorders such as dissociative and conversion disorders. While anxiety may be subjectively experienced and verbally expressed among adults, among children it may only be expressed through a variety of symptoms. It needs to be highlighted that an optimal level of anxiety may be necessary to prompt the child to excel in studies or sports.

Children who are brought to the attention of mental health professionals display a range of problem behaviours that create difficulties for the children themselves, their parents and those around them. A major group of disorders are subsumed under the headings of internalizing and externalizing syndromes (Achenbach and Edelbrock, 1978). Behaviours included under the externalizing syndromes are conduct disorders or juvenile delinquency, and are primarily reflected in conflict with the environment. Among problems which are commonly listed under this category are aggressiveness, temper tantrums, lying, stealing, truancy and other problems which are distressing to those around the child. Hyperkinesis is also often included under this category because the manifest symptoms are impulsivity and over-activity.

Included under the heading of internalizing syndromes are problems of depression, withdrawal, anxiety, fears, obsessions, somatic complaints and schizoid features. These are also associated with the traditional categories of neurotic and psycho-physiological (psychosomatic) disorders and the more favoured ICD-10 diagnosis of disorder of emotion. The internalizing syndrome is characterized by subjective distress rather than conflict with the environment.

In traditional classification systems such as DSM-III-R, externalizing disorders are divided into three categories as the 'group type', 'solitary aggressive type' and the 'undifferentiated type', while the ICD-10 conduct disorders are divided into four types, conduct disorder confined to the family context, unsocialized, socialized and the defiant oppositional type. Empirical studies adopting dimensional approaches have highlighted some essential features.

Aggressive behaviour in children has been described differently by different workers. The pioneering work of Hewitt and Jenkins (1946) delineated socialized delinquency and unsocialized aggressive behaviour as the two major components. Subsequently, the two dimensions were seen by Peterson

(1961) as conduct and personality problems, and by Achenbach (1966) as externalizing and internalizing syndromes. The externalizing syndrome was described by Quay (1964) as unsocialized psychopathic disorder, by Miller (1967) as aggressive disorder, by Conners (1970) as aggressive conduct disorder, by Kolvin, Wolff, Barber, et al. (1975) as conduct disorder and by Anniah (1981)in India as disturbance of conduct. As pointed out by Rutter and Gould (1985), though different researchers have worked with different populations, there has been an impressive consensus among them.

Although aggressive behaviour is seen more frequently in males than females, almost all children display aggressive behaviour to some degree at some point in their development. Aggression may be manifested physically through hitting, biting, kicking, scratching or verbally through abusive language towards other children and adults. Though aggression is common in childhood, the frequency and intensity of aggressive behaviour may vary. Based on teacher ratings of a large sample of preschoolers, Crowther, Bond, and Rolf (1981) report that 18 per cent showed moderate aggression and only 7 per cent showed high-severity aggression. However, marked aggressiveness in childhood is found to be reasonably stable over time and is also related to later delinquency.

Aggression has theoretically been explained from several angles. From the psychoanalytical perspective, aggression results from an instinctual drive. Ethological approaches tend to support the view of aggression as a self-perpetuating instinct. The frustration–aggression hypothesis links aggression to frustration. Learning models highlight the mediating effect of punishment or non-reward on the actual manifestation of aggressive behaviour. Aggression has also been explained through the social learning model as being learnt directly or vicariously from acts of aggression by others. Aggressive behaviours are always maintained through contingent reinforcement.

Juvenile delinquency is a legal term which may or may not be specified under criminal law, referring to a youngster usually below 18 years of age who is brought to the attention of the judicial system. Delinquency comes under the broad spectrum of conduct disorders. Aggression and antisocial behaviour, which come under the rubric of conduct disorders, may or may not be detected by the judicial system. Based on longitudinal studies, there is a growing body of evidence that juvenile crime has its roots in childhood conduct disturbance. The magnitude of research work in the area of juvenile delinquency is so vast that it cannot be justifiably dealt with in the present chapter. Hence, this chapter focuses essentially on work done in the area of conduct disturbance of childhood as prevalent in the community and psychiatric clinics, rather than its more severe forms in adolescence which are dealt with under the judicial system. A number of theories have been proposed to explain delinquent behaviour, each emphasizing the effect of biological/genetic, sociological and psychological variables. In the subsequent sections, these viewpoints are briefly dealt with.

As highlighted by Wolff (1985), clearly defined syndromes within the broad group of conduct disorder have not yet been delineated. Although special features of conduct disordered children are known to have particular implications for aetiology and prognosis, there is much overlapping between conduct disorders of all kinds in their presentation, background and outcome. Further, investigation into aggressive and non-aggressive disorders, occurring at home and outside, at different ages in children from different cultural backgrounds, is necessary. For example, in India, Rao, Srinath, and Sharma (1986) in a follow-up of 110 conduct disordered children found that fire-setting, trouble with the law and sexual promiscuity were not found in India. But going to the movies without informing the family, fighting, hitting, temper tantrums, being demanding and disobedient in the family context were frequently reported.

PREVALENCE RATES

Many studies have suggested different prevalence rates for psychiatric disturbance in general. Studies on prevalence rates of conduct disturbance have often been reported separately for boys and girls because of the significant differences between boys and girls in the ratios for various disorders. In the Isle of Wight study (Rutter, Cox, Tupling, et al., 1975), out of the total prevalence rate of 10.6 per cent for all disorders, 57 per cent were conduct disorders, and 34 per cent were neurotic disturbances. In the Inner Borough of London, a higher prevalence rate of 19.1 per cent—of which 51 per cent are anti-social and 38 per cent neurotic disorders—has been reported. Connell, Irvine, and Rodney (1982), reported 6.7 per cent conduct disorders in children aged 10–11 years. Offord et al. (1980), in a population of 1,329 boys in the age range of 4–16 years, found 8.1 per cent of conduct disturbance in the total prevalence of 19.2 per cent, while in the 1,345 girls in the same age range, it was 2.7 per cent. Bird et al. (1988), in a Puerto Rican population of 4–16 year-olds, reported a low prevalence of conduct disturbance at 1.5 per cent. McGee et al. (1984) in New Zealand, in a sample of 951 children aged 4–7 years, reported 89 per cent prevalence, with 60 per cent being conduct disordered and 32 per cent being neurotic. The Venables et al. study (1983) of 1,063 children in Mauritius in the age range of 7–8 years, reported a total prevalence rate of 23.3 per cent with only 39 per cent being anti-social and 52 per cent being neurotic; this being the only study to report higher rates of neurotic problems. The studies by Wang, Shen, Gu, Jia, et al. (1989) in China, Matsuura Okubo, Kato, et al. (1989) in Japan, and McGee, Silva, and Williams (1984) in New Zealand reported lower overall prevalence rates of around 8 per cent. The majority of them reported a high percentage of conduct disturbance. The Japanese study reported an overall prevalence of 3 per cent, 83.6 per cent of which were conduct disturbances. In the Puerto Rican population the overall prevalence is much less when compared to other psychiatric conditions. Though the general prevalence rates vary and the proportion of conduct disturbance varies within this range, all studies show that boys outnumber girls in presenting with conduct disturbance.

Sarkhel, Sinha, Arora, and DeSarkar (2006) reported that the prevalence of conduct and hyperactivity disorders in Kanke, Bihar in 1,690 school children (with 6.81 per cent in boys and 1.85 per cent in girls) was 4.58 per cent. About 73 per cent had childhood onset while 27 per cent had adolescent onset. Among the disordered children, 36 per cent had ADHD and 72.7 per cent had difficult temperaments.

A study by Chaudhury, Prasad, Zacharias, et al. (2007) in a retrospective analysis of 213 children attending a child guidance clinic found behaviour and emotion disorders in 23.06 per cent children and neurotic, stress-related somatoform disorder in 15.98 per cent, while 38.5 per cent showed mental retardation. In Asian countries, the intellectually disabled form a large proportion of the parents in the clinical settings.

A prevalence study by Anita, Gaur, Vohra, Subash and Khurana (2003) of 800 children from urban and rural areas revealed the prevalence of 4.5 per cent conduct disorder, anxiety in 2.87 per cent, psychosis in 1.87 per cent, enuresis in 1.13 per cent and somatization in 0.5 per cent. Total prevalence including mental retardation and others was 16.5 per cent. Prevalence was slightly higher in the urban areas. Conduct disorder was the commonest and most prevalent in boys.

In the Asian countries, there have been few reports. The Mahat (2008) study may be considered the best prevalence study in the Asian region. It is a two-phase study in 30 districts in Nepal covering a very large child population. It reports overall prevalence of 14.74 per cent with more boys with conduct disorders, and girls with emotion disorders. The study reports caste, region and age differences.

AGE TRENDS

In the general population and among clinic population, aggressive behaviour is fairly common in preschool children and declines in the early school years, rises at adolescence and declines again between 15 and 16 years (Masterson, 1967; McFarlane, Allen, and Honzig, 1954; Werry and Quay, 1971; Wolff, 1985). Trends of increased prevalence in certain age groups have also been noted in some Indian studies, for example in 5–10 year-olds (John, 1980; Parvathavardhini, 1983) with predominantly conduct disturbance. This was further confirmed by Shenoy (1992) in groups of boys and girls in the age range of 5–8 years, where 7 and 8 year-olds differed significantly from the younger children with higher prevalence rates. Studies by Dalal (1989), Kapur (1985) and Rozario (1988) for 8–16 year-olds showed a similar peaking of disturbance at certain points. These could be confirmed by longitudinal studies and studies of factors associated with exacerbation and remission.

There have been several psychosocial variables which have been reported to have strong association with conduct disturbance. These are: distal (distant and indirect) factors such as residential environment (being urban or rural) social class and proximal (closer and direct) factors such as family and relationships, mental ill-health in the parents, school- and peer-related factors and the child's temperament.

URBAN-RURAL RESIDENCE

The study by Rutter et al. (1975) reported a lower ratio in the Isle of Wight when compared to the Inner London Boroughs. The Ontario study of Offord, Boyle, Szatmari et al. (1987) had also reported lower rates for the rural population, while the Japanese study of Matsuura, Okubo, Kato, et al. (1989) reported no such differences. Parvathavardhini (1983) studied 309 rural children in the age range of 5–12 years. She found a prevalence rate of 10.6 for psychiatric disturbance, with 30.3 per cent being conduct disordered. In a community survey of the same rural catchment area, of 117 children, there was a higher prevalence of other psychiatric disorders and only a few children with conduct disturbances. John (1980) in a study of school children in a slum catchment area, reported a prevalence rate of 21.43 per cent with conduct disturbance being 3.06 per cent. In the Parvathavardhini study, there was strong association between psychiatric disturbance and scholastic backwardness, in particular with conduct disturbance. Whether such a link exists between conduct disturbance in schools catering to upper and middle class families is yet to be explored.

SOCIAL CLASS

In Britain and in the USA, several researchers have reported substantial social class differences in maternal and child behaviour. The parents belonging to lower social classes were more punitive, less nurturing and more restrictive. They also differed in fostering competencies, especially in language development and provided less verbal and more aggressive role models (Wolff, 1985). Though the majority of the studies implicate low socio-economic status in the genesis of conduct disorders, Robins (1966) has rightly cautioned that it is the inadequacy of the parents rather than socio-economic status which may be the causal factor. Robins and Lewis (1966) pointed out that it was the presence of anti-social fathers or other relatives, irrespective of whether they were white or blue collar workers that led to conduct disturbance in the children, particularly in boys. Thus, apparently it is the pathological child-rearing practices, whether affected or unaffected by the low socio-economic status that matters in the genesis of conduct disturbance.

In India, a study by Arulmani (1991) found that intact families fostered competent behaviour, while disturbed families contributed to conduct disturbance in school-going 16 year-olds from a slum population. This has special implications in third world countries such as India. Removal of poverty is neither feasible nor possible, while helping the families and children at risk could be planned at the community level.

FAMILY

Family Size

Strong associations have been reported between large family size and deviancy in developed countries (Lapouse and Monk, 1958; Shepherd, Oppenheim, and Mitchell, 1971). In Western studies, greater family size—usually defined as four or more children—has been reported to be associated with increased rates of conduct disorder and delinquency in boys (Rutter, Tizard, and Whitmore, 1970), but not in girls (Jones et al., 1980). Findings in developing societies have contradicted findings in the West and, in fact, very low rates have been reported to be associated with large family size by De Almeida-Filho in Brazil (1984) and Wang, Shen, Gu, et al. in China (1989). The above findings appear to suggest that social support of the family members seems to guard against development of disturbance.

Marital Disharmony

The role of marital disharmony in the parents of anti-social children has been studied very extensively and has been implicated in the genesis of conduct disorders (Whitehead, 1979). Rutter and Garmezy (1983) have reported that this is even more significant in boys. This association has been reported in India by numerous researchers (Bapna and Ramanujam, 1976; Daniel, 1989; Gowrie Devi, 1983). Uncongenial relations between the parents and children and inconsistency in disciplining have been found to be present in the families of conduct disordered children in several Western studies. In India, Gowrie Devi (1983) compared 30 conduct disordered and 30 normal children in the age range of 9–14 years and found significantly more indifferent or antagonistic attitudes at home and over-protectiveness by mothers among the conduct disordered children.

Robins and Lewis (1966) have highlighted the disturbed patterns of relationship between the child and the parents. Such a pattern is characterized by inconsistent discipline and/or lack of discipline. This has been supported by several studies such as those of Hetherington and Martin, 1979; McCord, McCord, and Howard, 1961; and Rutter and Giller, 1983. In India, too, researchers have highlighted similar trends (Baldev et al., 1972; Bapna and Ramanujam, 1976; Chacko, 1964; Hoch, 1967). Daniel (1989) found the parents of the conduct disordered to be significantly more hostile, rejecting, controlling and authoritarian compared to the parents of emotionally disordered, those with mixed disorder of emotion and conduct and normal children.

Mental Ill-health of Parents

Several Western and Indian workers have implicated poor mental health of parents as contributing to conduct disturbance in children. Sociopathy, alcoholism and psychotic illnesses in parents have been the point of focus. Daniel (1989), Gowrie Devi (1983) and Shenoy (1992) suggest that mental ill-health, particularly alcoholism in the father and anxiety and depression in the mother, appears to be a major predisposing cause.

Peer Interaction and Difficulties in School

The major studies by Mulligan et al. (1963) and Conger and Miller (1966), have shown that delinquents did poor school work, challenged the teacher's authority and were unpopular with their schoolmates. As in Western studies, Indian studies have also highlighted troubles in relationships with peers and at school. Daniel (1989) found that in her clinic sample of 33 conduct disordered children, peer relationship was intact despite trouble with teachers and studies, when compared to a sample of normal children. Thus, having good peer interaction may be considered a good prognostic indicator, a silver lining despite trouble at home and school in India as this is not reported in the Western studies. Figure 9.1 illustrates the family related factors behind externalizing (conduct) disorders.

PSYCHOSOCIAL STRESSORS

Despite the fact that conduct disordered children are disturbing to others in their environment, an analysis of psychosocial stressors faced by them, especially in the Indian context, appears to suggest that subjective distress may be at the root of the trouble in many conduct disordered children.

PARENTS	CHILD
Marital Discord Parental Attitudes • Hostile • Rejecting • Authoritarian • Controlling	Pre-Peri-Postnatal Problems Stress Academic Difficulties Outward Directed Aggression Sibling Rivalry Good Peer Interaction

Figure 9.1 Externalizing (Conduct) disorders

A file review of 2,927 child psychiatric cases at NIMHANS by Srinath, Bhide, and Kaliaperumal (1986) showed significantly more psychosocial stressors in conduct disordered children. The Arulmani study (1991) also reported a significantly greater number of stressors in conduct disordered 16-year-olds when compared to competent adolescents from a similar impoverished socio-economic background. In the Indian setting, it is essential to focus on the role of stressors at home, in the neighbourhood and at school in initiating and maintaining conduct disturbance. This, in turn, leads to the assessment of subjective distress in these children, which is of great importance in establishing a therapeutic alliance with them.

TEMPERAMENT

Temperament has been conceptualized as a set of inherited personality traits that appear in infancy (Buss and Plomin, 1984). The nine categories of temperament delineated by Thomas and Chess (1977) have been widely used for the study of infant temperament. Many researchers have studied the relationship between early temperamental characteristics and subsequent development of behaviour problems. Rutter, Maugham, Mortimer, and Ouston (1979) found the presence of irregularity of sleeping and feeding, irritability and poor adaptability to new circumstances even before behaviour disorders became manifest. Graham, Rutter, and George (1973) found similar negative temperamental characteristics in children from working-class homes where one parent had a psychiatric problem before the children had manifested behavioural problems. Kolvin, Wolff, Barber, et al. (1975) found that anti-social children differed significantly from normal children on all dimensions of temperament.

In India, Malhotra, Varma, Verma, and Malhotra (1986) found a strong relationship between difficult temperament and conduct disorders. A detailed study by Daniel (1989) investigated the relationship between conduct disorder and temperament in a clinic sample in 8–12 year-olds. In this study, the conduct disordered children were significantly more sociable than normals and had a high energy level. Yet they had greater distractibility, poor attention span and great irregularity in patterns of eating and sleeping. The conduct disordered children also differed significantly on all dimensions of temperament from children with emotion disorders and those with mixed disorder of emotion and conduct. The study by Shenoy (1992) of a group of five- to eight-year-old boys and girls found externalization to be highly correlated with activity, low threshold of responsiveness, high intensity of emotionality, high distractibility and low persistence. There was also a high correlation with the approach dimension, indicating that they were sociable and cheerful. It is worthwhile to note that in this group of young conduct disordered boys and girls, sociability and a cheerful mood may be protective factors and may perhaps be related to better prognosis.

THE CONTINUITY–DISCONTINUITY DIMENSION OF CONDUCT DISORDERS

Longitudinal studies offer the best perspective on the issue of childhood and adult disorders. Despite the methodological problems inherent in longitudinal studies, certain major trends have been reported. The Berkeley growth study (McFarlane, Allen, and Honzig, 1954) was pioneering in pointing out that most problems of children are age-specific. That is, a problem present at one age may

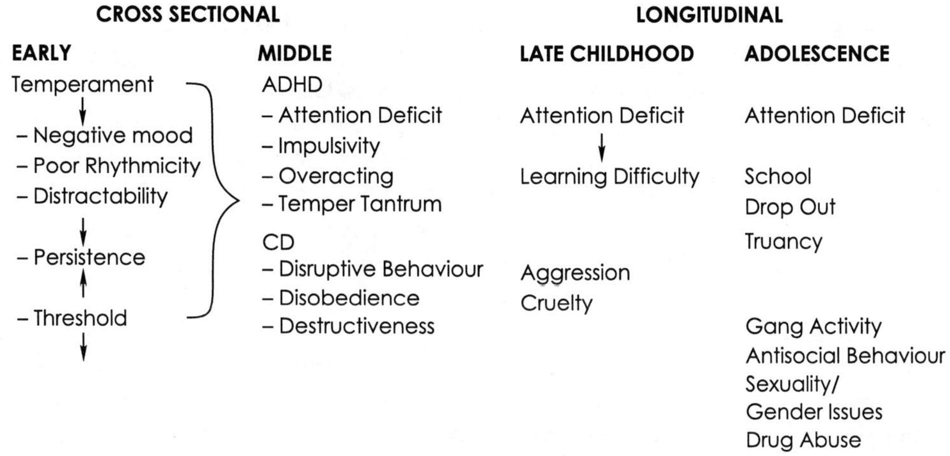

Figure 9.2 Phenomenology of conduct disorders in childhood and adolescence

not be found later, with the exception of destructiveness, demanding attention, jealousy, shyness and excess reserve. When these were present at the age of seven years, they were likely to be present at 13 or 14 years as well. Children with many symptoms at one age tended to also have many symptoms later. However, before the age of seven, symptoms had little predictive value. Figures 9.2 and 9.3 illustrate the trends reported in longitudinal studies on conduct disorders.

In a major study related to prognosis of delinquency by Glueck and Glueck (1968), where 500 delinquents and 500 non-delinquents were followed up to their early thirties, the outcomes were found to be worse for the delinquents. The delinquents had a higher number of convictions, poor employment and unstable family relationships. The number of serious offences, however, decreased with age. Similar later-life outcomes were reported by Robins (1966): 82 per cent of the males had been arrested for offences not related to traffic, 70 per cent females had got married early to men

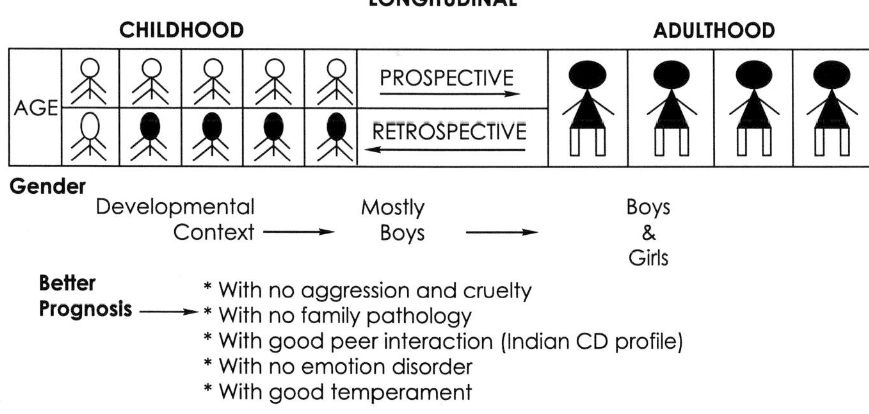

Figure 9.3 Trends reported in longitudinal studies

with high rates of criminal offences, while girls had higher rates of both unemployment and poor work records. More recently, Robins (1978) replicated the study in four different groups varying in geographic location, generation, race and ethnic backgrounds. Despite the differences, Robins concluded that childhood anti-social behaviour best predicted adult anti-social behaviour but that most anti-social children do not become anti-social adults. A study by Henn, Bordwell, and Jenkins (1980), predicted poor adult outcomes for different subcategories of delinquents.

The techniques of following the cases backward, such as the one use by Robins and the one by Pritchard and Graham (1966), reported that adults with sociopathy, when compared to other disorders, were often conduct disordered in childhood. Kellam et al. (1975) suggested continuity between hyperactivity-externalizing disorders and drug and alcohol abuse in their longitudinal studies. Though most of the studies suggest strong continuity between conduct disturbance in childhood into adulthood, they also point out that though all adult sociopaths were conduct disordered in childhood, not all childhood conduct disordered become sociopaths. Poor social class, a broken home and family pathology have low predictive power, while aggressiveness, anti-social parents and scholastic difficulty appear to lead to adverse outcomes. Sociability, presence of emotional disturbance and good academic performance are associated with better outcomes.Thus, several of these factors should be taken into account while planning treatment and evaluating outcomes.

A study in India conducted at NIMHANS by Daniel (1989) aimed at investigating the three groups of disorders, i.e. disorders of conduct, of emotion and of mixed disorder of conduct and emotion in the Indian context, with a control group of normal children in the age group of 8–12 years. The sample consisted of 33 children in each of the four groups and interactional patterns, attitudinal variables, cognitive, temperament, and personality variables were studied.

The conduct disordered were predominantly males in comparison to the emotionally disordered group. The groups did not differ with respect to the type of family (joint or nuclear) and size of the family. In the mixed disordered and the emotionally disordered group, there were significantly more first-borns. Lower socio-economic status was associated with conduct disorders, but not in the other two disorder groups.

The mixed and the conduct disordered had significantly high parental problems when compared to the normal and the emotionally disordered. In all the three groups, there was a significantly higher degree of parental ill-health than in the normal group.

Certain major trends were seen in the interpersonal variables in all the three groups. Marital disharmony in the parents was significantly higher in comparison to the normals. A significantly larger number of the fathers and mothers of the clinic groups were hostile and rejecting when compared to the parents of normals (an exception being the fathers of the emotionally disordered children). A greater number of the mothers of the three disorder groups manifested controlling, authoritarian and overprotective attitudes in comparison to the parents of normals. The parents of the conduct disordered were more hostile and rejecting, while those of the emotionally disordered and the mixed group were overprotective. In the three groups, there was significantly higher sibling rivalry when compared to the normals. The conduct disordered and mixed disordered had a significantly higher degree of sibling rivalry than the emotionally disordered. Peer interactions were significantly poorer in the emotionally disordered, while the conduct and mixed disordered were comparable to normal children in their peer interactions.

The visuo-motor perceptual organization of the three groups showed that the conduct disordered had the highest disorganization, followed by the mixed group, the emotionally disordered and then the normals. Similarly, conduct disordered had the lowest mean IQ (89) followed by mixed group with an IQ of 94, emotionally disordered with an IQ of 97.5 and normals with a mean IQ of 103.

The normals differed from the clinical groups in temperamental characteristics. The conduct disordered had significantly higher mean ratings than normals. The normals were friendlier, approachable and responsive, being high on emotionality, which consisted of mood and persistence and the energy factor which comprised activity and intensity, attentiveness or distractibility factor and rhythmicity factor. The emotionally disordered had significantly lower ratings on all these factors. The mixed group had low sociability and emotionality and were more irregular in their sleep and food habits but were comparable to the normals in their energy and attentivity levels.

On the Rosenzweig's Picture Frustration Test, the conduct disordered were extra-punitive, mixed disordered were impunitive like the normals, while the emotional disordered were intro-punitive, with aggression and hostility directed towards themselves.

CONDUCT DISTURBANCE AND OTHER PSYCHIATRIC PROBLEMS

Hyperactivity

There is evidence of a strong association between hyperactivity and conduct disturbance. Cantwell (1978) has commented that the data of various clinical, follow-up, family, laboratory and treatment studies indicate there is a relationship between the presence of hyperactivity syndrome in children and the development of anti-social tendencies in later life. However, many hyperactive children do not engage in antisocial activities. Thus, the specific characteristics of hyperkinesis and associated environment and factors which predispose a child for developing conduct disturbance need to be studied. Figure 9.4 illustrates the factors behind hyperkinesis.

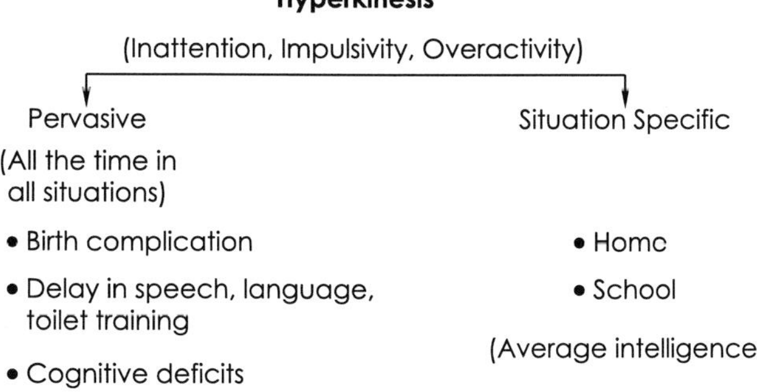

Figure 9.4 Factors behind hyperkinesis

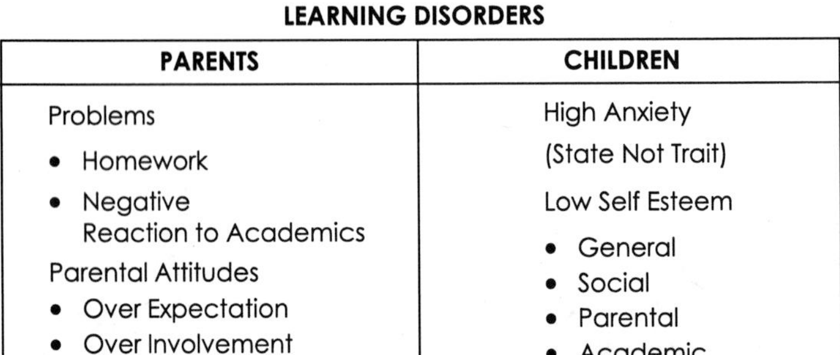

Figure 9.5 Factors leading to learning disabilities

Learning Disabilities

In recent years, several well-designed studies have suggested an association between persistent scholastic problems and delinquent behaviour. Incidence of reported learning problems has ranged from one-third to one-half (Offord, Boyle, Szatmari, et al., 1987) or even higher. Whether the problems of learning are primary or secondary, or whether both conduct disturbance and academic difficulties have a common unknown aetiology, is a matter of scientific debate. Indian studies have reported significantly lower intellectual quotients and perceptual-motor deficits in the conduct disordered when compared to normals and emotionally disordered children. Figure 9.5 illustrates the factors leading to learning disabilities.

Disorders of Emotion and Other Internalizing Problems

The Daniel study (1989) established conduct disorders as a separate category, while the mixed and the emotional group formed a separate category, the normal group being in the middle. Clinical impression supports the contention that the conduct disordered children with features of other disorders, particularly emotion and neurosis, respond better to intervention. Figures 9.6, 9.7 and 9.8 illustrate this section in detail.

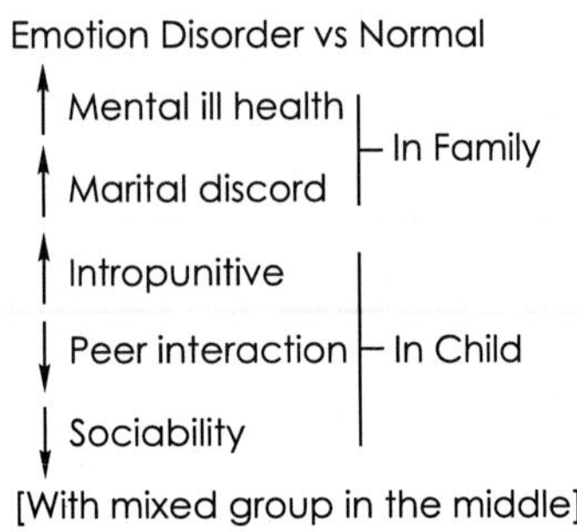

Figure 9.6 Disorders of emotion

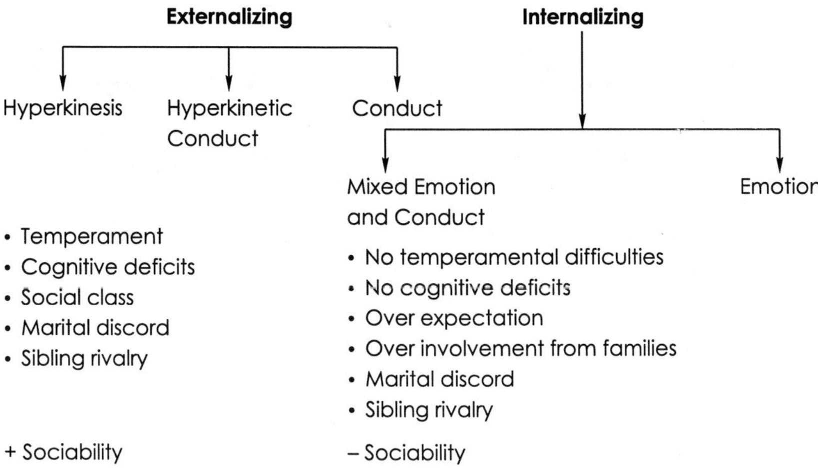

Figure 9.7 Disorder and normal children

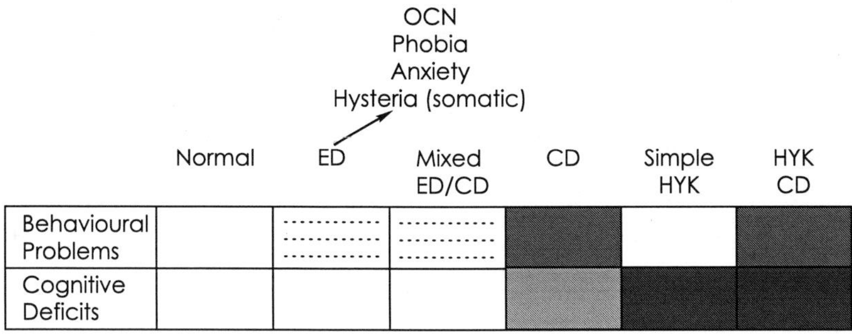

Figure 9.8 Behavioural problems and cognitive deficits

SUMMARY

The conduct disordered had the most severe pathology of the three groups because of the number of adverse bio-psycho-social factors which acted on them with an additive effect. Such children are found to present increased evidence of peri-natal difficulties, adverse temperamental traits characterized by distractibility, increased activity levels, and irregular sleep and feeding patterns and had significant perceptual-motor dysfunctions, slightly lowered levels of intellectual functioning, and a personality profile characterized by outward-directed aggression. They came from poor socio-economic settings with punitive, hostile and rejecting parents who had a higher incidence of mental illness and marital discord. Good peer interaction in these children appeared to be a silver-lining. Conduct disorders may also be associated with hyperactivity, language disabilities and emotion disorders.

CHAPTER

10 Internalizing Disorders: Anxiety, Phobias, Social Withdrawal

Internalizing disorders are characterized by anxiety and include the following conditions: (*a*) anxiety, phobias (fears) and obsessive compulsive disorders—similar features as found in adults, are found less frequently among children; (*b*) emotion disorders—manifested by shyness, social withdrawal, fearfulness, timidity, weepiness and so on; psychosomatic, somatoform dissociative and (*c*) conversion disorders—wherein the disorder has physical symptoms indicative of psychological distress or anxiety and it may or may not have an organic basis.

ANXIETY AND FEARS

Anxiety and fears in a child depends on her/his age. In infancy, anxiety may be a sensory experience of loud sound and sudden movements. In the first and second year, fear or anxiety may be of separation from the mother or fear of strangers. In early childhood, it may be a fear of real or imagined objects or beasts. In late childhood, it may be anxiety about one's performance and, finally, interpersonal anxieties in early and late adolescence. It is crucial to note that the child's levels of cognitive and emotional development decide the nature of her/his anxiety or fear. Some fears may be temporary and pass off as the child gets older.

Anxiety in childhood may be attributed to genetic predisposition, cognitive and affective development and learning. Anxiety may vary in severity but its fundamental nature remains the same.

Phobias and separation anxieties are the major types of anxiety in childhood. Depressive disorders are also considered anxiety disorders at this time. In childhood, obsessive compulsive disorders and physical disorders are considered neurotic disorders. The manifestation may be very similar to that seen in adults. Functional impairment is an important criterion of diagnosis in childhood.

From the psychoanalytic perspective, anxiety is at the core of psychoneuroses. It is possible to support the same postulate about the important role of anxiety in the disorders of emotion, with or without espousing the construct of the 'unconscious'. It is always necessary to go beyond mere identification of symptoms to an analysis and meaning in terms of association with other symptoms and links with prior circumstances, environmental precipitants and exigencies (Rutter and Garmezy, 1983).

In order to enhance our understanding of internalizing disorders, they may be classified according to the framework offered by Miller (1983), which also encompasses the traditional classificatory systems.

1. Anxiety-related conditions:
    - Anxiety reaction
    - Obsessive-compulsive neurosis
    - Hysterical (conversion and dissociation) reaction
    - Traumatic reaction
    - School avoidance (Type 1 and Type 2)
    - Phobia (physical injury, natural events, social anxiety)
2. Depression (manifest and masked)
3. Social withdrawal
4. Somatization (headache, stomach-ache and others)

DSM-III-R lists four sub-types of anxiety, i.e., separation anxiety, avoidant disorders, overanxious disorders and adjustment disorder with anxious mood. Depression is classified under affective disorders, as in the adults. In the ICD-10, the categories are: disorder of emotion—onset specific to childhood, as separate from neurotic disorders; and anxiety disorder, which is further categorized as phobic anxiety disorder, social anxiety disorder and sibling rivalry disorder. The neurotic and somatoform disorders share the adult classificatory system. The category of disorder of social functioning specific to childhood and adolescence consists of elective mutism, reactive attachment and disinhibited attachment disorders of childhood.

In the following sections, disorder of emotion and hysteria are dealt with at length as these two are the commonest internalizing disorders encountered in the Indian setting.

DISORDER OF EMOTION

The prevalence of emotion disorder compared to conduct disorder has already been reported in Chapter 9. The prevalence of emotion disorder or of internalizing disorders renders reporting of prevalence figures a difficult task. The following section also reflects this ambiguity for the same reason. The predominance of girls in the emotion disordered group, in comparison to the conduct disordered which consists mostly of boys, has been reported by several Western workers (Rutter and Garmezy, 1983). In India, Balan (1970), Baldev, Jain, and Manchanda (1972) and Murthy, Ghose, and Varma (1974) have reported similar trends.

In India, Daniel (1989), in a clinic sample of 33 conduct disordered, 33 emotion disordered and 33 with mixed disorder of emotion and conduct found the ratio of boys to girls to be 3.2:2.3 in the emotion disordered and 9:2 in the conduct disordered and 2.3:1 in the mixed disorder of emotion and conduct. Shenoy (1992), comparing externalizers and internalizers, found the ratio of boys to girls to be 3:2 in her epidemiological study of 1,535 children in the age range of five–eight years. There were 178 boys and 103 girls who were disturbed. The boys had significantly more externalizing and learning problems and girls had significantly more internalizing problems. Figure 10.1 illustrates some of the factors behind internalizing (emotion) disorders.

PARENTS	CHILD
Marital Discord Parental Attitudes • Hostile • Rejecting • Over Protective Disciplining Pattern • Inconsistent • Inadequate (Fathers are not involved)	Poor Sociability Poor Interaction with Peers Sibling Rivalry

Figure 10.1 Internalizing (Emotion) disorders

AGE TRENDS

In earlier studies on child guidance populations, the children who improved belonged to the group of neurosis, as seen in the study by Cunningham, Westerman, and Fischoff (1956), wherein the psychosomatic and neurotic reported the most improvement after one- or two-year follow-up. Masterson (1967) reported a better outcome in neurotic adolescents on a five-year follow-up when compared to anti-social and psychotic adolescents. Warren (1965) reported similar improvement in children with onset of neurotic disorders before the age of 15 years.

Based on an epidemiological survey, Verhulst and Akkerhuis (1986) reported that stability was associated with academic and social functioning, though difference in overall score was not significant. Koot and Verhulst (1992), in a study of four-year stability based on a population of 1,052 children in the age range of 4–12 years, found internalizing problems to be fairly stable, though less so than externalizing problems. However, nearly half the children across age and gender were stable in their manifestation of psychopathology.

SOCIAL CLASS

Though several socio-economic variables have shown strong association with conduct disturbance, the majority of the Western studies do not reflect such trends in the emotionally disordered groups (Cullen and Boundy, 1966; Lapouse and Monk, 1958; Rutter, Tizard, and Whitmore, 1970). In India, the disorder of emotion as defined by the ICD classificatory system has hardly been reported as a separate diagnostic category. However, the term has been used as a blanket category, suggestive of disturbance (of both externalizing and internalizing kinds). Daniel (1989) found the parents of emotion disordered children to have similar income and occupation status as the parents of the normal children, although normal parents had higher educational qualifications. The parents of the mixed disordered group were comparable to those of the normal group; the parents of the conduct disordered showed significantly lower income, occupation and education than the parents of normals as well as the clinic groups.

PERI-NATAL PROBLEMS

Taylor, Everitt, Thorley, Schachar and Weiselberg (1986) found that peri-natal problems were implicated in their sample of conduct and mixed disorders. Daniel (1989) also reported that though the normals had fewer peri-natal problems compared to mixed and conduct disordered groups, the emotion disordered were similar to normals.

FAMILY FACTORS

Mental Illness in the Parents

Western studies (Buck and Laughton, 1959; Jonsell, 1982) have reported significant parental ill-health in the emotionally disordered group. In India, Sharma et al. (1980) have reported similar trends. Daniel (1989) reported higher prevalence of mental ill-health in the parents of the emotionally disturbed when compared to normals. Shenoy (1992) found high neuroticism in the mothers of internalizers and alcoholism in the fathers.

Marital Disharmony

The parents of the emotionally disordered were reported to have marital disharmony in several Western studies (Hess and Camara, 1979; Porter and O'Leary, 1980; Rutter et al., 1970). Boys in particular were shown to be more vulnerable to marital disharmony in the parents. A study of non-clinical population in four–seven year-olds in the community by Block, Block, and Morrison (1981) even went on to suggest that while parental disagreements have a negative effect on boys, they have the beneficial effect of increasing resiliency in girls. In India, several studies (Bapna and Ramanujam, 1976; Geetha, Shetty, and Venkataramaiah, 1980) have suggested a strong association between emotion disorder and parental marital disharmony. The finding of greater marital discord in the parents of the emotion disordered compared to the parents of conduct disordered, as reported by Taylor, Schachar, Thorley, and Weiselberg (1986), is not supported by the Daniel (1989) study in India.

Parental Attitudes

While several Western studies report pathological parental attitudes, several Indian workers (Agarwal, Saksena, and Singh, 1978; Bapna and Ramanujam, 1976; Hussaini, 1975) have also reported faulty parental attitudes as contributing to disorders of emotion. Daniel (1989) has reported that a significantly larger number of mothers and fathers in the groups of emotion, mixed and conduct disordered were hostile and rejecting when compared to the normal fathers. But within the clinic groups, the fathers of the emotion disordered were less hostile and rejecting than the fathers of the conduct and the mixed disordered groups. It appears that the parents of the clinic groups in general were not only hostile and rejecting but were also overprotective. Shenoy (1992) found parental characteristics such as rejection and inadequate or inconsistent disciplining to be significantly less in the parents of normal children. Generally the fathers were less involved with disciplining. These attitudes appear to be a fertile ground for 'enmeshment' and 'ambivalence' in the context of parent–child relationship, indicating a pathological over involvement.

Sibling Rivalry

Sibling rivalry in conduct disordered children has been reported extensively in the West and in India. Yet there are hardly any studies on this in the emotion disordered group. Daniel (1989) found significantly greater sibling rivalry in the emotion disordered in comparison to the normals, though they had significantly less sibling rivalry than the conduct disordered and the mixed disordered children. On the continuum of sibling rivalry, the normals had the least, then came the emotion disordered, followed by mixed disordered, and the conduct disordered, who had the most severe rivalry. Shenoy (1992) too reported significant sibling hostility in the disturbed children.

PEER RELATIONSHIPS

Difficulty in social interaction is the hallmark of emotional disturbance and forms a descriptive category in the classificatory systems. Several workers have reported poor peer relationship in these children. Muste and Sharp (1947) found that children with low scores on aggression had poor scores on social participation. In India, Daniel (1989) reported significantly poorer peer interaction in the emotion disordered when compared to normal, conduct disordered as well as mixed disordered groups.

SCHOLASTIC ACHIEVEMENT

In the West, the emotionally disordered, in general, have been reported to have average intelligence. Daniel (1989) found some association between academic difficulties and emotion disorder despite average intelligence in these children. However, the strength of this association is not as high as the one between conduct disturbance and scholastic backwardness. Shenoy (1992) reported strong association between disturbance and scholastic backwardness, particularly in the externalizers. Robins (1974) has reported that academic difficulties are associated with poor prognosis in the emotion disordered. In India, there is a need to study the relationship between academic difficulties and emotional disturbance.

PSYCHO-SOCIAL STRESSORS

Psycho-social stressors, moderated by age, sex and socio-economic strata, are less frequent in emotional disorders when compared to the conduct and the mixed disordered in the West as studied by Rutter and Garmezy (1983). Absence of sensitive age-appropriate perspectives and the interplay of vulnerability and social support in the presence of stressors renders it a fascinating yet formidable challenge for research in India or elsewhere in the world.

TEMPERAMENT

There have been many studies of temperament in relation to conduct disorder in the West and only a few in India. Daniel (1989) found the emotion disordered to be less sociable, less adaptable, more moody, less active, with irregular biological functions and also less distractible. They had inwardly directed aggression in comparison to the conduct disordered—who had outwardly directed aggression, and mixed disordered—who were impunitive in handling aggression. In the Shenoy study (1992), externalizers were significantly withdrawn, underactive and less adaptive. Thus, it appears that the emotional disordered as reflected in the Indian studies are cognitively adequate, with no biological vulnerabilities except inhibited temperament, but with significant interpersonal problems in the context of parents, siblings and peer groups.

The clinical picture of childhood neuroses is often multi-symptomatic and often not amenable to nominal and unidimensional classification. In clinical practice, it is common to find that an obvious or ostensible symptom masks several other difficulties. Thus, multiplicity of symptoms belonging to different diagnostic categories—caused by multiple bio-psycho-social aetiological factors which respond to multimodal treatments—is a rule rather than an exception, particularly in the internalizing disorders. The various syndromes in this group are not mutually exclusive and are merely symptoms of distress in a child. This notion would provide a better perspective in planning the treatment strategy.

The issue of continuity and discontinuity amongst emotional disorders was aptly described by Hersov (1977), when he stated that some emotional disorders are strong precursors of adult disorders while others constitute rather different types of conditions carrying a much better prognosis. Conduct disorders, obsessive compulsive disorders and phobias have a more enduring quality.

Anxiety and Fears. Fear and anxiety have been universal experiences of man at every age and stage of development. Yet there is very little empirical evidence and clear understanding of childhood fears and anxieties. Fear, anxiety and phobias are subjectively felt, with feelings of misery and unhappiness and a heightened sense of uncertainty. Fear is a normal physiological reaction to a genuine threat and disappears with the withdrawal of the threat. Anxiety is a response to an internal cue without obvious external threat. In phobia, the anxiety becomes attached to external objects or situations which by themselves are not dangerous.

Characteristics of Anxiety in Childhood

1. Anxiety in children may be manifest or latent. When anxiety is not manifest, symptoms such as hyperactivity, aggressive behaviour, enuresis, encopresis, social withdrawal, stammering and learning disabilities, may all arise out of latent anxiety. This construct is very helpful for the clinician in understanding a child who presents different psycho-pathological complaints.
2. Anxiety may be a primary or secondary diagnosis. Sometimes anxiety produces the symptoms, while at other times the symptom may, in turn, produce anxiety. Anxiety is common in most of the psycho-pathological disorders, though less in aggressive conduct disorders and more in internalizing disorders. Anxiety, thus, can be present in children with developmental delays, organic brain dysfunction, neurotic and psychotic problems (Chess, 1973).
3. Anxiety is age-related in its causes and consequences. Although the experience of anxiety or fears may be similar, the causes and consequences may be very different across ages.
   The clinical and experimental evidence clearly demonstrates that the source of the content of anxiety and fears changes with age and stabilizes around the age of six years.
   Sources of anxiety may vary accordingly in the age of the child, for example, excessive or unexpected sensory stimuli, loss of support, loud noises at six months; fear of strangers, novel stimuli, masks, heights, etc. at nine months; fear of separation, injury, toilet in the first year; imaginary creatures, death, robbers in the second year; dogs, being alone in the third year; darkness in the fourth year; while a fear of school, injury, natural events and social anxiety are common at 6–12 years.
   In general, the specific number of stimuli which give rise to fears also increases with age. This in turn may be related to the ability to reason, abstract and generalize. Graziano et al. (1979) proposed that, in clinical practice, fears were to be defined as those with a duration of **over two years**, or that which had an intensity debilitating to the child's lifestyle.
4. Anxiety as a state or a trait: Whether the child is anxious by nature when anxiety is a chronic condition, or whether a child is extremely anxious and the condition acute, is yet another distinction that should be made and understood in the context of developmental stages, unlike in adults, where trait and state anxiety are clearly defined and understood. A temperamental dimension of being anxious would, thus, be an equivalent of trait anxiety.
5. Anxiety and depression: In children, depression, like anxiety, is a nebulous concept and may be manifest or latent, primary or secondary. In very young children, depression is characterized by extreme withdrawal, particularly in the context of separation from the mother, institutionalization and under-stimulation. Spitz (1946) called it anaclitic depression. Bowlby (1980) studied depression which follows separation from the caretaker in early years of childhood and manifests itself through numbness, protest, despair and detachment. However, after early childhood, depression manifests in older children with all adult aspects of depression, with disturbances in affective, cognitive, motivational, vegetative and psychomotor functions (Kovacs, 1987). The only difference may be that dysphoric mood may not be the primary symptom as it is in adults. Achenbach and Edelbrock (1978) reviewed studies using multivariate statistical techniques and suggested the presence of symptoms of anxiety and depression in children and that the symptoms were intermixed. Both anxiety and depression existed at the manifest level and were part of a general inhibition (internalizing) syndrome.

There are the two major theories of anxiety. In the psychoanalytic framework, conscious anxiety is experienced by the person as a result of unconscious anxiety produced by conflict between the id, the ego and the superego. The social learning theory specifies respondent conditioning, operant conditioning and the two-factor theory of conditioning. Each of these assumes that anxiety is learned. According to the respondent theory, any neutral stimulus that happens to make an impact on the child at the time that a fear reaction occurs will subsequently evoke a fear reaction. Operant theory postulates that behaviour that is rewarded tends to occur again, while behaviour that is not rewarded is extinguished. The two-factor theory combines the respondent theory and the operant theory and holds that anxiety occurs through fear reaction and is unpleasant; consequently, avoidance of the fear-arousing situation reduces the anxiety.

There are theories which explain childhood anxiety and fears, focusing on the stages of cognitive and emotional development of the child. For example, fear of a snake will come after the child's cognitive ability makes him understand that snakes are dangerous. Separation from the mother produces anxiety in a year-old child, but not in a 12 year-old and this is related to the phase of emotional development of the child. It is important that the clinician views the cause of anxiety in a child from the perspective of the child in the context of interaction with his environment. Furthermore, anxiety in children may be a product of several factors and may not be explained adequately by the simplistic explanations provided by some of the traditional theories.

School Phobia

Many of the phobias seen in adults may also be present in children. The most interesting and typical phobia in children is school phobia wherein the child refuses to go to school. School phobias are divided into two types: Type I and Type II (Kennedy 1965). Type I occurs in the younger group and has an acute and traumatic onset. It is attributed to separation anxiety and generally occurs in a child who is functioning well in all other areas. In the Type II phobia, unlike Type I, the onset is in adolescence and is gradual. Disturbance is more pervasive and the condition more resistant to treatment.

Hersov (1960), in his study of 50 cases of school refusal, found 74 per cent of the school phobics to be timid and fearful when they were away from home, but wilful and dominating at home. The younger children had less experience in coping with parental absence and tended to be overprotected. Mothers were overcontrolling and fathers, though good providers, were inadequate in nearly half the sample. Neurosis was also present in the families of school phobics.

Shapiro and Jegede (1973) suggested a four-dimensional approach to school phobia.

- The first criterion is the age or the developmental stage: When a younger child, for example, has separation anxiety it is normal. The same in an older child is pathological.
- The second criterion concerns external forces such as parental attitude to school, peer relations, punitive school system and socio-cultural values.
- The third criterion is the child's intra-psychic organization, defences and conflicts.
- The fourth dimension is how the child perceives his anxiety. For example, a neurotic child does not go to school because of anxiety, though he wants to go, whereas a truant avoids school and does not bother about it.

Thus, it is essential to identify whether school refusal is due to voluntary withholding by the parents, due to separation anxiety, phobic manifestation, aspects of depression, a psychotic disorder, or personality disorder (Hersov, 1977). The management rests on the identification of the causes. It is essential that the child is returned to school at the earliest, as the longer the absence, the poorer the prognosis.

Hersov (1960) found that in his group of school phobics, 68 per cent had returned to school in a year's time. Recovery was not related to age, sex, IQ, duration of symptoms or quality of relationships.

PHOBIAS

Phobias in children are severe and unreasonable fears of specific persons, objects and situations, varying from very intense to mild but persisting beyond two years. Miller, Barrett, and Hampe (1974) define phobia as anxiety which:

- Is attached to a specific non-threatening stimulus
- Is out of proportion to the demands of the situation
- Cannot be reasoned or explained away
- Is beyond voluntary control
- Leads to avoidance of the feared situation
- Persists over an extended period of time
- Is unadaptive
- Is not age- or stage-specific

Kessler (1972) suggests that phobias may develop in five different ways. First, the parents' warning about something may create a fear about it. Second, some phobias may develop through classical conditioning, in which a neutral object elicits fear by its association with a feared object. Third, it could be the child's own imagination that gives rise to misunderstandings. Fourth, a child might develop a phobic reaction by modelling the behaviour of someone with whom the child has positive identification. Finally, classical psychoanalysis views phobias as a defence against the unconscious impulses striving for expression.

Another reason could be family conflicts or stressors. Hence, management has to be determined by the actual causes of phobia. Treatment consists of behaviour therapy, psycho-dynamically oriented individual therapy, family therapy or supportive measures.

Obsessive-Compulsive Disorder

Obsessive-compulsive disorder is relatively rare in childhood. Judd (1965) reported a prevalence rate of 1.2 per cent in the child psychiatric population. Hollingsworth, Tanguay, Grossman, and Pabst (1980), in a later study in the same setting, established it to be 0.2 per cent. Typically, the obsessive child is above average in intelligence and this disorder occurs more frequently in children of middle socio-economic status. It must be remembered that some obsessive-compulsive rituals are normal at certain ages, such as avoiding cracks on the roads, touching lamp-posts and preoccupation with numbers of vehicles on the road. These are innocuous, non-intrusive and transient, and are not distressing to the child or his family.

It is useful to distinguish whether the child yields to compulsion or resists it. Yielding to the compulsion offers primary gratification. Based on extensive psychotherapeutic work with obsessive children, Adams (1973) considered the syndrome as one of cognitive pathology.

Several workers have commented on the higher incidence of psychological disorders in families (Hollingsworth et al., 1980; Judd, 1965), where parents frequently showed obsessive-compulsive neurosis themselves. Marital discord, schizophrenia, depression and serious mental illness among parents have also been reported. Pollak (1979) suggested an association between obsessive-compulsive personality in the parents and in the offspring. In India, Khanna and Srinath (1988) studied 16 cases of obsessive-compulsives and found fewer obsessions and more compulsions, especially washing rituals, in their sample. The obsessions consisted of religious thoughts, fears of harm and impersonal images. In traditional settings, compulsive behaviour may not strike the parents as pathological, because they merge in the compulsive ritualistic background.

A relationship between obsessive-compulsive neuroses, the Tourette syndrome and conduct disorder has been reported and has led to the postulate of a neurological basis of behaviour. Treatments have generally been psychodynamic, behavioural and, in more recent times, pharmacological.

Selective Mutism

Another neurotic condition that is not as frequent is selective mutism. It may be transiently present in young children when they first join school. Hayden (1980) classified the syndrome into three groups based on a sample of 60 children. In the first group, where the child and the mother had a symbiotic relationship, the children used their silence to control their environment; in the second group were the phobic mutes who were afraid to hear their own voices; and the third group consisted of those who reacted to trauma with muteness, for whom silence was a passive–aggressive weapon. Reed (1963) suggested that those who were manipulative and attention-seeking should be treated by behavioural methods, while those who were tense and anxious, with low self-esteem, should be treated by counselling about the source of anxiety.

SUMMARY

Internalizing disorders or disorders of emotion are characterized by subjective distress in the child. Disorders of emotion are characterized by feelings of inferiority, self-consciousness, social withdrawal, shyness, anxiety, crying, hypersensitivity, depression and sadness. These also include symptomatology similar to adult neuroses such as anxiety states, depressive disorders, obsessive-compulsive neurosis, phobias, hysteria and hypochondriasis. The diagnosis of disorder of emotion is based on whether the child has a psychiatric disorder as judged by (*a*) persistent disturbed behaviour; (*b*) emotions and relationships which are accompanied by impairment in personal or social functioning; and/or (*c*) a distortion of the developmental process. The diagnosis has to be based on the total pattern of symptoms and not on any one symptom alone. The so-called neurotic traits of childhood such as nail-biting, thumb-sucking, food fads, stammering or bedwetting are not valid indicators of emotion disorder.

CHAPTER

Physical Symptoms of Psychological Origin and Chronic Physical Illness

The definition of 'health psychology' has three key components. Health psychology as a sub-discipline of psychology emerged in 1978 in the West. Earlier, over the years, the Cartesian dualism of body and mind had been perpetuated by medical technology. In India, especially in the medical tradition of Ayurveda in ancient India, the dualism of body and mind, man and universe, never existed. In the West, though mechanistic approaches have been successful in conquering acute infections, they have failed to address problems of chronic diseases such as cardiac illness, stroke, cancer, diabetes and HIV/AIDS. This has been more so in the field of prevention. By the late 1960s and early 1970s the need for a comprehensive approach to the diagnoses, treatment and prevention of chronic diseases became evident. This included:

1. The examination of the relationship between behavioural, cognitive, psycho-physiological, social and environmental factors in the establishment, and the maintenance and decline of health.
2. The integration of psychological and biological findings in the designs of empirically-based interventions for the prevention and the treatment of illness.
3. The evaluation of physical and psychological status before, during and after medical and psychosocial interventions.

In *Child and Adolescent Psychiatry: A Comprehensive Textbook*, health psychology was described as 'paediatric psychology' by Logan Wright in 1967. It is an interdisciplinary field addressing the interaction of physical, behavioural and emotional development in health and illness issues affecting children, adolescents and families, within the larger field of health psychology. The focus is not only on children and adolescents but also on the contexts of the child within the family, the school, and in medical settings. The emphasis is on the normative development of adaptation to stress resulting from physical conditions, medical treatment and psycho-social interactions with the family and peers rather than the psycho-pathological view of children in adjustment and disease.

Three groups of conditions have received attention from the perspective of health psychology. These are:

1. Interventions for enuresis, encopresis, vomiting, food refusal, chronic abdominal pain, failure to thrive, anorexia and attention deficit disorders

2. Appreciation of psychological principles to understand and intervene with behavioural and psychological constraints of disease, disabilities and medical procedures
3. A focus on healthy development in conditions such as cancer, AIDS, diabetes and asthma

The strength of health psychology lies in its holistic approach and the emphasis on empirical validation. Perhaps this is an approach we need to adopt for child psychiatric disorders in general and psychosomatic disorders in particular.

The term 'psychosomatic disorders' is no longer in vogue in the Western world. Yet the fact remains that body and mind continue to interact constantly. Some of the popular diagnoses like hysteria have fallen by the wayside while terms like psycho-neuro immunology have gained currency. These symptoms of body and mind continue to interact and produce a spectrum of disorders. However, some of the somatic manifestations of 'dissociative and conversion' disorders as expressions of distress are very common in the Asian context. Functional fits, abdominal pain in younger children and headaches in older children and adolescents are some of the common manifestations in India. These disorders are often seen more frequently in general hospitals and primary care settings. Mass hysteria in schools has been encountered with some regularity in rural India.

SOMATIC PROBLEMS

Anxiety includes both fear and bodily symptoms which are part of autonomic responses. The symptoms include abdominal pains, nausea, vomiting, headache, frequent micturition and diarrhoea. These are physical symptoms which are psychologically caused.

There is yet another set of bodily symptoms which is not triggered by the autonomic nervous system, while having emotional origins. These include psychologically caused paralysis, abnormality of gait, disorders of sensation such as blindness, deafness, aphonia, pain, along with pseudo-seizures and fugues. These are explained in terms of 'dissociation' and 'conversion'. They are often responses to acute stressful conditions and come under the rubric of hysteria.

The third set of conditions, namely, psychosomatic conditions, are initiated and maintained by chronic emotional distress, conflict and anxiety.

All the three groups may be seen as body language expressing distress. It is thus possible to conceptualize somatic problems with traditional hysterical disorders at the psychological end of the continuum; psychosomatic disorders such as ulcers, migraine, chronic and recurring pain with a large emotional component and vague physical basis in the middle; and psychological associated problems with identifiable physical basis towards the physical end of the continuum. Severity and management are influenced by psychological variables (as in the case of asthma or diabetes) at this point of the continuum. Chronic physical illness, which also requires psychological adaptation for optimal adjustment, falls at the physical end of the continuum. Figure 11.1 illustrates the interactions between the body, mind and environment that result in such somatic problems.

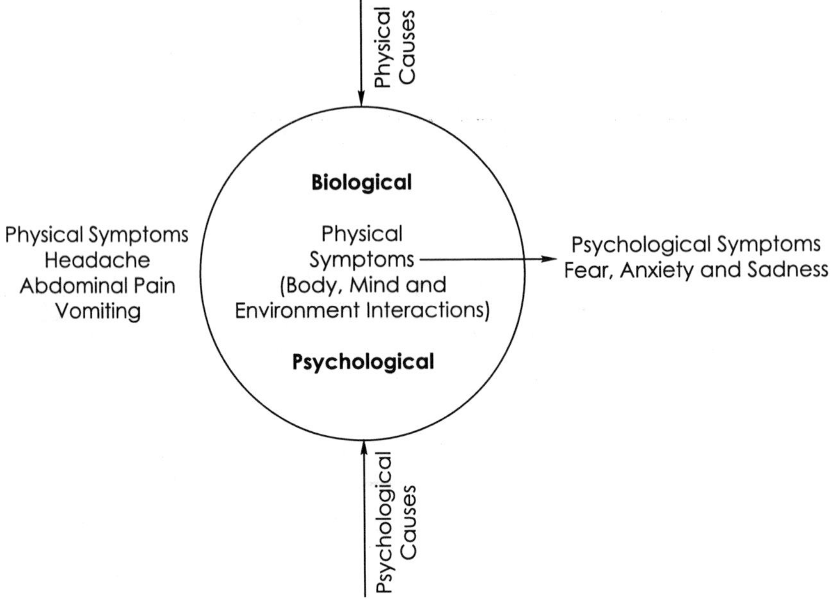

Figure 11.1 Somatic Problems

PSYCHOSOMATIC OR PSYCHO-PHYSIOLOGICAL DISORDERS

Theoretically, psychosomatic relationships are explained by psychoanalytic concepts and deal essentially with the complex, yet integrated, nature of interaction between the body and the mind. Subsequently it has been suggested that conscious and unconscious intra-psychic conflicts are not the important causes. Social stressors occurring in the family and environment, however, have a significant role in the aetiology and maintenance of the symptoms. Thus, the study of acute and chronic stressful events and their role in psychosomatic disorders has been of interest in recent decades.

Some of the disorders which are encountered more frequently in children shall be discussed briefly in this section.

Failure to Thrive

A small number of young children may be brought for medical attention because they are well below average in height and weight. This condition generally does not have any organic basis. There is an overwhelming likelihood that a child presenting with failure to thrive will be suffering from adverse psycho-social factors. Management consists of identifying a suitable diet and counselling the parents as to how to meet the emotional needs of the child in a sensitive manner and how to provide cognitive stimulation. In India, a variant of this condition has been reported. Hoch (1967) reported six children in the Indian setting who were diagnosed as having psycho-physical infantilism that may also be referred to as 'failure to thrive' in the current usage. Retarded physical, emotional and mental development was also noted in these children; it was not the potential for growth that was lacking but the speed of actualization that was inhibited. Hoch attributed this to general immaturity which the child could catch up on under favourable circumstances.

Anorexia and Bulimia

Although obesity is reckoned to be one of the most common disorders in developed countries and there is a large volume of research on the subject, considerable uncertainties remain about its definition, aetiology and treatment (Graham, 1985). The condition is seen less frequently in children belonging to the lower strata of society within developing countries, which consists of the majority of the population in India.

Anorexia in the young is found in the second generation of Asian immigrants in Europe. In Asian countries the syndrome was rare earlier—now it is not. During her 32-years stay in India, Hoch reported (personal communication) to have seen only one case which was probably 'genuine'. Others, in which anorexia played a role, were more akin to catatonic reactions or exaggerations of the 'normal' Indian reaction of going on 'hunger-strike'. In the West, there is (or was?) the theory that such girls do not accept the feminine role. In India, a woman, though still suffering from discrimination, can become important by distinguishing herself in her biologically female role, i.e., by having children. Perhaps the syndrome only occurs when other ways of 'distinguishing themselves' are not open to females in a culture. Another observation by Hoch was that at times one finds pre-adolescent or adolescent boys in India who starve themselves almost to the scale reminiscent of anorexia nervosa. The reason they give is that they want to reduce the production of energy so as to prevent the waste of it in sexual practices (for example: masturbation, *svapna-dosh*, i.e., wet dreams, etc.). Hoch has also more often heard boys saying they would prefer to be girls (as this would relieve them from much responsibility!), than girls who said they would like to be boys. Phenomena of this kind may still exist today, but one would have to look for them very selectively in traditional Indian settings.

Anorexia is not seen very often in Indian psychiatric practice and is even less frequently associated with bulimia. Anorexics, as a rule, are treatment-resistant and often have to be treated at in-patient facilities because of their poor nutritional status, often leading to fatal results. Management consists of psychodynamic and behavioural measures and alert medical regimentation of nutrition.

Asthma

Childhood asthma is primarily due to an inborn vulnerability causing hyperactivity in the bronchi. The asthmatic attacks may be precipitated by infection and allergens. In a large number of children, anxiety and excitement appear to be precipitating factors for the attacks. Emotional distress has a less important role as an aetiological factor. Matus (1981) pointed out in a review that emotional factors which precipitate the attacks should be identified and efforts should be made to improve communication in the family, apart from medical treatment which is essential during the attacks.

Chronic Abdominal Pain

Stomach-aches are common complaints among children with non-specific emotional disorders. Organic pathology should be ruled out; weight loss and pain at night may be suggestive of organic pathology. Pattern of child–parent communication of anxiety and preoccupation with body symptoms in the family may be important in the understanding and treatment of this disorder.

Chronic pains, such as headaches and body-aches, can also be the manifestation of emotional disorders, particularly in older children. Emotional distress could also be manifested through cyclical vomiting and other gastro-intestinal problems. While abdominal pain is common in younger children, other kinds of pain are often seen in older children and adolescents.

CHILDREN WITH CHRONIC OR SERIOUS PHYSICAL ILLNESS

Children with physical handicaps, chronic or serious illnesses like diabetes or cancer require psychological help in the management of their problems in order to better adjust to their condition. The new field of behavioural medicine essentially focuses on these issues. In the management of psychosomatic problems, guidelines by Minuchin and his co-workers are useful to the clinician. Minuchin et al. (1975) studied three disorders, namely asthma, anorexia nervosa and juvenile diabetes. They suggested that the development of severe psychosomatic disorders was associated with certain patterns of family organization and functioning, which were:

1. **Enmeshment:** Family members are over-involved with one another with little regard for individual autonomy, independence and privacy.
2. **Overprotectiveness:** Family members exhibit a high degree of concern for each other with considerable nurturant and protective response.
3. **Rigidity:** Such families are committed to maintaining the status quo and experience difficulty when change and growth are necessary; the family members often deny any other problems apart from the child's medical problems.
4. **Lack of conflict resolution:** There is a low threshold for overt conflict and direct confrontations are avoided or defused; consequently, such families live in a chronic state of submerged conflicts with associated stress and tension.
5. **Use of the patient's symptoms as a conflict 'detouring' mechanism:** The patient is involved in parental and family conflicts. The family's focus on the child's symptoms serves to reduce the intensity of family conflicts.

The three patterns in which the sick child is involved are described as: (a) where the child has divided loyalty and cannot side with either parent; (b) where the child aligns with one or the other parent; and (c) where the parents show a united front in protecting or blaming the child.

The above description of a psychosomatic family fits into what often passes as normal interaction in traditional Indian families. Thus, management of psychosomatic problems, medical or otherwise, should consist mainly of behavioural and family therapy, especially along the lines of the Minuchin model.

HYSTERIA

Hysteria as a syndrome seems to be on its way out in Western psychiatric practice. Some workers like Taylor (1986) believe that it is essentially a Third World syndrome. The belief that hysteria is a fast-disappearing syndrome is reflected in the current classificatory system and the sparse and dwindling number of studies reported from the West. In the DSM-III-R classificatory system, the term 'hysteria' is not used and is considered under somatoform disorder as conversion disorder, along with body dysmorphic disorder, hypochondriasis, somatization disorder and undifferentiated somatoform disorder. Dissociative disorder is dealt with as a separate disorder. Thus, only sensory and motor and no psychic manifestations are included. There seems to be an antipathy to the use of psychoanalytic constructs which can effectively explain the phenomenology and the aetiology of hysteria. The ICD-10 classificatory system uses the terms 'dissociation' and 'conversion' instead of 'hysteria'.

Hysterical conversion and dissociative reactions have a special place in medical history. Hysteria may manifest in numerous ways—as amnesia, fugues, narcolepsy, stupors, dissociative symptoms of different kinds and conversion symptoms of sensory, motor or somatic types. On occasion, psychotic or depressive episodes and mono-symptomatic hallucinations may be seen. Hysteria can thus mimic several neurological, psychosomatic and psychological disorders.

The psychodynamic explanation, which is equally applicable in India as elsewhere, postulates that hysterical symptoms have an important function in symbolically expressing intra-psychic conflicts (which may or may not be sexual or aggressive) and defences against these impulses. At the same time, the symptoms serve multiple purposes. The primary gain lies in the reduction of the anxiety associated with the conflict. The secondary gain is achieved by getting the attention of family members.

In the West, a very low prevalence of hysteria has been reported by some workers (Robins and O'Neal, 1953; Rutter et al., 1975), while slightly higher rates have been reported by others (Proctor, 1958; Rock, 1971). In general, studies have reported higher prevalence in girls than boys and more in adolescents than in younger age groups (Kanner, 1957; Proctor, 1958; Rock, 1971). In the younger age groups the sex ratio is the same. There are very few studies in the West on the prevalence of hysteria in children. Proctor (1958) stated that this is related to the diagnostic criteria set forth by the authors and the type of population studied. Rae (1977) found that conversion reactions were rare in the general population but were frequently encountered at in-patient medical facilities, which ranged from 5–24 per cent of the referrals, with no significant difference between blacks and whites. In Europe, Eggers (1986) reported a prevalence rate of 1.4 per cent of the total number of 900 patients of the child psychiatric unit for a duration of five years.

Regarding age trends, some studies have reported hysteria in very young children (Eggers, 1986; Goodyer, 1981; Proctor, 1958), while others like Robins and O'Neal (1953), Rock (1971) and Seltzer (1985) have reported a greater number of hysterics in the post-puberty period.

Uncommon presentations such as possession are reported by Chandrashekar et al. (1980). 30 cases of possession states were found to be in the age group of 10–15 years with no cases of possession states below the age of 10 years. Earlier studies had also reported possession states to be uncommon in children (Teja et al., 1970; Varma et al., 1970). Sultana et al. (1982) reported that 12 per cent cases were in the age range of 12–15 years.

Several studies have also been conducted on the child population in India with regard to hysteria. In an epidemiological survey Dubey (1976) reported hysteria in 25 per cent of the total sample of 8,035 children. Chacko (1964) found hysteria in 30 per cent of the 70 cases; Hoch (1967) in 9 per cent of the 208 cases seen over 6 years; and Mishra (1976) in 6.93 per cent of the children with emotional problems. Manchanda and Manchanda (1978), in a sample group of 49 neurotic children, found hysteria in 71 per cent children. Sharma et al. (1980) similarly reported 66 per cent of 30 cases to be hysterics. Srinath et al. (1991) reported that of the 640 out-patient and 143 in-patient case records in a year, 30.8 per cent had been diagnosed as hysterics. Of these, 37 per cent were in the age group of 5–11 years, 63 per cent in the age group of 12–16 years, with 48 per cent females, 74 per cent from urban areas and 74 per cent school-going children. An ICMR study (1984) found hysteria in 23 per cent of 1,835 child psychiatric cases. Uma and Kapur (1987) in a retrospective review of 100 cases, found the peak occurrence to be in the age range of 8–12 years and equally common in both boys and girls. Precipitating events, presence of a model and primary and secondary gains were often recognizable. Ninan and Kapur (1989) found the hysterics as having average intelligence in comparison to normal adolescents of 12–16 years. Studies in India have generally found social class and urban-rural residence to be non-contributory in the child population (Srinath et al., 1991; Uma, 1988).

In children, hysterical traits such as suggestibility, vivid fantasy life and attention-seeking behaviour can be normal features, as highlighted by Kessler (1972). Symonds (1973) suggested that conversion and dissociative symptoms may fall into different diagnostic categories.

The findings of Indian studies are equivocal as they have been done on fairly small samples without normal controls (Florence, 1983; Singh et al., 1979; Somasundaram et al., 1974).

The common causal factors of hysteria in children fall into three categories. These are:

(a) Clear precipitating factors such as personal loss, examination, failing in exams.
(b) Primary gain: Here the symptom itself offers a solution to the problem. For example, when the child finds going to the school unpleasant or traumatic because of being beaten by the teacher or bullied by other children—a symptom of 'inability to walk' provides a solution.
(c) Secondary gain: Because of the illness, parents become affectionate, give in to all the demands and teachers too act kindly towards the child. This prompts the child to cling on to the symptoms because of the secondary benefits.

Psycho-social Stressors

The presence of stressors causing distress has been considered as one of the diagnostic criteria by Rock (1971) and Friedman (1973). Several Indian studies have reported precipitating events. Rangaswamy and Kamakshi (1983) studied life events in a group of 30 hysterical adolescents and found that in 88 per cent the onset was preceded by unpleasant personal experiences. The life events in this group were physical illness, failure at school, lack of recreation, increased arguments between parents, death of relatives, etc. Ninan and Kapur (1989) found a significantly larger number of stressors in a sample of hysterical adolescents when compared to normals.

Cognitive Functioning

Uma and Kapur (1987) found that 95 per cent of the children diagnosed as hysterics had average intelligence. Ninan and Kapur (1989) found 18 hysterical adolescents to be of average intelligence, though their intelligence level was significantly lower than that of normal adolescents.

Family Characteristics

In Western literature, there are no conclusive or consistent findings about the relationship between family characteristics and children with hysterical disorders. Rock (1971) found the mothers of hysterical children to be overprotective and the fathers to be ineffectual, and reported that such parents were unwilling to view the child's problems as psychological. Yates and Steward (1976) commented on the generalized inhibition of anger in the family. Laitman (1981) commented on enmeshed boundaries in these families. Gilpin (1981) found the mothers of hysterical children to be very religious, with narcissistic and hysterical traits. Gilpin also reported inappropriate physical closeness of the fathers to their daughters and marital infidelity in the fathers of hysterical children.

In India, Shetty (1975), in a sample of 30 hysterics in the age range of 4–14 years, found overt marital discord, impaired decision-making, diminished communication and decreased interaction between the child and the father in families with hysterical children, when compared to families of normal controls. Uma and Kapur (1987) found familial over-involvement, inadequate disciplining, and discordant intra-familial relationships in the families of a sample of 100 hysterical children. Geetha (1976), in a small sample of 10 hysterical children, found less interaction between the parents, with increased warmth and interaction between the child and the father, as observed in the hospital setting.

Phenomenology

A study was carried out by Uma (1988) on 70 hysterical and 70 normal children in the age range of 8–12 years. This aimed at establishing the nature of phenomenology and correlates of hysteria in the Indian context.

Symptoms such as unresponsiveness, falling to the ground, abnormal movements of the body (functional seizures), giddiness, pain in a specific part of the body, headache and abnormal behaviour were frequently reported. Symptoms such as possession state, abnormal behaviour, pulling sensation of the body, attacks of 'shivering' appear to be unique to the Indian setting (Uma, 1988).

Primary gain was evident in 52.6 per cent of the children, while secondary gain could be identified in 90 per cent of them. Hysteria was also associated with other disorders of emotion and conduct, with sleep problems, poor appetite, scholastic backwardness, sadness and inappropriate talk in some cases.

The majority of the hysterics were comparable to normals in their interpersonal relations with parents and siblings, but had significantly more problems with teachers, as reported by the mothers and children themselves. On the fifth axis of the multi-axial system, the hysterical children had significant stress at school, were exposed to inadequate and inconsistent parental control, discordant intra-familial relationships, familial over-involvement and anomalous family relationship with multiple parenting (these children came from larger families with multiple disciplinary figures). There was no evidence of mental illness in their families when compared to normals and this is at variance with some of the Western reports (Goodyer, 1981; Robins and O'Neal, 1953). Child-rearing attitudes of the mothers of hysterics differed significantly from that of normal mothers. Mothers of hysterics were dominating, overprotective, and did not treat the child as an individual, giving her/him a subordinate role. The mothers often had faulty attitudes to child-rearing.

Hoch (personal communication) offers insight into brief episodes and hysterical personality. Hysterical reaction is a kind of makeshift emergency solution, which is superficial because there is no time to 'construct' something more deep and solid. On the other hand, a comparatively flimsy, superficial solution can serve as a long-term solution of a problem if the patient's 'health consciousness' is poor and the tolerance for this kind of demonstrative deviation is high. A symptom is always partly 'revealing' and partly 'concealing' in hysterical reactions; the 'revealing' portion is relatively high, either because one did not have time to 'cover up' more efficiently, or because there is no need for concealment. What is more important as a base for hysterical reactions is the 'level of consciousness', i.e., the span of openness to or awareness of the world, and introspective reflection, of oneself. In hysterical reactions, the span of awareness and the ability for introspective reflections are limited.

CHRONIC CHILDHOOD ILLNESS

Chronic childhood illness may be physical like diabetes, asthma, epilepsy, haemophilia, kidney malfunction, leukaemia or even AIDS. All the chronic illnesses in children pose special problems:

1. Adherence to treatment may not be carried out either by the parent or by the child. The reasons may be that these are expensive, painful, produce unpleasant side-effects, have social implications of being made fun of, etc. It is important to find out the reasons for non-adherence and deal with it effectively in the context of child-care and the family.
2. Problems arising at school which could include absenteeism, disciplinary issues and school performance.
3. Serious psychiatric disorders occurring independently or arising out of a physical illness, too, can be problematic. Depression is particularly common in children with chronic disorders.
4. Some related problems may be increased mortality, the threat of sudden death, threat of recurrence, impairment of brain function, deterioration of functioning of various bodily systems, limitation of scenario inputs, personality alteration, stigma, effect on appearance and body image.
5. Psychological burden of care on the families is immense. In addition, there are practical burdens of labour, cost, access to treatment and so on. These are more important considerations especially in the developing countries. In the long run, community and financial support to the family becomes even more important than provision of care directly to the child. If the family is not cooperative, the child may be denied care.

DEALING WITH DEATH AMONG CHILDREN

Fears of one's own death or the death of siblings or parents often cause severe psychological problems in children. Children's understanding of the above depends on their age. It is reported that better family functioning and better psychological outcome for the children include openness of communication, positive approach to illness, good emotional support, healthy parental marital relationship, family cohesiveness, and religious faith. Family income is also a crucial factor, especially in low income countries with poor access to health care.

SUMMARY

Anxiety gives rise to both fear as well as bodily symptoms such as abdominal pain, nausea, vomiting and headache. There are also physical symptoms caused by stress acting in the conscious and unconscious mind, that produce symptoms which mimic neurological symptoms such as fainting, paralysis, etc. In addition, physical symptoms themselves can lead to emotional distress and make it worse. All these disorders point to the close and complex interaction between the body and the mind.

SELF-EVALUATION

Short-answer Questions

1. Name five physical symptoms of anxiety.
2. Name five physical symptoms of stress.
3. Name five physical illnesses that can produce emotional distress and make it worse.
4. What are the problems caused by chronic physical illnesses in childhood?
5. What are some of the common manifestations of Hysteria (Dissociative Disorder) in the Asian countries?

Multiple-choice Questions

1. The relationship between body and mind
   a. Does not exist
   b. Is interactive and complex

c. Is unrelated
d. Is imaginary
e. None of the above

Answer: b

2. Health psychology examines the roles and interactions among the following factors:

a. Behavioural
b. Cognitive
c. Psycho-physiological
d. Social environmental
e. All the above

Answer: e

3. Body symptoms caused by anxiety in childhood:

a. Abdominal pain
b. Nausea and vomiting
c. Headache
d. Frequent urination
e. All the above

Answer: e

4. Psychosomatic conditions:

a. Ulcers
b. Migraine
c. Chronic recurring pain
d. Asthma
e. All the above

Answer: e

5. Some of the family organization and functioning typically described in the psychosomatic conditions are:

a. Over-protection
b. Rigidity
c. Lack of conflict resolution
d. Conflict 'detouring'
e. All the above

Answer: e

CHAPTER

12 Pervasive Developmental Disorders and Childhood Psychoses

This chapter is a mixed bag of disorders. It talks about syndromes of autism, schizophrenia, affective disorder, disintegrative psychosis and reactive psychosis. In short, it contains mention of all the serious psychiatric disorders of childhood. A word of caution is that these disorders need to be handled by an experienced mental health team. These cannot be handled by counsellors. **The information is to enable the reader to refer the cases to appropriate agencies**. Since these are to be referred, a brief note on interventions is given here instead of in Part III to sensitize the reader.

Existence of psychoses in childhood was noted by Kraeplein and Bleuler in the beginning of the century and till the 1930s it was believed that there were no differences between adult and childhood forms of psychoses. It was Kanner, in the 1940s, who first argued that there exists a unique and qualitatively different syndrome of childhood psychosis which should be differentiated from schizophrenia (Kanner, 1957). He described 11 cases in great detail. They were normal in cognitive potential and the onset of psychosis was in infancy. He described their inability to relate to people as 'autistic' aloofness. The cases had language deviance—manifested in delayed acquisition, echolalia and mutism. They also had excellent rote memory, repetitive stereotyped play activities and an obsessive desire to maintain sameness in the environment. Kanner named the syndrome 'infantile autism', and it was eventually called Kanner's Syndrome by others. Subsequently, several studies (Kolvin, 1971; Makita, 1966; Rutter, 1978) have highlighted the differences between infantile autism and childhood schizophrenia.

The age distribution for the onset of serious childhood psychiatric disorder was bipolar, falling most frequently before three years of age in the case of infantile autism or in early adolescence in the case of schizophrenia or affective disorders. Kolvin (1971) found significant differences between early and late onset of psychiatric disorders in the phenomenology, in terms of parental social class, family history of schizophrenia, frequency of cerebral dysfunction, speech patterns and levels of intelligence quotient.

Phenomenology of infantile autism has several characteristics, which are now widely recognized (Ritvo and Freeman, 1977). The core symptoms include age of onset prior to 30 months of age, disturbances of speech and language and impaired social relationships. Other symptoms, such as insistence on sameness, disturbances in developmental sequences and disturbances in responses to stimuli have been considered important.

PREVALENCE

The prevalence of early infantile autism is estimated to be about four to five cases per 10,000 of the population (Lotter, 1966) and this may be so all over the world (Ritvo and Freeman, 1977). Most investigators agree that 70 per cent of autistic people have mental retardation (DeMeyer, Hingten and Jackson, 1981). Several investigators have reported that autism occurs more frequently in males than in females and the reported ratio is 4:1 (Kolvin, 1971; Rutter and Lockyer, 1967).

Other conditions to be differentiated from autism are mental retardation, developmental language disability and schizophrenia. Autism and retardation are two different, though overlapping conditions. Autistics do not use language for social purposes and use less symbolic play. Schizophrenia differs from autism and rarely develops before the age of 10 (Ross, 1980). In about 70 per cent of autistic children, intelligence is below average and there is also a failure to form relationships in the first place.

AETIOLOGICAL SPECULATIONS

Psycho-social Factors

Some theories have stressed unusual personality traits in parents including emotional coldness and superior intelligence which could be transmitted genetically (Ounsted, 1970) or determine the child's response to the parents' personalities. Others have suggested pathological parent–child interaction, consisting of poor maternal communication, too much or too little stimulation or early parental rejection (Bettelheim, 1967).

The psycho-social factors implicated may be grouped under four categories as suggested by Cantwell, Baker and Rutter (1978):

1. Severe stress and traumatic events early in the child's life, particularly in the first two years
2. Parental psychiatric disorder or deviant personality characteristics
3. Parental intelligence quotient and social class
4. Deviant parent–child interaction

However, despite the various speculations on aetiology, there have been an equal number of studies denying the role of psycho-social factors.

Neurological Correlates

Decreasing emphasis on psychogenic theories in the last two decades has been accompanied by increasing research on the possible role of brain dysfunction. Several studies have reported increased incidence of pre- and peri-natal complications (Kolvin, Ounsted and Roth, 1971). The presence of soft neurological signs has been reported in 40–100 per cent of cases depending on the sample studied (DeMeyer et al., 1974). Autistic symptoms have been seen in conditions associated with central nervous system infections and brain damage. Abnormal electro-encephalograms (EEGs) and epileptic seizures have been reported in 20–30 per cent of autistic children (Kolvin, 1971). Ornitz and Ritvo (1976) suggested a maturational defect on the basis of neuro-physiological findings. There are neuropsychological speculations suggesting over-arousal of the reticular activating system, perceptual inadequacy of vestibular nuclei of the brain stem, dysfunction of the limbic system and cognitive deficits associated with hemisphere dysfunctions. These speculations are often based on isolated behaviours, such as stereotyped movements and other disturbances found in autistic children.

Sanua (1986), in a review of studies claiming the organic aetiology of autism, traced many of the major articles and highlighted the dubious nature of the samples and tentative nature of the conclusions drawn. Thus, it has been conceded that definite evidence for the organic aetiology of autism is as elusive and tentative as it was for psychogenic aetiology two decades ago.

There are workers who go beyond the conventional notion of causes of autism and postulate fundamental functions in terms of cognitive, perceptual, linguistic and emotional deficits which make the autistics behave in the manner they do.

Hermelin and O'Connor (1970) suggested that active social avoidance was due to poor communication skills based on underlying perceptual and cognitive deficiencies. Bartak, Rutter and Cox (1975) particularly highlighted a child's communication disability which extends beyond spoken language to include both gesture and inner language. Hermelin (1978) has argued that autism is related to an inability to form an internal representation of external events, including play, and forming stable relationships, all of which depend on symbolic functioning. DeMeyer et al. (1972) postulated a lack of ability in autistics to imitate their own or other people's motor actions due to both auditory and perceptual visual-motor deficits and in their inability to communicate in verbal and non-verbal modalities.

Continuity and Discontinuity. Autism is considered to be a stable condition in which an autistic child grows up to be an autistic adult who is quite unlike an adult schizophrenic. High IQ and linguistic skills are associated with better prognosis. In the 1960s, the prognosis was considered to be poor, with the majority of autistics being under institutional care. However in recent years, the prognosis is much better in countries where better training facilities are available. For example, Venter, Lord and Schopler (1992), in an 8-year follow-up study of a Canadian sample of 58 high-functioning autistic children, reported that verbal skills were the strongest predictor of social adaptive functioning and a positive relationship existed between intellectual functioning and academic attainment. The authors related better outcome to better educational opportunities offered, which were not available in the 1960s.

AUTISM IN THE INDIAN SETTING

One of the earliest reports from India is that of Bassa (1962) which gave a male-female prevalence rate of 3:1 in child guidance population, 1:1 in psychiatry departments and 1.7:1 in private clinics. An in-depth study of a sample of 17 autistic children was reported by Hoch in 1967. This classic report consisted of astute phenomenological observations and aetiological speculations. To paraphrase Hoch, disturbances in the close relationship between mother and child may occur either because of the child's excessive sensitivity or a faulty maternal attitude. As such disturbances occur fairly early in infancy, they may leave a permanent weakness of what one calls the 'ego boundary', which is the ability to identify oneself as a separate unit which faces the outside world.

In unravelling the mysteries of bio-psycho-social causes, Hoch reported an interesting exercise of analysing the approximate ratios of the loading of biological and psychological factors. Of the 17 children, she reported more organic loading in three cases, more psychogenic loading in six cases, and equal organic and psychogenic loading in eight cases. She also stated that considerable variations are possible in factors, from neurologically demonstrable brain damage to the absence of the same, from seemingly average to an accumulation of severely unsettling emotional factors. In her sample, the male-female ratio was 3:1.

The author (Kapur, 1986) did an in-depth study of six cases of children who presented autistic features and in whom the illness was precipitated by severe psycho-social stressors. It was suggested that reactive pervasive developmental disorder or reactive infantile autism needed to be considered as a separate diagnostic entity as it carried better prognosis if managed with psycho-dynamically oriented therapy. This group of autistic children could be understood better from a developmental perspective.

In this sample, the age of onset was between one and a half and three and a half years, which is a critical period for cognitive, emotional, social and language development. The children had normal developmental history, with speech delay in two who had attained normal linguistic skills at some point in their development. They had adequate self-help skills. Neurological examination showed no deficits, including soft signs. Pre- and peri-natal history was non-contributory. Family history was also non-contributory. Parents had consanguineous marriages in three of the six cases.

The onset of illness was precipitated by marked psycho-social stressors leading to severe disorganization in previously normal children who were empathic and sensitive to those around them. The onset occurred in the Piagetian stage of pre-causal logic, after bonding had occurred with the mother, but before, individuation and separation could take place (as evidenced by the absence of peer interaction in all of them). In these families, there was emotional isolation of the mother and the child, overt marital disharmony, depression in the mother, and family conflicts had led to neglect, social isolation and under-stimulation of the child.

Transient disturbances in the developmental processes were seen in these children. Some of the developmental processes included:

1. Specific developmental problems: Speech and communication disturbances despite normal acquisition of speech and language skills, inattention, over-activity, impulsivity and learning difficulties were observed.
2. Transient developmental problems: Problems such as sleep disorders, feeding problems, secondary enuresis and encopresis occurred, lasting from a few weeks to months.
3. Normal cognitive, linguistic and emotional functioning was seen in the context of the family and significant others. They would respond to praise, toys and outings like normal children. They could also express emotions of anger and happiness.

4. Though they could communicate using symbolic language, they failed to communicate with others in an effective manner because they chose not to.
5. Despite normal functional skills, they failed completely in peer interaction, though they often had a clinging relationship with one or two caretakers.

These children responded well and quickly to psycho-dynamically oriented approaches like play therapy, family and marital therapy in conjunction with some behavioural techniques. While conventional methods of intervention of autism are behavioural and psycho-educational, the focus of the therapy of the reactive autistic children consisted of establishing rapport and normal communication with the child.

Vythilingam (1991) conducted the first systematic research in India on a group of autistic children. She studied several biochemical parameters and psycho-social stressors, using paediatric controls for the former and mentally retarded controls for the latter. The sample consisted of 24 autistic children. One child had myopia, one had microcephaly and one had hypothyroidism. Four children had seizures, nine had hyperkinesis. The rest had no neurological and physical abnormalities.

The male-female ratio was 2.4:1, while Gillberg, Steffenburg and Schaumann (1991), reported a ratio of 4.5:1 in a recent report from the West. Vythilingam reported a greater proportion of pre- and peri-natal injuries in these children. On the biochemical parameters, lowered dopamine, serotonin and tryptophan levels were found, and she suggested that this could be considered for drug management. She also found a significantly high number of psycho-social stressors, especially inadequate stimulation and migration. There were seven nuclear families who had migrated to the Middle East and subsequently had to face social isolation. Significantly higher representation of high socio-economic status was reported in the study. Despite reports of lowered levels of certain neurotransmitters, behavioural concomitants could not be obtained, and actual implications of the findings could not be gleaned. It is interesting to note that from 1967 to 1991, the research methodology has become increasingly sophisticated, yet the syndrome has remained as elusive as ever.

Three types of intervention have been used with autistic children. These are psycho-dynamically oriented therapy, behaviour therapy and drug management. The intervention should, however, be guided by the possible aetiology in a particular case and the worker should make use of the package available, to suit the needs of the child. The first level of diagnosis should be whether the autistic child has average or above average intelligence and linguistic skills. If the child is mentally retarded, the recommended techniques for the training of such children could be effectively used. In a high functioning autistic, efforts should be made to carry out a fine-grained analysis of various associated factors. In the absence of evidence of brain damage (neurological soft signs, epilepsy, pre-/peri-natal injuries, etc.), the presence of psycho-social stressors, particularly around the time of onset, should be explored. The focus should be on the likely impact of these events on a young child who is cognitively well-equipped to handle the event but is deprived of the emotional support normally available to a young child. Such a group of autistics benefits from psycho-dynamically oriented therapy. However, it is necessary to keep an open mind about dynamically oriented therapies, particularly in autism of purely psychogenic origin.

Interventions involving behavioural management are the most commonly used techniques of management with autistic children. The techniques are directed to many aspects including self-injurious behaviour; aggressive behaviour; self-stimulatory behaviour; enhancing verbal and non-verbal communication/social skills; encouraging the development of self-help skills; generalization and maintenance of behavioural change; parent-teacher training; and classroom instructions.

Behavioural interventions have been influential in improving a wide variety of behavioural and educational skills and in decreasing self-injurious, self-stimulatory and aggressive behaviour. A comprehensive intervention package which often consists of training parents and teachers makes institutional care unnecessary.

The third form of intervention is drug treatment. There has been an increased emphasis on this in recent years. Drug treatment in autistic children is used particularly in those with aggressive and self-injurious behaviour. Yet, biological interventions are probably less effective with autistic children than with other psychotic conditions. Carefully monitored use of drugs can be a useful adjunct in some cases.

CHILDHOOD PSYCHOSES OF LATE ONSET

Schizophrenia

Kanner (1957) stated that the older the child is at the onset of psychosis, the more closely the clinical picture resembles that of adult schizophrenia. The symptoms include disturbances in thought processes and affect (e.g. thought insertion and thought broadcast), hallucinations (e.g. voices in the form of running commentary, visual and somatic hallucinations) and well-formed delusions (e.g. of grandeur or persecution). While auditory hallucinations are common in adults and in children, visual hallucinations are more frequently reported in children. Eggers (1978) and Kolvin (1971) documented mood abnormalities which include inappropriate giggling, incongruity, blunting of affect, perplexity, rage, self-directed aggression and ambivalence. Blunting and incongruity of affect were reliable discriminators between childhood schizophrenia and autism. Avoidance of contact with people, which is a central characteristic in autism, is not as frequently seen in schizophrenia.

Prevalence rates for childhood schizophrenia are unknown, although it is thought to be rarer than autism. Kolvin (1971) reported a male-female ratio of 2.6:1. The age of onset in Kolvin's sample was seven years or older. Eggers (1978) has reported that those with the age of onset below 10 years were likely to run a more chronic course and less likely to have an eventual remission. In the early onset, the course is often insidious. Though lowered intelligence quotients were reported in these children, half the children scored in the normal range and were distinctly superior to the autistic children. The schizophrenic children were better at school and were more responsive to therapy and educational programmes. Kolvin (1971) and Eggers (1978) reported that schizophrenic children with above average IQ were more likely to show favourable outcomes.

While most investigators agree that schizophrenia is in part organically based, no consistent organic deficit has yet been found in childhood schizophrenia. Kolvin, Ounsted and Roth (1971) have reported epilepsy in a minority of cases and pregnancy and birth complication in 12 per cent of the cases. Biochemical studies have been few and suffer from unclear diagnostic criteria. It is now generally agreed that in most cases a genetic predisposition is a necessary, but not sufficient prerequisite for the development of overt schizophrenia.

Eggers (1978) reported that 33 of the 57 schizophrenic children lived in a 'disturbed family atmosphere'. However, the family environment was not of prognostic value, as in the rest of the 24 cases it was normal. It was also suggested that difficult family interaction could be due to the child's illness. It is likely that schizophrenia is a result of a complex interaction between genetic, intra-uterine and family factors. A clear understanding of the aetiology of schizophrenia has not been established.

Continuity-Discontinuity. Eggers (1978), in a long-term follow-up of 57 childhood schizophrenics, found that 20 per cent had complete remission, 30 per cent had relatively good social adjustment and 50 per cent had moderate to poor outcome. Early age of onset (before 10 years), shy and introverted personality and low intelligence were predictive of poor outcome. Adverse family environment and family history of schizophrenia were not related to the prognosis.

In a review of European research, Tsiantis, Macri and Marotos (1986) highlighted issues in research on diagnosis, classification and differential diagnosis, and found the boundaries of the all-encompassing term childhood 'psychosis' to be unclear and overlapping. It was pointed out that the Russian approach favoured a unitary concept of psychosis as opposed to the bipolar model supported by the British group of workers. Developmental factors have been singled out to explain relative crudeness and simplicity of symptoms at an early age versus the complexity and systematization with the progress of age. Most European authors agreed on a nature–nurture interactional model rather than a purely biological model.

Affective Disorders

The nature and prevalence of affective disorders in children was, till recently, a much-debated issue. Recent longitudinal studies, such as that of Kovacs (1987), have used adult diagnostic criteria for affective disorders in children. Kovacs found that the background factors, such as broken homes, separation and developmental trauma were non-contributory when compared to the control group. The depressive disorders were divided into adjustment disorder with depressive mood (11 children), major depressive disorder (48 children), and dysthymic disorders (28 children). She showed evidence that depression in children was not short term and that the stage of cognitive development modified the symptom manifestation. In fact, younger children had more severe depression and expressed feelings of worthlessness more often. Older depressed children were more likely to be aggressive and act out their aggression than younger ones; suicidal ideas were common in both the groups.

Recovery from depression in a time span of one and a half years was found in 92 per cent in major depression and 89 per cent in dysthymic disorder with a chronic course. Rapid recovery was common in adjustment disorder with depressed mood and in major depressive disorders. Age of onset of the first episode of major depression and dysthymic disorders were inversely related to recovery, possibly because of strong genetic loading. When the two conditions are superimposed, the risk of subsequent episodes was relatively high.

Aetiologically, family history of affective disorders is important, and suggestive of genetic aetiology. Family history studies suggest an even higher percentage when more than one first-degree relative suffered from an affective disorder, and also when early onset bipolar illness had a stronger genetic loading (Weissman et al., 1984).

In India, Prakash (1987), in a sample of 3,659 psychiatrically ill children, found 2.2 per cent to have minor depressive disorders. Of these, 12 were cases of neurotic depression, 29 of adjustment reaction (19 of brief depressive type and 10 of prolonged depressive type), 6 of depressive disorder, and 39 of emotional disorder with misery and unhappiness. In another study of a sample of 20 children with depression, who were taken up for psycho-dynamically oriented individual therapy and family counselling, Prakash reported that there was a preponderance of psycho-social disadvantages such as discordant family relationship, mental illness in the parents (depression in the mother and alcoholism in the father, anomalous family situation, etc.). In the Indian setting, over-expectation from the parents, leading to lowered self-esteem was an important issue. Out of 1,989 cases, Srinath and Bavle (1987) reported 53 cases of depression, 31 with mania, 15 with depression and 7 with both mania and depression, and with only one female in the sample. Both the studies report male preponderance, though in Western countries the male-female ratio in depression is 2:1. In India, males have a significantly higher prevalence. Management has been generally pharmacological with use of lithium prophylaxis.

In the Indian setting, Reddy (1991) studied a sample of 50 cases of childhood psychoses consisting of 24 males and 26 females in the age range of 10–16 years. Out of these cases, he reported mania in 21, depression in 13 and schizophrenia in 9, with 5 cases of atypical psychosis.

Schizophrenia: In the schizophrenics, the symptoms were similar to those of adult schizophrenics. Auditory hallucinations were the commonest symptom, unlike the Western population, where 44 per cent have catatonic features. Delusions and thought disorders were reported less frequently.

Mania: Symptoms reported in adults could be found in children. Pressure of speech was present in 90.4 per cent of cases. Irritability was present in 80.9 per cent followed by elation in 76.2 per cent. Expansive mood was present in 92.8 per cent of cases. There were some symptoms which overlapped between mania, schizophrenia, attention deficit disorder and conduct disorders. Psychotic symptoms (61 per cent) which were mood incongruent tended to be present, particularly in the early onset group (before 12 years of age).

Depression: The features of adult depression were found equally frequently in children. Appetite disturbance was the most common symptom, present in all the cases, followed by loss of interest (92.3 per cent), psychomotor retardation (92.3 per cent), depressed mood (84.6 per cent), decreased concentration (84.6 per cent), and sleep disturbances (84.6 per cent). However, guilt, hypersomnia, death wishes and suicidal ideation were reported only in a small number of cases. Fifty-nine per cent of the depressives were psychotic and had mood incongruent psychotic features. Features of depression were found in mania and schizophrenia. The atypical psychosis was quite similar to schizophrenia and could possibly be a variant of the same.

In this study, adverse temperamental traits were not reported in schizophrenics, but eight children with affective disorder were head-strong, stubborn and independent, while four were reported to be very sensitive and two were unusually sociable. The majority of the subjects did not have pre- and peri-natal problems or developmental delays. Forty-five per cent of the sample had a positive family history of mental illness, the majority of them (68 per cent) were those with affective disorders. Male-female ratio in schizophrenia as well as mania was 2:1, and in depression it was 3.3:1.

The two major themes emergent in the study were: first, that adult criteria could be used for diagnosis of childhood psychoses, and second, that multiplicity of symptoms which belong to different diagnostic categories, such as mania, depression, schizophrenia, hyperkinesis and conduct disorders, could overlap to make the clinician's task difficult.

DISINTEGRATIVE PSYCHOSIS

This psychotic condition does not belong to any of the psychotic conditions described earlier. The condition is associated with gross disorganization of behaviour, especially with a drop in the developmental milestones which have already been achieved. The onset may or may not be associated with physical illness. It is considered to be biological in origin, with very poor prognosis, and arrest in the deteriorating course is an exception to the rule. Drug and behavioural management to reinstate the lost skills is essentially aimed at making the child more manageable. Marked improvement or recovery on follow-up renders the diagnosis of disintegrative psychosis untenable.

REACTIVE OR HYSTERICAL PSYCHOSIS

These are psychotic conditions which are essentially related to stress and can be diagnosed under the adult classificatory criteria of reactive psychosis. Management is essentially psychosocial, consisting of dynamically oriented individual psychotherapy and family therapy.

INTERVENTION IN SCHIZOPHRENIA AND AFFECTIVE DISORDERS

Intervention consists of a combined approach using drugs, behavioural techniques, special education, social skills training, supportive psychotherapy, family counselling, and structuring of the child's environment and rehabilitation, particularly in chronic cases.

Drug management, especially on a long-term basis, is beset by problems of non-compliance due to distance from the clinic, poverty and lack of motivation on the part of the family. Ensuring a good follow-up is an important factor. The general trend in India is to administer electroconvulsive therapy (ECT) to psychotic children, as is done with adults. A study by Jagdish (1990) appears to suggest that in these cases, such as stuporose, catatonic or severely depressed and withdrawn conditions, where ECT is indicated according to Western criteria, one or two ECTs over the span of 2–3 weeks may suffice.

Education and counselling of the family is important with regard to marriage, child abuse and rehabilitation, particularly for those children who enter with chronic phases of illness. In illnesses where the phases are clear-cut, as in affective disorders, monitoring the symptoms and anticipating a future attack can be done by sensitizing the family.

CASE ILLUSTRATION OF A CHILD WITH REACTIVE AUTISM

Kittu, an 8-year-old boy came from a Hindu joint family of rural background. He was the third of four siblings and was brought with complaints of repeating words and sentences, talking irrelevantly, talking to himself and telling others to do something which he wanted to do. He had had these symptoms since the age of three.

The father, a 40-year-old clerk, had been drinking alcohol for 10 years. For the past three years he had been having an extramarital relationship with a widow at his workplace. He would visit his family in the village once a week. He was reported to be short-tempered and irritable. The mother (30 years old), was irritable and had depressive features because of her husband's extramarital relationship. The relationship between husband and wife was severely strained due to the father's alcoholism and extramarital relationship. The children had witnessed their drunken father beating the mother to unconsciousness a number of times. But when sober, he was reported to be overindulgent with the children.

Kittu's birth was after full-term and normal. Developmental milestones were normal except for speech delay, but he could speak in sentences at the age of five and a half years. In school, he did not mix with other children. He used to sit with his hands covering his ears. He did not learn to read or write in the three years he had been in the first standard. He was teased and laughed at by other children at school and did not play with anyone at school or at home.

The onset of the symptoms was sudden and the course was continuous and progressively deteriorating. It was apparently precipitated by the family's transfer from Chennai to Bangalore. It started en route in the train, with Kittu screaming and crying for no apparent reason, followed by withdrawal, refusal to eat food, incontinence and being fearful of noises. Around this time, the fourth sibling was born and Kittu started clinging to the mother. The psycho-social stressors at this point of time were: moving from one town to another; birth of a sibling; joining a new school; and serious marital conflict due to the father's alcoholism and extramarital relationship.

Kittu often repeated what others said in a mechanical way, talking irrelevantly, and referring to himself in the third person. He was not interested in other children or games, would avoid eye contact, would talk, laugh, cry to himself and would sometimes give no sign of recognizing his family members. He would appear to be deaf, would rotate continuously, and rock back and forth while sitting. He would run forward and backward many times, and would wave a stick or fingers in front of his eyes. The predominant mood was one of happiness. Attempts by the family members to teach him self-help skills had failed.

On psychological assessment, Kittu was found to have average intelligence. During therapeutic management, the therapist actively sought to play with Kittu, forcing him to make eye contact and play. His daily activities were structured, and because of his fondness for groundnuts, these were used as positive reinforcements along with a smile and a word of appreciation. The mother was trained to start working on his self-help skills after breaking them sequentially into small steps. To enable the mother to function more effectively, several sessions were spent with her, allowing her to vent her distress and enabling her to learn to distance herself from the husband's problems. The siblings were encouraged to play with Kittu rather than to ignore him, as they had done earlier. Kittu's fondness for music was capitalized upon by making him sing, making him listen to music and so on. He was also encouraged to play with other children in the ward, who were specially instructed to play with him despite his reluctance. In fact, a couple of over-active and playful children virtually forced him to play with them. The mother was instructed by the speech pathologist in dealing with Kittu's deviant communication. At the end of 10 sessions, on discharge from the in-patient facility, his mother reported him to be 60 per cent better. He had regained his self-help skills, was not as withdrawn as earlier, and would make eye contact and smile. Siblings were instructed to continue to talk to him and actively encourage him to play. On six-week follow-up, he had recovered a good deal with the cooperation of his mother and the rest of the family.

As discussed in this chapter, autistic features may cross-sectionally present themselves in a similar fashion whether the disorder is of biogenic or psychogenic origin. Much of the work consists of improving eye contact, verbal communication and social skills, reduction of disruptive behaviour, and training the mother to carry out the programmes tailored to improve deficits in the child. In biogenic autism, counselling the mother would be of a supportive kind. In a child with psycho-social aetiology, the series of events which lead to the child's illness in terms of under-stimulation, the changes which upset the child and the parental conflicts have to be dealt with from a psychodynamic angle. The therapist has to virtually act as a catalyst for communication between the child and the mother. Play remains the main tool of therapy along with behavioural and linguistic training.

SUMMARY

Autism in infancy and early childhood may occur due to psychosocial and biological causes. Examining the longitudinal bio-psycho-social history is essential. Earlier onset before the age of one, in the absence of psycho-social adversities, is likely to be biologically determined while later onset between 2–5 years is caused by psycho-social adversities. Careful examination of the nature of onset, caretaking history and the child's temperament are essential. In later childhood and adolescence, adult like symptoms of schizophrenia and affective disorders may emerge.

SELF-EVALUATION

Short-answer Questions

1. According to Kanner's description, what are the main features of autism?

2. What is infantile autism characterized by?

3. Name any five psycho-social conditions associated with autism.

4. Name five physiological/neurological correlates of autism.

5. What can be the interventions for autism?

Multiple-choice Questions

1. Psychosis of childhood in comparison to adults is:

a. Same
b. Different
c. Same in the older children
d. None of the above
e. Different in the younger children

Answer: e

2. Psychosis of childhood can be understood by the use of:

a. Cross sectional examination
b. Longitudinal examination
c. Both cross sectional and longitudinal examination
d. Neither cross sectional nor longitudinal examination
e. Comparing to symptoms of adult psychoses

Answer: c

3. Disorders that resemble autism are:

a. Mental retardation
b. Developmental language disability
c. Schizophrenia
d. Disintegrative psychosis
e. All the above

Answer: e

4. The psychotic disorders that may be encountered in childhood and adolescence are:

a. Autism
b. Depression
c. Mania
d. Schizophrenia
e. All the above

Answer: e

5. Disorders that may be mistaken for autism are:

a. Intellectual disability
b. Delayed language development
c. Developmental dysphasia
d. Extreme withdrawal
e. Any of the above

Answer: e

CHAPTER

13 Nature, Causes and Patterns of Disorders in Asian Countries

In the earlier chapters, various specific disorders of childhood have been described. In the present chapter, the focus is on the prevalence and pattern of these disorders in different settings in the South-east Asian region. Most of the studies have been from India and other regions are unrepresented due to the paucity of published studies from the region. However, it can be assumed that Indian studies across settings will perhaps reflect the trends likely to be typical of South-east Asian and other developing countries. The studies will be brief, and in a tabular form to make them easily understandable.

The studies have been carried out at the child guidance clinics, community and school settings across age, gender, ethnic and socio-economic groups. Tables 13.1, 13.2 and 13.3 portray the studies conducted (*a*) in community settings (*b*) in school settings and (*c*) of specific disorders.

Most of the studies have thrown up varied results because of the following differences in their approaches:

1. Sampling
2. Case definition
3. Tools used
4. Multiple sources of information such as parents, teachers, peers and examiners in different settings such as home/school/community
5. Data analysis

Largely, the studies are head-counts of psychiatric categories along with some demographic and biographic details about the subjects and their families. This kind of data gives approximations of the percentage of different kinds of cases across different settings. This data is very useful at the policy level and for the planning of delivery of services to the children who need them.

There has been little effort at providing services as part of epidemiological services. In the countries where services to child population are neglected, it is desirable that interventional epidemiology should take precedence over simple head counts. (Two studies by the author that attempt this are reported in the chapters dealing with studies in the school setting, in Part IV). Interventional epidemiology means that when the cases are identified while studying a population, attempts should be made to provide services for them.

This could be done by:

- Providing counselling services directly
- Referral to appropriate agencies such as child guidance clinics, primary care centres, psychiatric, paediatric, speech and language clinics

Table 13.1 Prevalence Rates in Community-based Studies

Authors	Setting	Age Range (years)	Number of Students	Tools	Prevalence Rate (%)
Surya et al. (1966)	Urban	0–15	2731	Screening schedule, Clinical interview	0.70 (MR)
Sethi et al. (1967)	Urban	0–10	540	Interview schedule	9.44 (Total) 5.74 (MR) 2.55 (Enuresis)
Dube (1971)	Mixed	5–12	8035	Interview schedule, Clinical interview	11.69 (Total) 7.70 (MR) 0.62 (Neurosis) 0.12 (Psychosis)
Elnager et al. (1971)	Rural	0–14	635	Interview schedule, Clinical interview	1.30
Sethi et al. (1972)	Rural	0–10	877	Clinical interview	8.09 (Total) 6.84 (MR) 0.55 (Epilepsy) 0.22 (Neurosis)
Verghese & Beig (1974)	Urban	4–12	747	Mental health item sheet, Clinical interview, ICD-7	8.17 (Total) 8.70 (b); 7.60 (g) 5.22 (Enuresis) 2.01 (MR) 0.81 (Behaviour disorder) 0.13 (Sleepwalking)
Nandi et al. (1975)	Rural	0–11	462	Case detection schedule (p), Clinical interview	2.60 (Total) 2.24 (b); 2.93 (g) 1.29 (Epilepsy) 0.87 (Neurosis) 0.22 (MR; Enuresis)
Thacore et al. (1975)	Urban	0–15	1191	Interview schedule (p), Clinical interview	6.90
Lal & Sethi (1977)	Urban	0–12	272	Clinical interview, DSM-II	17.27 (Total) 2.94 (MR) 2.57 (Behaviour disorder; Enuresis) 1.84 (Neurosis)
Shah et al. (1980)	Urban	< 14	1089	Interview schedule & checklist (p), Clinical interview	0.83

Authors	Setting	Age Range (years)	Number of Students	Tools	Prevalence Rate (%)
Kurup (1980)	Rural	5–12	451	RQC	16.40
Singh et al. (1983)	Urban	1–14	279	Clinical interview, ICD-9	29.40 (Total) 25.10 (Special symptoms) 8.60 (CD) 4.70 (MR) 1.10 Developmental delays) 0.40 (Hyperkinesis; Conversion)
Sen et al. (1984)	Urban	0–14	NR	Case detection schedule (p), Clinical interview	0.56 (0–4 yrs) 3.12 (5–14 yrs)
Mehta et al. (1985)	Rural	< 14	2012	IPSS (p), Clinical interview	1.84 (Total) 2.52 (b); 1.12 (g)
Nandi et al. (1986)	Rural	0–11	551	Case detection schedule (p), Clinical interview	0.48
Sachdeva et al. (1986)	Rural	0–14	660	Case detection schedule (p), IPSS (p)	1.06
Banerjee et al. (1986)	Urban (tribal)	0–14	320	Interview schedule (p), Clinical interview	0.00 (0–4 yrs); 1.15 (5–14 yrs)
Premarajan et al. (1993)	Urban	0–12	273	IPSS (p), Clinical interview, ICD-9	5.86 (Total) 6.87 (b); 4.93 (g)
Hackett et al. (1999)	Rural	8–12	1403	CBQ (p & t), IW interview, ICD-10	9.40
Nandi et al. (2000)	Rural	0–11	1173	Case detection schedule (p), Clinical interview	2.73
ICMR (2001)	Mixed	0–16	4389	Screening checklist (p), CBCL (p), CBQ (t), DISC (c & p)	12.50 (Bangalore centre) 12.10 (Lucknow centre)
Malhotra et al. (2002)	Urban & Rural	6–14	400	CBQ	16.5
Prashan-tham et al. (2004)	Tsunami-affected	Juvenile Survivors	523	CBCL (Modified Tamil version)	70.7% PTSD (Post-traumatic Stress Disorder)

Abbreviations: NR: not reported; b: boys; g: girls; p: parent; c: child; t: teacher; MR: mental retardation; CD: conduct disorder; CBQ: Children's Behaviour Questionnaire (Rutter, 1967); CBCL: Child Behaviour Check List (Achenbach and Edelbrock 1983); DISC: Diagnostic Interview Schedule for Children (NIMH, 1992); IPSS: Indian Psychiatric Survey Schedule (Kapur et al., 1974), IW interview: Isle of Wight Interview (Rutter et al., 1981); RQC: Reporting Questionnaire for Children (Giel et al. 1981).

Table 13.2 Prevalence Rates in School-based Studies

Authors	Setting	Age Range (years)	Number of Students	Tools	Prevalence Rate (%)
Rao (1978)	Urban	13–16	428	GHQ-60, Clinical	19.62 (Total) 18.80 (b); 22.80 (g)
John (1980)	Urban	9–12	98	CBQ (t), Clinical interview	15.31 (t) 21.43 (p)
Jiloha & Murthy (1981)	Rural	5–12	715 (b)	Questionnaire (t), RQC (p), Clinical interview; ICD-9	20.70 (Total) 8.80 (Enuresis) 5.87 (MR) 2.10 (Stammering) 1.67 (Emotional disturbance) 1.60 (Epilepsy)
Parvatha-vardhini (1983)	Rural	5–12	309	CBQ (t)	10.60 (Total)
Sekar et al. (1983)	Urban	9–14	90	CBQ (t)	35.55
Kapur (1985)	Rural	10–16	353 (b)	CBQ (t)	25.00
Rozario et al. (1990)	Urban	12–16 4–12	1371	CBQ (t) CBQ (t)	6.42 (Total) 11.27 (b); 1.47 (g)
Bhargava et al. (1988)	Urban		6199	Questionnaire (p, t), DSM–II	32.60 (p) 38.10 (t)
Dalal et al. (1990)	Urban	12–16	665 (g)	GHQ-30 (c)	30.92
Sarkar et al. (1995)	Urban	8–11	408	CBQ (t)	10.54 (Total) 8.96 (b) 12.43 (g)
Deivasig-mani (1990)	Urban	8–12	755	CBCL (p) CBQ (t), Clinical interview (p&c) ICD-9	16.16 (t); 33.70 (p & c) 43.44 (b) 35.29 (g) 14.30 (Enuresis) 11.13 (CD)
Uma & Kapur (1990)	Mixed	2.10–3.8	155	PBCL (p)	2.91 (MR) 1.72 (Hyperkinesis) 3.23 (Total)
Mehta et al. (1991)	Urban Rural	6–12	2055	CBQ (t)	3.70 (Urban); 2.97 (Rural) 13.28 (Total) 14.53(b) 10.20(g)
Ruckmini (1994)	Rural	6–12	271	PBCL (p) CBQ (t)	13.60 (Total) 13.10(b) 14.50(g)
Sarkar et al. (1995)	Urban	8–11	408	CBQ (t) CBCL (p)	10.54 (Total) 8.96 (b) 12.43 (g)
Shenoy et al. (1996)	Urban	5–8	1535	CBQ (t); CBCL (+) CBCL (p)	19.80 (t) 22.47 (b) 16.83 (g) 27.17 (p) 21.98 (b) 32.97 (g)

Authors	Setting	Age Range (years)	Number of Students	Tools	Prevalence Rate (%)
Banerjee (1997)	Urban	8–10	460	CBQ (t), Clinical interview (p) ICD – 9	33.30 (Total) 41.90 (b) 19.80 (g) 13.50 (CD) 5.40 (MR) 4.00 (Enuresis) 3.10 (Disturbance of activity)
Sidana & Nijhawan (1999)					2.70 (Relationship problems) 27.67 (Total) 26.00 (b); 29.33 (g)
Dash et al. (2000)	Urban	8–11	—		
Bhatia et al. (2000)	Urban	3–5	100	PBCL (t)	20.54 22.00 (Total) 23.30 (b) 20.00 (g)
Mishra & Sharma (2001)	Urban	12–18	1097 (g)	YSR (c)	13.76
Gupta et al. (2001)	Urban	9–11	957	CBQ (+), Clinical interview, ICD-10	36.50 (Total) 10.17 (t) 7.48 (p)
Malhotra et al. (2002)		4–11	963	CBQ (t) CPMS (p) Clinical interview ICD-10	36.50 (Total) 1017 (t)
					7.48 (p) 6.33 9.23 (b); 4.43 (g)
Sarkhel et al. (2006)	Urban	10–16	240	K-SADS-PL DSM-IV	4.58 CD with ADHD
Mahat P (2008)	(Rural Nepal)	6–18	2999	CBQ CBCL YSR	Overall 14.74 LD = 6.67 25.7 (b); 11.7 (g)

Abbreviations: NR: not reported; b: boys; g: girls; p: parent; c: child; t: teacher; y: years; m: months; MR: mental retardation; CD: conduct disorder; CBQ: Children's Behaviour Questionnaire (Rutter, 1967); CBCL: Child Behaviour Check List (Achenbach and Edelbrock, 1983); DICA: Diagnostic Interview for Children and Adolescents, revised version (Reich et al., 1991), GHQ–30: General Health Questionnaire (Goldberg, 1972); PBCL: Preschool Behaviour Check List (McGuire and Richman (1986); RQC: Reporting Questionnaire for Children (Giel et al., 1981); YSR: Youth Self Report (Achenbach, 1991).

Table 13.3 Prevalence Rates in Studies of Specific Disorders

Authors	Setting	Age Range (Years)	Number of Students	Tools	Disorder	Prevalence Rate (%)
Mohan et al.. (1978)	School	14–16	2256 (b)	Questionnaire(c), Checklist (t)	Substance abuse	34.20
Gada (1987)	School	5–10	321	Rating scale (p), Clinical interview, DSM-III	ADHD	8.10 (Total)
Singh & Kamal Preet (1981)	Community	12–20	444	Questionnaire (c)	Substance abuse	15.54 (Tobacco) 13.96 (Alcohol) Others 20.61
Venugopal & Raju (1988)	School	9–10	137	PRS (t)	Learning disabilities	8.50
Chawla & Sahasi (1989)	School	6–12	2,160	Checklist (t)	CD	4.67
King & Bhugra (1989)	School	14–23	580 (g)	EAT-26(c)	Eating disorder	29.00
Kushwaha et al. (1992)	Community	10–18	10,187	Questionnaire(c)	Substance abuse PTSD	25.00 (Slum) 15.00 (College)
Servan-Schreiber et al. (1998)	Community Refugee	8–17	61	Questionnaire (c), Clinical interview DSM-IV	Depression	11.50 (Total) 16.60 (b) 6.70 (g)
Kumar et al. (1999)	(Refugee)	13–16	1,100	C-YBOCS(c), DICA (c)	OCD	1.45 (Total) 2.01 (b) 1.00 (g)
Sinha et al. (1999)	School	14–15	685 (b)	GHQ-30 (c) YSR (c)	ED	5.69
Bhola & Kapur (2000)	School	13–16	446 (g)	GHQ-30 (c) YSR (c)	ED	10.99
Anita et al. (2002)	School	6–14	2000	—	CD MR Anxiety Enuresis Psychoses Depression Somnambulism Pica Somatization	4.5 3.25 2.87 1.13 1.87 0.37 1.13 0.88 0.5

Authors	Setting	Age Range (Years)	Number of Students	Tools	Disorder	Prevalence Rate (%)
Chowdhury et al. (2007)	Urban and Rural	0–15	213	—	MR ADHD Dissociative Anxiety Somatoform CD Epilepsy Psychosis Acute/Transient Sch. M.R. Depr (Of the 47 listed disorders)	7.85 11.28 8.92 2.82 2.35 0.94 6.57 2.82 1.41 0.47 0.94 1.86

Abbreviations: NR: not reported; b: boys; g: girls; p: parent; c: child; t: teacher; ADHD: attention deficit hyperactivity disorder; CD: conduct disorder; ED: emotional disorder; Sch: schizophrenia; MR: mental retardation; Depr: Depression OCD: obsessive compulsive disorder; PDD: pervasive developmental disorder; PTSD: post-traumatic stress disorder; DICA: Diagnostic Interview for Children and Adolescents (Herjanic & Reich, 1982); EAT: Eating Attitudes Test (Garner et al.., 1982); PRS: Pupil Rating Scale (Myklebust, 1981); C-YBOCS: Yale-Brown Obsessive Compulsive Scale-Children's Version (Goodman et al., 1986); CPMS: Indian Adaptation of CBCL and DISC (Diagnostic Interview Schedule for Children).

SUMMARY

The studies reveal that in India the earliest study was in 1966. Studies in clinical settings have more serious disorders and a wider range of disorders while in school settings these are mostly hyperkinesis, conduct and emotion disorders. Most of the tools are modified Western tools in regional languages and thus reflect the bias in the tools. Learning disorders, though encountered commonly in clinical and school settings, are not reported in these studies. Age and gender trends have also been reported. The above studies definitely indicate the need for provision of services in India as well as other developing countries where these are almost nonexistent. Apart from India, Nepal seems to have some epidemiological studies. Otherwise, the number of studies on children's psychological problems appears to be rather limited.

CHAPTER 14

Developmental Psychopathology in the Indian Context

In this concluding section of Part II, some of the important issues with reference to phenomenology, assessment and aetiology will be dealt with, albeit briefly.

PHENOMENOLOGY

Various studies mentioned earlier have suggested that the following features are perhaps unique to the Asian child population:

1. Attention deficit may occur in children who are anxious or suffer from emotion disorders, with or without over-activity.
2. There may be sub-cultures where hyperactivity disorder may not exist at all, for reasons as yet unknown.
3. Emotion disorder or quiet withdrawn behaviour may often be mistaken for good and socially appropriate behaviour, especially amongst girls.
4. When compared with Achenbach's norms for externalizing and internalizing behaviour, Indian children score much below the Western norms. This might indicate that these children may indeed be less disturbed or that they may have some other symptoms. This illustrates the point that many of the Achenbach items are not applicable in the Indian context. Similarly there could be symptoms that are not included which may be indicative of disturbance such as somatic symptoms in the Indian culture.
5. The conduct disordered children in India have better peer interaction, possibly indicating better socialization and better prognosis in the long run.
6. Symptoms of hysteria or dissociative syndromes in the clinics as well as mass manifestation of hysteria in the community—especially in schools, are fairly common.
7. Stress-related severe manifestation of psychotic-like transient symptoms can occur too—close to a dissociative spell rather than chronic conditions.
8. Reactive 'autism'-like syndromes, too, have been encountered.
9. Multiple syndromes occurring together are more common than a single and independent diagnosis.

ASSESSMENT

Great caution needs to be exercised in indiscriminately using Western tools in the Indian context. Most tools are used in the elite, English-speaking school population where the original norms may apply equally for the Western and the Indian population. However, almost over 90 per cent of children not exposed to the English language and Western cultural influence may perform exceedingly poorly. For example rural children in Classes I to IV perform at 'defective' level on Raven's Coloured Progressive Matrices. Many of the arithmetic and vocabulary tests are totally inapplicable. Thus, development of appropriate and suitable tools independently in the local languages becomes essential. Similarly, study of temperament in India following the Chess and Thomas model required modifications appropriate to the cultural ethos.

It must be noted that a number of good questionnaires cannot be used because of illiteracy.

AETIOLOGY

Various constellations of factors associated with disorders such as pre-, peri- and post-natal complications, parental discord, sibling rivalry, disciplinary pattern and other stressors have been reported. This lends strength to the contention that the causes are many and may often occur together. These may be at biological, psychological and social levels. But they produce the symptoms together in a complex interaction. Thus, there is no single cause for any disorder.

CONTEXT

Developmental psychology rests on the contexts in which development occurs. Age, gender and socio-cultural context play a crucial role in the presentation of symptoms, aetiology and interventions. Thus, the Developmental Psychopathology Check List (DPCL) attempts to combine all the above aspects to give an integrated profile.

Our experience proves that DPCL does provide a comprehensive framework for the formulation of the case as well as the intervention strategies in the Asian context. The fact that multiple aetiologies obviously require multiple strategies of management will be elaborated upon in Parts III and IV.

PART III

Counselling Techniques

CHAPTER

15 Play Therapy

Though play is a universal activity of childhood, Indian parents and teachers tend to view it as a purposeless and useless activity. However, it is one of the firmly established principles of psychology that play is very essential in the development process of a child. Through play, children develop their intellectual, emotional, perceptual, motor and social skills (Schaefer and Conner, 1983). If one looks at any of the games played by children in India, one would be astounded by the fine-grained tasks required in playing marbles or hopscotch, or the sensori-motor skills required to execute the traditional art of drawing *rangoli* (decorative line drawings) in front of the house in South India. Psychologists and educators now take play very seriously and are engaged in extensive research to uncover its full potential in normal child development.

Play and games promote all the domains of development. The role of play in the physical domains is very obvious. For example, fine motor and gross motor skills, visuo-motor coordination, kinaesthetic and tactile skills are essentially exercised in play, thus ensuring their promotion and development.

Play promotes the basic skills of attention and memory, advanced skills of problem solving, analysis and synthesis, planning of steps and planning ahead. In short, play promotes intelligence, creativity, language skills and communication. Social development is promoted by games with rules, where cooperative play, not cheating and waiting for one's turn are promoted. Emotional development is a realm that is enhanced to a great extent in play therapy and will be dealt with at length in the following section.

Apart from its growth-producing role, play is also of therapeutic value to children with emotional and behavioural problems. Erikson (1963) considered playing as the most natural healing process in childhood. There are many creative aspects of play, such as:

1. Play releases tensions and pent-up emotions.
2. Play allows for compensation for loss, hurt or failures in fantasy.
3. Play facilitates self-discovery of most adaptive behaviour.
4. Play promotes awareness of conflicts revealed only symbolically or through displacement.
5. Play offers the opportunity to re-educate children.
6. Play alters behaviour through role-play and story-telling.
7. Play is a medium of expression, learning, relationship and catharsis. Additional aspects of play consist of practising and trying out new forms of behaviour which enhance creativity rather than adaptation.

The therapeutic usefulness of play lies in the fact that it is a natural mode of a child's self-expression. It also helps in the establishment of rapport and contact with peers since it is interesting, enjoyable and provides for a natural relationship. All this is particularly important in view of the largely passive–receptive nature of present-day recreation, in particular television and video. Play has been used by many therapeutic approaches, including psychoanalysis, structured therapy, relationship therapy, group therapy and behaviour therapy. Extensive use of play has been made by Klein (1937) and Anna Freud (1946) in the psychoanalytic framework. Levy (1939) advocated a 'structural' approach which used case-history material to identify the problem areas. One of the major approaches in 'relationship' therapy focuses on the genuine concern of the therapist for the child. Axline (1947) highlighted the importance of steps in play therapy based the principles of client centred therapy for adults:

1. Establishing rapport
2. Accepting the child completely
3. Establishing feelings of permissiveness
4. Recognition and reflection of feelings
5. Maintaining respect for the child
6. The child leads the way
7. Therapy cannot be hurried
8. Setting of limits

With this particular model it is especially easy to initiate a novice therapist into the world of play therapy, and it is also well-suited to the Indian setting. Even non-professionals can use this approach. Play can also be used in therapeutic groups. Behaviour therapy principles can be used in eliciting the desired behaviour where play is not the therapeutic end itself.

PURPOSES OF PLAY IN CHILD THERAPY

Relationship Function

- To establish a trusting relationship
- To establish a special relationship

Disclosure Function

- To facilitate diagnosis
- To facilitate assessment
- To allow expression of feelings
- To act out unconscious material
- To act out fears

- To allow expression of the forbidden
- To allow the expression of needs/affects
- To allow the expression of conflicts
- To reconstruct conflicts
- To reconstruct experiences

Healing Function

- To provide an arena for intervention
- To provide a sense of direction
- To deal with defences
- To resolve resistances
- To relieve tension
- To facilitate catharsis
- To provide corrective emotional experiences
- To teach coping skills
- To experiment with new behaviours

PLAY MATERIALS

Though not absolutely essential, it is good to have a play therapy room. Even a play corner in an office or materials packed in a briefcase would suffice.

For therapeutic play, selection of play material is essential. Some toys elicit self-expression, while others elicit cooperative social play (cards, checkers) and still others tend to result in isolated play (jigsaw puzzles, crayons, etc.). In general, the toys should be simple, durable (non-mechanical) and capable of being adapted for different purposes. They should also be familiar and within the child's cognitive and manipulative skills. The toys generally recommended are:

1. Toys representing the child's family and physical environment (doll house, doll family, puppets, animals, cars, trees, costumes, etc.)
2. Art materials (paints, crayons, etc.)
3. Toys that can be manipulated (blocks, plasticine, clay, water, sand, etc.)
4. Special-purpose toys (feeding bottles, doctor sets, etc.)

The *Handbook of Play Therapy* by Schaefer and Connor (1983) is an excellent sourcebook on play therapy for children with different types of disturbances.

Play therapy does not mean one simply keeps the child engaged in play. Several centres in India make this mistake. In India there have been small-scale research studies using play therapy. The following is a brief account of the use of play as a therapeutic method in India. In 1992, Raman studied the effects of nondirective play therapy in a group of 5–6 year-olds with emotion disorder. The group was divided into two—a control group and an intervention group. The group that received 11–15 sessions of play therapy significantly improved with reduced symptoms, increased positive attitude towards love, and interaction with the therapist. They played out their conflicts during the sessions and showed reduced aggression.

In a study by Raman (1998) both play and behavioural intervention were carried out with 30 emotionally disturbed 4–10 year-olds. Shashi et al. (1997) used 10 sessions of nondirective play with 10 children with disturbance in the age group 9–10 years. The families were counselled in both the intervention and the control group. There was significant reduction of symptoms and changes were observed in terms of how the child depicted self, aggression fears and conflict resolution through play.

The above studies are examples of how play therapy can be used for children with emotional disturbance.

Finally I would like to conclude with the Asian context. Axline's book *Play Therapy* would give sufficient background material to prepare a novice play therapist to work with children. However, some modifications become necessary with regard to the materials to be provided. For example, some photographs of family dolls for use in Karnataka in India are given. (See illustrations on inside cover). Such changes need to be made appropriate to each region.

Important Tenets of Play Therapy

- Provide space and material
- Do not instruct
- Do not criticize or mock the child
- Appreciate
- Encourage
- Ask the child to describe situations
- Clarify feelings
- Always explore with the child but establish the facts with the family

SUMMARY

Play promotes overall development in all the domains. These domains are physical, cognitive, language, emotional, social and moral development. Play therapy is a technique used across such varied approaches as psychoanalytic, behavioural and nondirective techniques. Nondirective play appears suited to the Asian countries while other techniques require rigorous training and supervision.

SELF-EVALUATION

Short-answer Questions

1. What does the natural play of childhood promote?
2. What are the four common approaches where play is used?
3. What are the features of Axline's play therapy?
4. Name some of the essential material for play in the Asian setting.
5. What are the uses that pioneer workers would have for play?

Multiple-choice Questions

1. Play promotes the following domain of development:
   a. Physical
   b. Cognitive
   c. Emotional–social
   d. Language
   e. All the above

Answer: e

2. Play therapy is generally recommended for:
   a. Emotional disorder
   b. Autism
   c. Obsessive compulsive disorder
   d. Hyperkinesis
   e. Schizophrenia

Answer: a

3. Play therapy promotes:
   a. Emotional catharsis
   b. Conflict resolution
   c. Reduction of psychopathology
   d. Problem solving
   e. All the above

Answer: e

4. Client centered approach in play was pioneered by:

a. Anna Freud
b. Melanie Klein
c. Virginia Axline
d. Margaret Mahler
e. None of the above

Answer: c

5. Time spent in play is viewed in Asian countries as:

a. Non-productive
b. Purposeless
c. Better used for school work
d. Waste of time
e. All the above

Answer: e

CHAPTER

16 Art Work

Play and art are both natural and spontaneous activities of children. When the word 'art' is mentioned, it must be made clear that it does not represent the aesthetics or artistic merit of the product. Art is an expression of thought, feelings, perception and reaction to the environment that is communicated through drawing and painting. When we look at art as a form of communication, it can be understood how it might be used for counselling. Art work by children not only represents creativity but also the normal developmental phases of the child.

There is an emphasis on the use of drawings as aids in the assessment process, taking them as unique expressions of personal experience which can offer insights which are of diagnostic and therapeutic value. Drawings have become an excellent source for measuring current functioning and for expressing present concerns and conflicts. Art is also seen to have curative value. In therapy, art work is valued as a healing process. It can also be a means of resolving emotional conflicts and of fostering awareness and personal growth.

Art work is being used with children with a focus on expression and communication. One of the pioneers of the use of art in therapy, Naumberg (1966) suggested that art therapy could be used effectively with emotionally disturbed children and adolescents with its advantages being the production of visual images.

In the clinical setting there are records of case studies of children suffering from various emotional–behavioural disorders and abuse where art therapy has been used successfully. In the Indian clinical setting a study has been conducted on the art work of Indian children with mental health problems, the results of which indicated progress in terms of reduction of psychopathology and enhancement in emotional development (Chandani, Kapur and Hirisave, 1999).

Art therapy is also being used in schools as an aid to education, especially in the face of emotional, behavioural as well as learning problems. Art work has been used effectively with school children with problems ranging from low self-esteem and peer-related problems to anxiety and depression.

Art for a child is primarily a means of self-expression. Art expression changes as the child grows. Between 2–4 years, the child is at a scribbling stage. Between 4–7 years, the first representational efforts are made. Between 7–9 years, the child achieves a firm grasp of concepts. Between 9–12 years comes the dawning of realism. Between 12–14 years is the age of reasoning. Adolescent art between the ages of 14 and 17 is a period of decision. At all these stages art may promote emotional, intellectual, physical, perceptual, social, aesthetic and creative growth.

Thus it may be seen that art represents:

- Different domains of growth
- Different stages of development
- A mode of communication

In addition, it also provides insights into not only normal development but also abnormal development. Understanding the abnormality enables one to use art for healing.

Some of the well known approaches to interpretation of art products are:

The **psychoanalytic approach**, where art is used as a projective technique and for discovering internal conflicts or describing experiences (Machover, 1951). Being allowed to draw or paint freely is considered therapeutic. But one has to guard against one's own interpretation which may completely ignore what the child sees in the picture.

As opposed to the psychoanalytic approach there is the **behavioural approach**. Here the drawing indicates the child's understanding of the activity at hand. The art product is judged against pre-established criteria involving perceptual motor skills, colour harmony, spatial relationships and awareness of proportion. For example, Florence Goodenough used human figure drawn by the child to arrive at the level of intelligence. As finer details are drawn, higher scores are obtained.

The third is the **developmental approach**, where the child's performance reflects what is expected at that stage. This is very important for anyone who works with children.

The fourth approach is an **artistic** one. Though important in terms of creativity, a counsellor needs to treat all art by children as expression of their communication of their inner world.

The present chapter looks at art as play. The adult is only a facilitator, a catalyst and not an instructor. The counsellor has to establish a good relationship with the child to start with, and have a good understanding of the child's history after obtaining it by interviewing the parents.

Spending time with the child doing activities that are non-threatening and interesting is essential to establishing a relationship. This could be done in a very relaxing environment using clay, puppets, toys or paper and crayons. As one is talking to the child, these activities keep the child absorbed. One child may respond with interest to dolls or clay and another to art work. The main idea is that the child is allowed an activity of his choice the way he wants it. Thus the child shows his preferred mode of communication. Many children use art as the preferred activity.

When one starts working with the child using art as a medium, one of the guidelines is that children with emotional disorder or those with other disorders but overshadowed by emotional disorder appear to respond well to art work as they find verbal communication more difficult.

ART WORK: THE PROCESS

The following materials can be provided to the child.

- Drawing sheets

- Stationery items: pencils
- Colouring materials: box of paint, crayons, colour pencils, sketch pens, water colours
- Paint brushes and palettes

The following themes may be provided to the children, though not sequentially, upon which they could base their drawings.

- Draw yourself and your family doing something you enjoy doing together.
- Draw a picture of your most important festival. Be sure to include your family and you enjoying this festival.
- Draw your picture when you play. What do you like to play?
- Draw your picture at school. What do you like about school?
- Can you draw a safe, happy house for the animal you have been given? (Each child can be asked to choose a toy animal).
- Draw a picture of yourself doing something that makes you happy.
- Draw what you would do tomorrow if you had the choice to do anything you wanted to.
- Draw a picture of what you want to be when you grow up.
- Draw a picture of what you have to do to achieve this goal.
- Have you ever been in a boat? Draw your picture in a boat and where you had gone.

The above themes were drawn from work of Chandani, Kapur and Hirisave (1999). In addition, some of the following topics may be provided:

- What do you fear? Can you draw a picture of what you fear?
- Draw yourself and your family at the dining table.

These themes can help in reaching the children, personally enabling them to open up and freely express the concerns of their inner world. However the children should be given the freedom to reject the themes if they so choose. Verbal description of the drawings should be encouraged, and encouragement, appreciation, positive feedback and reassurance (if deemed necessary) should be freely practised by the researcher.

The objective of the study by Tyagarajan (2000) was to conduct art work with emotionally disturbed school children with an emphasis on the therapeutic value of art. A sample was taken of 10 children between the ages of 8–12 years. They were found to be emotionally disturbed on screening. Children were assigned to study and control groups, each consisting of five children. The study group had 10 individual sessions of art work. One or two sessions of counselling were also conducted with the parents and the teachers.

Results were analysed quantitatively, revealing statistically significant reduction of symptoms in the study group. Qualitative analysis revealed consistent changes, reflecting positive emotiona growth.

Steps of Artwork Therapy

- Assessment (recognition of moods and feelings, interpersonal information, conflicts and problems) leading to diagnosis and planning of therapy.
- Free emotional expression by recreating past and present experiences, release and mastery of conflicts.
- Growth (rapport, problem-solving, creativity, learning new skills, self-esteem and goal directedness).

SUMMARY

Art work is an important method of communication for children. From the art product of a child one can assess the child's developmental stage and understand particular domains such as perceptual, cognitive, emotional and social development in addition to creativity and imagination. When one uses art for therapy it is not viewed from the angle of beauty or aesthetics. Art when used as a medium of communication can be used to detect abnormal experiences and as a treatment mode facilitating healing.

SELF-EVALUATION

Short-answer Questions

1. What are the different stages that children pass through from early childhood?

2. What are the domains of development promoted by art?

3. The development of which skills can be promoted by art?

4. What are the ways in which art can heal?

5. What are the functions of art in therapy?

Multiple-choice Questions

1. Art work with children has the following components:

a. Supplemented by verbal description

b. Encouragement

c. Non-critical
d. Exploratory
e. All the above

Answer: e

2. Art therapy is generally used for:

a. Emotion disorder
b. Conduct disorder
c. Dissociative disorder
d. Stress related disorder
e. Any of the above

Answer: e

3. Art therapy promotes:

a. Emotional catharsis
b. Conflict resolution
c. Reduction of psychopathology
d. Problem solving
e. All the above

Answer: e

4. Art is used for different purposes—but only one is helpful in art therapy:

a. Aesthetic art
b. Modern art
c. Copying art
d. Commercial art
e. Free art

Answer: e

5. Art in childhood is a natural mode of:

a. Emotional self expression
b. Communication
c. Emotional Response
d. Healing
e. All the above

Answer: e

CHAPTER

17 Psychodynamic Techniques

Interest in the effectiveness of psychotherapy is of recent origin. The USA saw the establishment of child guidance clinics throughout the country from the mid-1900s and services for the disabled even earlier. In India, even today, there are very few child guidance clinics and psychological services for children though there are a sizable number of facilities for the care and training of children with disabilities.

In the West, the early works of Sigmund Freud and Anna Freud gave an impetus to psychoanalytic work with children. This in turn led to psychodynamic approaches to psychotherapy. On the other hand, the learning and conducting experiments in the 1950s gave rise to behavioural approaches based on learning theories.

The psychodynamic approach anchors the therapy to uncovering the deeply embedded unconscious and conscious causes of the symptoms and removing them. The behavioural approach anchors the treatment to conscious unlearning of all the learnt behaviour that is presented as symptoms.

Psychodynamic therapies or counselling use verbal communication as it is the medium to carry out the intervention. Some important factors in the psychodynamic approach include the relationship between the counsellor and the client.

Therapist variables:

- Warmth
- Empathy
- Verbal encouragement
- Characteristics such as gender, ethnicity, etc.

Client variables:

- The presenting problems
- Level of motivation
- Level of pro-social functioning
- Temperament
- Intelligence

These theories focus on emotional and social development. The foremost among them are psychoanalytical theories. The most influential of all psychoanalytical theories was proposed by Freud in 1923. His theory of psycho-sexual development consists of oral, anal, phallic and genital stages of development of the libido. The infant, whose mental apparatus works on the 'pleasure principle' dominated by the absence of a capacity to differentiate between self and others, develops into an adult who has the capacity for genital sexuality and adult balance of the Ego, Superego and Id.

Anna Freud (1946, 1966) proposes a phasic theory of psycho-sexual development integrated with a theory of aggressive drive. Her description of ego development in relation to deployment of ego defences is her special contribution. In addition, she propounds the notion of developmental 'ties', beginning with the biological unit of mother and child, to the last step of adolescent struggle of loosening infantile ties, and libidinal ties being transferred to objects of the opposite sex outside the family. Klein (1937) stresses unconscious fantasies created in infancy which affect subsequent life. Mahler (1968) focuses on the symbiotic relationship between the infant and the mother, and divides it into autistic, symbiotic and separation–individuation phases. Separation anxiety is the result of infringements on the biological mother–infant tie. Erikson (1963) proposes a theory where each stage is seen as a developmental crisis imposing certain tasks on the developing organism. In his model, psychoanalytical concepts of aggression and sexual drives are integrated with social and cultural factors. The child passes through the stages of 'trust versus mistrust' in infancy, 'autonomy versus shame and doubt' in toddlerhood, stage of 'initiative versus guilt' in early school age, 'industry versus inferiority' in middle school age and 'identity versus identity diffusion' in adolescence.

On the foundation of psychoanalytical theories, Bowlby (1980) proposed a model of interaction between infant and the mother leading to healthy emotional development. He introduces the term 'attachment' to describe this 'bond' between the infant and the mother. Ainsworth (1973) defines attachment as an affectionate tie that a person or animal forms between himself and another specific one, a tie that bonds them in space and endures over time. According to Bowlby, attachment behaviour is characterized by:

- behaviour that initiates interaction such as greeting, touching, embracing, calling, reaching, smiling, etc.;
- behavioural response to mother's interactional initiative;
- behaviour responses aimed at avoiding separations by clinging, crying, etc; and
- entering new situations in the presence of the mother and withdrawal and fear in her absence.

Development of attachment to a specific individual occurs around the age of nine months (in the majority of infants). By the eighteenth month they would form attachments with more than one figure. The age at which specific attachments occur appears to be related to the infant's early interaction with his mother as well as her/his level of cognitive development.

Many short-term and long-term effects have been noted in the case of insecure attachment or absence of attachment. 'Separation anxiety' and 'stranger anxiety' are two widely recognized conditions. Several studies focus on harmful effects which go beyond childhood in the form of lack of ability to form relationships in adulthood. However, the concept of attachment has been criticized on the grounds that it may not be truly predictive of later difficulties, and that it is an interactional process between the infant and the mother, not a biological bond. But the importance of the quality of caretaking in early childhood as a critical factor has not been questioned. In the Indian context, the effect of multiple caretakers needs to be examined.

Psychoanalytic therapy as practised by Anna Freud, Melanie Klein, Erickson and other pioneers is very elaborate, time consuming and expensive and most importantly requires long-term supervised training and personal analysis by an analyst. Unless the above conditions are fulfilled this book does not recommend the novice counsellor to independently follow these techniques.

The client centered (humanistic) therapy as opposed to the psychoanalytic approach advocates positive regard, warmth and affection for the client and focuses on the 'here and now' experience of the client. Although early practice was with children, most of its theoretical framework deals with adults.

In the Asian context, it is suggested that we could use psychodynamic approaches to understand the pathology and use it with discretion along with other approaches in an integrated fashion while counselling. One could say that the psychodynamic approach probes into how a problem developed against the background of the child's upbringing, child's nature, environmental disadvantages, etc. These could be mostly at a conscious level. However, the role of the unconscious cannot be overlooked. But this requires some background readings of the works of Sigmund and Anna Freud.

SUMMARY

Psychological therapies that use verbal communication are psychodynamic and client centered methods. Psychodynamic approaches—which emerged out of psychoanalysis—delve into the past history of the person to understand his problems in order to heal. The client centered approach focuses more on the therapeutic relationship and the present. The primary goal is to enable the child to fulfil her/his potential. In both the approaches symptom removal is secondary.

SELF-EVALUATION

Short-answer Questions

1. What are the key characteristics of client centered counselling?
2. What is attachment behaviour in infancy and childhood characterized by?
3. What are the conditions under which psychoanalytic therapy can be practised?
4. What are the three key factors of client centered counselling?
5. What are the crucial client variables?

Multiple-choice Questions

1. In psychodynamic approach the focus of therapy is in the:

a. Past
b. Present
c. Future
d. All the above
e. None of the above

Answer: a

2. In the client centered approach the focus is on:

a. Conscious processes
b. Unconscious processes
c. Past conflicts
d. Childhood fantasies

Answer: a

3. According to Freud, three dynamic processes of personality are:

a. Only conscious
b. Only unconscious
c. Only subconscious
d. None of the above
e. All the above three (a, b, c)

Answer: e

4. The difference between psychoanalytic and client centered approaches is:

a. In the techniques
b. In the nature of therapist client relationship
c. Focus on the conflict
d. Focus on the present
e. All the above

Answer: e

5. Applicability of psychoanalysis to Asian countries is:

a. Hampered by time constraints
b. Hampered by paucity of trained personnel
c. Financial constraints
d. Compromised by differences in the socio-cultural contexts
e. All the above

Answer: e

CHAPTER

18 Behaviour Therapy and Cognitive Behaviour Therapy

Both behaviour therapy and cognitive behaviour therapy have their roots in learning theories. These approaches follow a set of working conditions (Kazdin, 1990).

- All the behaviour of children and adolescents is learned unless there are genetic or biological indicators to the contrary.
- Maladaptive behaviour is independent of other such behaviour unless there is proof to the contrary.
- Behaviour problems are situation specific.
- The causes of behaviour are situated in the present (here and now)—consequently a history of the child's problems is of less importance.
- Reduction or removal of the problem behaviour is the aim of therapy.
- The unconscious has no role to play in understanding or treatment.

Behaviour therapy and cognitive behaviour therapy (CBT) differ in that CBT emphasizes on **cognitive processes** as mediators. These cognitive processes are the child's feelings, thoughts, attributions, self-statements and other cognitive variables (See Fig. 18.1). In contrast, behaviour therapy approaches typically focus on the **directly observable behaviour** in the child's immediate environmental setting that may be modified (See Fig. 18.2).

Figure 18.1 Cognitive Behaviour Therapy (CBT)

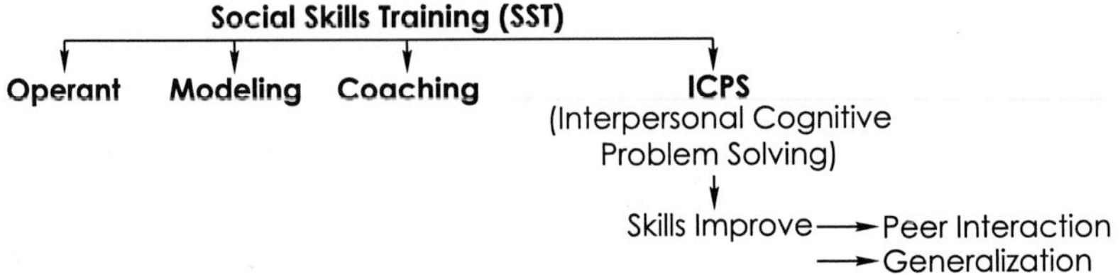

Figure 18.2 Behaviour Therapy

Behaviour modification with children dates back to Watson and Raynor's experiments with Little Albert in the 1920s. Yet, child behaviour therapy as a specialty has emerged only in the past three decades. Behaviour modification techniques in use with adults are anchored firmly in laboratory settings and in learning theories. Work with normal and disturbed children, however, reveals that their behaviour seems governed largely by the environmental settings where they are observed. Establishing a relationship between complex events in the environment and the child's specific behaviour is too complex a process and often yields simplistic equations. There are at least three other reasons for modification of existing techniques being used with children. These are:

1. The analysis of current behaviour, of antecedent behaviour and of consequences has to be done in the context of behaviour in natural settings. Some behaviour can be observed easily and a chain of events can be established, such as in the case of temper tantrums. In other cases, such as stealing or fire-setting, it is hard to establish such a link.
2. Symptoms often occur in clusters, each symptom has its own chain of events.
3. Symptoms undergo changes as the child goes through the lifespan and some of them remit over a period of time, such as thumb-sucking, sleep disturbances and bedwetting.

Behaviour modification techniques need to be carried out by those around the child in her/his natural setting, such as the parents and siblings at home, or teachers and peers at school.

Thus, training significant others in the child's environment is essential, particularly in the 'here-and-now' context of what initiates and maintains problem behaviour.

One dictum is that the younger and the more severely disturbed the child (as in autistic or psychotic children), the more behavioural control has to be managed with the help of caretakers and by actual environmental manipulation. With older (over six years of age) and more cooperative children, techniques of self-control and self-monitoring can be used effectively. In fact, by not involving the child in the planning of strategies or in deciding upon reinforcements and the rationale, an older child might become resistant to the programme and fight against the regimen suggested for her/him.

Thus, the caregiver, the child and the therapist have equal roles to play. One of the crucial issues affecting the outcome of behaviour modification in childhood disorders is generalization of the learned behaviour.

For example, a child who is trained to say thank you to the counsellor may not say it in other similar situations with teachers, parents or strangers. Improvement in one situation thus may not generalize to other situations.

SOME CONCEPTS UNDERLYING BEHAVIOUR MODIFICATIONS

Positive reinforcement is central to solving children's behaviour problems. The parent or teacher should provide social (a smile or praise) and material (a chocolate or TV viewing time) reinforcers so that only the child's desirable behaviours are reinforced. This implies that for dealing with undesirable behaviours such as temper tantrums or aggressive behaviours, punishment (because of ethical issues) is considered only under certain conditions. Only certain forms of punishment, for example, 'time-out' and 'response-cost', are used for suppressing problem behaviours.Both are used as temporary loss of reinforcers, contingent on the occurrence of the problem behaviour. For example, in 'time-out', every time the child throws a temper tantrum, he is removed from the company where he throws his tantrum and sent into a room where he is isolated for a brief period of 5–10 minutes. Or whenever an aggressive child hits at people, he loses his privileges (such as chocolates) which he has earned through good behaviour as the 'response cost'. But it is important that these techniques should be used consistently. Both forms of punishment should be covered by a contract drawn up by the therapist, the child and the parents at the beginning of the therapy. But punishment, when used, should be seen as a temporary measure in situations where extinction is not possible with time-out or response-cost, as one cannot ignore self-injurious behaviours (head-banging) or behaviour injurious to others (hitting or biting). Positive reinforcement always represents a stable, long-term ingredient of a successful treatment programme. The observation by Hoch (1970), that Indian parents prefer methods of immediate control of children's behaviour, not taking into account the long-range objectives, is to be noted in planning strategies in the Indian setting.

Behaviour modification techniques have been used very successfully for minor problems such as temper tantrums and severe disturbances of autistic children. Whether one believes in orthodox learning principles or not, behaviour modification techniques have contributed a great deal to the effective management of behaviour problems. Symptom removal is carried out efficiently in many of the conditions. However, if one views the symptom as a manifestation of distress in the child in the context of his family, a dynamic understanding of symptom formation is essential. Dealing with dynamic issues in symptom formation may, in fact, enhance the effectiveness of behaviour modification techniques in symptom removal.

Low socio-economic and educational status of parents in the West is seen to reduce the effectiveness of the parents as mediators in behaviour management. The experience in India reveals that actual demonstration of techniques, without technical jargon, can be practised very effectively by parents belonging to low socio-economic strata. In our experience, a combination of behavioural techniques with dynamically oriented individual and family therapy gives the best results.

Effectiveness of Behavioural Approaches

Kazdin (1990) noted that psychotherapy appears more effective than no treatment at all. Treatment differences, when evident, tend to favour behavioural rather than non-behavioural approaches. Some of the studies in India have demonstrated the efficacy of behavioural methods. However outcome research on children are very few. A study comparing behaviour therapy with play therapy in the case of children, found behaviour therapy superior in some respects and not in others (Raman et al., 2001).

SUMMARY

Behavioural approaches emerged out of laboratory experiments of animal learning. The early applications of the learning models when applied to clinical conditions were found to be particularly effective in the removal of symptoms. When the focus is on behaviour in the situational context and its relationship to the problem, it is termed behaviour therapy. Behaviour approaches have been increasingly used in the West and are gaining a foothold in Asian countries as well.

SELF-EVALUATION

Short-answer Questions

1. What are some of the behavioural approaches?

2. Name some of the disorders treated with behavioural approaches.

3. According to Kadzin, what are some of the sets of working conditions?

4. Which people are supposed to carry out behaviour modification in children?

5. Which are the conditions for which behaviour modifications have been successfully used?

Multiple-choice Questions

1. Behavioural approaches are based on:

a. Psychoanalytic theory
b. Humanistic theory
c. Learning theory
d. Psychodynamic theory
e. Attachment theory

Answer: c

2. Behavioural approaches consider it most important:

a. To remove symptom
b. Change the personality
c. To examine the past
d. To establish therapeutic relationship
e. All the above

Answer: a

3. Behaviour therapy focuses on:

a. Directly observable behaviour
b. Inferred behaviour

c. Unconscious conflicts
d. Past history of stressors
e. None of the above

Answer: a

4. Cognitive mediating processes are accommodated in:

a. Behaviour therapy
b. Cognitive behaviour therapy
c. Psychoanalysis
d. Client centered therapy
e. None of the above

Answer: b

5. As believed in the West, low socioeconomic and education status of the parents in the Asian countries:

a. Does not permit the practice of behavioural techniques
b. Allows the practice of behavioural techniques
c. Behavioural approach is more effective than a dynamic approach
d. Dynamic approach is more effective than a behavioural approach
e. Combination of the two works best

Answer: e

CHAPTER

19 Supportive Measures

Supportive measures are the most widely used ones in India, yet they are the least reported in published literature. Supportive techniques should be the most used approach in developing countries for the following reasons:

1. These are the most obvious techniques: easy to use in terms of intervention.
2. These techniques lend themselves to a wide range of situations.
3. They act not only as first aid, but also take a holistic perspective of a difficult situation.
4. The techniques combine all strands that go into the making of effective therapy.
5. This is the most economical approach with reference to financial, time and manpower resources.

Supportive measures view psychological disturbance against the background of stress, coping, social support and developmental characteristics of the child. In one sentence, supportive measures can be described as 'treat the situation rather than the child'. Children face numerous stressors at home and school. While children who are resilient do not break down, some others do. These are the vulnerable children who succumb to stress and manifest psychological symptoms. Obviously, removal from the stressful situation will produce symptom relief. 'Developmental stressor' is a very useful context. There are unique stressors at each developmental phase. For example, separation from the mother on entering school or an adolescent's close friendship with the opposite sex are typical stressors at each developmental phase.

Supportive techniques include the following:

1. Reassurance
2. Suggestion
3. Environmental manipulation
4. Psycho education
5. Parental training
6. Remediation for attention and learning problems
7. Encouragement and praise

8. Strengthening adaptive responses
9. Emphasis on strengths and talents
10. Emotional abreaction/catharsis
11. Limit setting

While all except limit setting are positive approaches, limit setting is very crucial in child management as children tend to go completely out of control if there are no strict rules or dos and don'ts. Figure 19.1 lists some simple guidelines to decide what should be the criteria in the use of different techniques.

Thus, work with the child needs to be carried out at three levels:

1. In-depth work with the child has been dealt with in the earlier chapters when the work is entirely carried out with the child.
2. When the child is unmanageable because of the disorder: conduct, hyperactivity, autism, etc., the parents need to be made aware of the need for structuring the child's daily schedule. Some environmental manipulation requiring change of school may be necessary. Children with low achievement and self-esteem may require much reassurance, encouragement and praise.

   Those with hyperactivity and conduct disorders may require 'limit setting'. Children with learning difficulties or disorders may require remedial work for attentional and learning problems. Psychological disorders in a child with temperamental difficulties may necessitate education of parents regarding the nature of the child and how to deal with it.
3. Some children may require direct work as well as supportive measures.

One solution is to work with parents to handle the behaviour problems of children. Parents have to be trained to handle children with different disorders ranging from attention-deficit disorder to autism. In other cases where the child is problem-free, the parents need counselling in order to foster better development, play and positive parent–child interaction. The work with parents can be done within the individual family or with a group of parents whose children face similar difficulties.

Child's condition	Choice of technique
Child is mature with good temperament, intelligent and competent	In-depth dynamic work directly with the child
When the child is unstable and poorly integrated due to: o Disorder o Disability o Temperament o Chronic physical problem	Only supportive measures
When the child falls somewhere between the above two	In-depth dynamic and supportive measures
A very young child	Greater reliance on supportive measures

Figure 19.1 Flow chart of choice of techniques

The parent training differs along the developmental life cycle of the parents. The training of young parents with a toddler differs entirely from training for older parents with a child in middle school or high school. In India, other significant people might also be involved. A grandparent, an uncle or aunt, siblings and even the domestic helps who act as caretakers for long hours can enhance or undermine treatment. Hence, the family matrix of relations needs to be examined completely before instituting suitable techniques.

Parental counselling may be guided by different theoretical orientations focusing on behaviour, cognition and emotion. But as these dimensions interact, the counselling, too, needs to include all the three key aspects. Cultural variations attributed to caste, religious and ethnic differences need to be recognized and kept in mind.

SUMMARY

Supportive techniques are the main forces of therapy in children as their problems are yet to be crystallized. Supportive counselling techniques are the most widely used ones in India. These consist of providing a support structure to the child to enable him/her to cope better and could be in the form of suggestion, reassurance and encouragement. These could also consist of bringing about changes in the uncongenial environment by attempting to alter it. There are also a series of techniques to enable the child to cope better through attention enhancement and remediation for learning difficulties. Supportive techniques may also be used along with other techniques directly with the child, parents, family or even the school. Despite all efforts to help the child in a positive way, 'limit setting' remains an important technique while working with children.

SELF-EVALUATION

Short-answer Questions

1. Name five supportive techniques.
2. Give five examples of environmental manipulation.
3. Give five examples of remediation.
4. Give five examples of limit setting.
5. Give five examples of catharsis or emotional release.

Multiple-choice Questions

1. When a child is severely compromised due to disorders or disabilities, the choice techniques are:
   a. In depth dynamic approach

b. Behavioural techniques
c. Play
d. Art
e. Supportive techniques

Answer: e

2. The younger the child, the more appropriate are:

a. Supportive techniques
b. In depth dynamic therapy
c. Direct behaviour therapy
d. Family therapy
e. Client centered approach

Answer: a

3. Supportive techniques are best used with children:

a. Who are poorly motivated
b. Whose symptoms interfere with daily living
c. Who are developmentally delayed
d. Who live in grossly disturbed environment
e. All the above

Answer: e

4. Supportive therapy can be effectively combined with:

a. Behaviour therapy
b. Psychodynamic therapy
c. Play/Art therapy
d. Client centered therapy
e. All the above

Answer: e

5. Supportive techniques are the most popular in counselling practice in Asian countries because:

a. They are obviously easy
b. They lend themselves to a wide variety of situations
c. They provide first aid as well as a holistic approach
d. They are most economical in terms of financial, time and manpower resources
e. All the above

Answer: e

CHAPTER

20 Working with the Families

FAMILY THERAPY

Family therapy does not owe its beginnings to any single person. In the 1950s, John Bowlby noted that problems presented by the child often reflected the tension between members of the family (Bowlby, 1949). The shift in theory from the individual child to the parent-child relationship and to the whole family unit is a relatively recent phenomenon in the Western context. Several workers dealing independently with the child, parents, the family and other agencies are gradually becoming disenchanted with the slow progress in finding solutions. However, in India, due to the presence of strong family ties, the family is the main unit the therapist has to work with, if not by choice, then by necessity. The closely linked family system offers ideal opportunities for family therapy. For example, in the in-patient unit at NIMHANS, a child is always admitted together with a significant adult member, and often other relatives are also involved in therapy if it is deemed necessary by the therapist. Indian families do not require introduction to the idea of family therapy as the Indian psyche automatically accepts the family as a primary unit and the child as embedded in it. Figure 20.1 illustrates the basis of family therapy.

The majority of theories developed on the adult population apply equally to the child population. Boszormenyi-Nagy and Spat (1973) developed a conceptual framework to bridge individual psychodynamic and family therapy. It is a complex model of family dynamics, and focuses on the need for autonomy and relatedness. Many of the problems in the West, particularly of an inter-generational nature, may also be found at the heart of family conflicts in India. Minuchin et al. (1975) focused on changing the structure of the family in terms of emotionally very close or distant emotional interactions, which again are very relevant to the Indian family subsystems. Family therapy offers a briefer, more effective and more economic method. It often becomes imperative to effectively combine individual therapy with family therapy, and in addition carry out marital therapy separately with the parents. Additionally, this holistic approach offers the opportunity for environmental manipulation at home, in school and in the neighbourhood with the help of the family members.

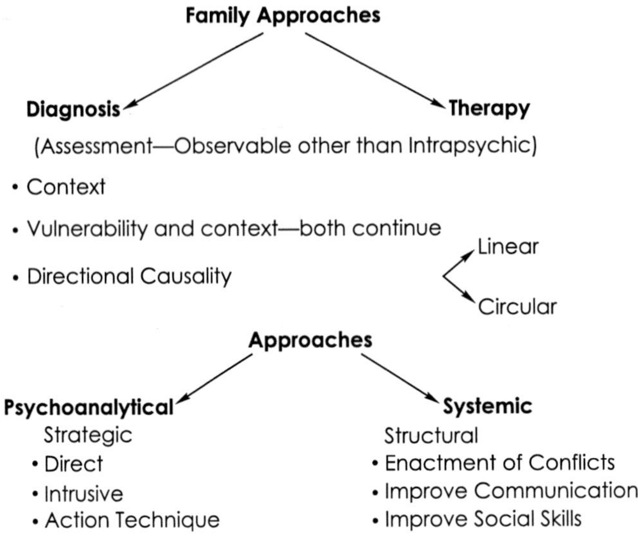

Figure 20.1 Basis of family therapy

Family therapy consists of the following:

1. Understanding the meaning of the presenting symptoms of the child in the family homeostasis: For example, a family with multiple problems would rally round the index child and her/his symptom to maintain a homeostasis.
2. Assessing the family schedule (daily schedules of all family members in the important interactions).
3. Assessing the flexibility of the family structure and acceptability of alternative patterns.
4. Uncovering the family's developmental stage: Young couple with toddlers to middle-aged parents with teenaged children.
5. Analysing internal conflicts in the family and the degree of cohesion or dissociation in the family.
6. Recognizing sources of external stress and support.

Thus, family therapy is a process of understanding why the child has a symptom in a particular family context, what triggers off and maintains the symptom in that system, and how it can be changed by engaging the whole family.

Families in India are to be viewed from an entirely different angle than that suggested by Western perspectives. As Hoch (1993) warns rightly, families cannot be understood by examining them in a static manner such as joint and nuclear. The family is a constantly evolving dynamic unit. Family problems are usually analysed according to the Western notions of interpersonal relationships and family dynamics. One assumes that the basic unit involved is the person, well-defined and limited within himself, entering into a relationship with another equally well-determined unit as seen by Western eyes. In contrast, the traditional Indian family has a strong family boundary within which the individual members hardly develop any ego boundaries. Transactions with outsiders are carried out by the family as a whole. Thus, in a counselling set up there is a need to examine whether the family is traditional or not.

There is no single method of child-rearing that can be called good or bad for all times and at all places as long as a socio-cultural system remains intact and child-rearing and later roles and tasks of the child remain in tune with each other. Interventions and rapid changes may disturb this.

Thus, working with families is one of the most important approaches to child counselling. Yet it is the most difficult one to approach for the teachers and other workers who work *exclusively* with children because, in any child guidance clinic or child psychiatric centre, parents and other family members voluntarily turn up at the clinics as they consider the family and child as a single unit.

Some of the common features noted in the East and the West to a greater or lesser extent are:

- Role reversal: Where the child takes on parental responsibilities (the eldest one in a parentless family, a slum child with alcoholic or mentally ill parents).
- Alliance and splitting: A child aligns with one parent and distances oneself from the other parent.
- Conflict detouring: For example in a traditional Indian family, the mother is the conduit through whom conflicts are communicated.
- Scapegoating: One child becomes targeted to relieve the frustration of several family members by being labelled the 'black sheep' of the family.
- Separation and individuation: One member may move out of the family bonding aiming to function independently. Any such effort is strongly opposed within Indian families while it is encouraged in Western families.
- These could be intergenerational problems. For example in India it is the parents-in-law undermining the disciplining efforts.

The three approaches to family therapy are outlined here. Figure 20.1 at the beginning of the chapter illustrates the three approaches and what they entail.

SYSTEMS APPROACH

Systems approach adopts a holistic perspective that is based on general systems theory. It proposes that all dynamic units are inter-connected and work together as a whole. Family therapists focus on patterns at different levels. Some work at the behaviour assuming that the changes in behaviour will be followed by changes in belief. Others address patterns of belief, assuming that changes in belief will automatically cause changes in behaviour.

Some of the techniques used to understand family relations can be tried out by the counsellor himself/herself with his or her own family. These include:

- Inter-generational family tree
- Current relations among those who live in the family
- The place of the individual child in this scheme

- In India, it is common that families may maintain strong psychological bonds although they live separately and therefore this, too, needs to be included. For example, women bonding with the maternal family.

STRUCTURAL APPROACH

This approach emerged out of Minuchin's work with poor families. The therapy includes action techniques such as an actual enactment of the conflict and possible new resolutions. Some family traits are described, such as enmeshment, over-protectiveness, rigidity, absence of conflict resolution and the psychosomatic symptoms. The Minuchin concepts seem to be most applicable in the Asian context, especially as the family characteristics mentioned are very common in Asian families.

STRATEGIC APPROACH

The strategic approach aims at brief therapies focusing on resolution of the problem, emphasizing the inherent resilience of people that is depleted due to stressors at that point of time. The steps in therapy consist of:

- Identifying family members motivated in the treatment
- Noting details of problems and solutions attempted in the past
- Setting specific goals
- Making plans to promote change
- Interventions for the solutions that have failed
- Interventions that are successful
- Termination of treatment

As may be seen, each of the three approaches offers useful insights in the Asian context. For example:

- Genograms and family maps are excellent ways of assessing family relations.
- Dealing with family conflicts in the family therapy setting is a very useful means of conflict resolution.
- Focusing on brief and effective solutions is the most crucial aspect in the Asian scenario in view of the paucity of manpower and functional resources.

Family therapy methods approach counselling problems in the .ontext of both intimate relationships and the wider social network of which the family is a part. Family therapy essentially uses a 'Systemic Approach', which is characterized by the notions that:

- o All the members of the family are intimately connected and the focus of intervention is on these connections rather than on the perspective of any one person.

- o Those who live in close proximity for a long time develop patterns of interactions that are relatively stable.
- o The cause and effect of the problem is seen as the 'fit' or 'misfit' between the family and its member.
- o The problems thus result from inappropriate adaptation. Some environmental change is often required.

While in the West, the unit of treatment may be rarely more than two people, in India one often includes several members of the family, extended family and, if necessary, people from the social network to which the family belongs.

Families in the West have undergone changes to include divorced, separated, foster, adopted, and single-parent families. In India, loss of support from joint families, young and inexperienced working parents, single parents, broken families, and poverty seem to be the common cause of family discord. Family therapy has received a substantial boost regarding its efficacy in recent reviews.

In Indian families, because of psychological closeness and dependence, the family is the most appropriate agency for child counselling. The three major schools of family therapy developed in the West are 'systems', 'structural' and 'strategic' modules of therapy. The fourth is the Milan approach developed in Italy. However each of these schools requires the counsellor to undergo rigorous training, supervision and practice.

Now, some of the observations regarding Indian families may be of interest. Girimaji (2001), using the Baumrind model of child-rearing practice, observed that Indian parents were high on nurturance, authority, protection, affiliation, discouraging aggression and encouraging pro-social behaviour while being low on communication and stimulation.

Thus, maladaptive parenting is characterized by:

- Overprotection/over-indulgence
- Exercise and inappropriate use of authority
- Polarization of rearing function: For example, the father is the sole disciplinarian and the mother is the sole nurturer
- Inconsistent use of authority
- Under-stimulation

The rearing practices could be explored using the following lines of enquiry:

1. Child's daily routine and who does what for the child.
2. The parent's responses to the child's misbehaviour.
3. How the parents were themselves brought up by their own parents and reflect on whether the same is evident in their interactions with their own children.
4. Identify problem areas.
5. Identify the link between the child-rearing practice and the problem.

Just explore, examine and float your suggestions about the positive links. But never take a dogmatic position. Allow the family to draw the obvious conclusions instead of suggesting what they should be doing. Dealing with families is a very sensitive issue and should be approached with caution.

SUMMARY

Working with families is the most complex yet effective way of dealing with childhood problems. In the West, several methods of family therapy have evolved, including systems, strategic and structural approach. Though effective, these are neither very popular nor widespread in use. In India, on the other hand, the family structure lends itself ideally to family therapy by neatly fitting into the cultural ethos of the nation. Re-establishing and facilitating communication among family members seems to be the key to therapy.

SELF-EVALUATION

Short-answer Questions

1. Name three well-known family therapy approaches.

2. Name some characteristics of family therapy.

3. Name some common features of family characteristics in the West and the East.

4. Name some features of strategic approach.

5. Name some maladaptive features of Indian (Asian) families as observed by Girimaji.

Multiple-choice Questions

1. In family therapy the focus is on:

a. Only family
b. Only includes one member
c. Therapist
d. Society
e. All the above

Answer: e

2. The child in India is seen predominantly as:

a. An independent member
b. A part of the family unit
c. A part of the society
d. None of the above
e. All the above

Answer: b

3. Important indices of child rearing practices in India to be explored:

a. Child's daily routine
b. Who does what for the child
c. How do parents respond to the child's misbehaviour
d. How the parents themselves were brought up
e. All the above

Answer: e

4. Techniques/approaches especially useful in assessing families in Asia:

a. Genograms and family maps
b. Dealing with family conflicts in the family therapy setting
c. Focusing on brief and effective solutions
d. Offering privacy to the needs of each member including the child
e. All the above

Answer: e

5. Advantage of the child being seen as a part of the family unit in the Asian countries:

a. The conflict resolution occurs in the family context
b. The family sees itself as responsible for the child
c. Leads to better communication between the family and the child (which often does not occur in the traditional families)
d. Solution by the child alone is strengthened by the family support
e. All the above

Answer: e

CHAPTER

21 Working with Groups

GROUP THERAPY

Though essentially described as American, group therapy has its roots in religious movements, ancient Greek theatre, and group work with parents and children. Group therapy represents a broad range of psychological therapies where group processes are an essential component. Groups may comprise different diagnostic categories, and can therefore be either homogenous or heterogeneous. They may be open or closed, educational (or strongly insight-oriented) or therapeutic. The therapeutic effects may be stronger than those in individual therapy, and help can come from multiple sources. This sort of therapy provides a practice-ground for the 'generalization' of new modes of behaviour acquired in individual therapy. One of the major advantages of group therapy is that it is economical—requiring relatively less time and manpower resources. It is particularly advantageous in the Indian setting as people tend to be happier and more receptive in a group encounter. People in India are used to a community approach to healing, as seen in religious settings, in traditional healing, and even in the out-patient medical facilities.

Often, it is helpful to have a few sessions with parents in 'open' group settings where they discuss the problems they face and their ways of coping with those problems. Such open group settings are the only possible form of group work with the majority of the parents of children who come as out-patients. On the other hand, closed groups can work effectively in an in-patient facility where the parents form a captive audience. At NIMHANS, short-term group work (4–5 sessions) in an out-patient setting has been conducted with moderate efficacy for parents of mentally retarded, autistic, and conduct disordered children as well as for parents of children with specific learning disabilities. This generally consists of educating the parents about the nature of their children's problems, and uses the parents' own experience in effectively coping with those problems. Group therapy may be viewed as being of two kinds, educative and experiential. Group work can also be carried out with adolescent patients, though the experience with this in a clinic setting is rather limited.

Although working in groups in India has several effective therapeutic possibilities, it remains the least explored technique in the Indian context. Working in groups is culturally most accepted, as confidentiality and privacy are basically Western and urban phenomena. Time need not be spent preparing the ground by introducing members to each other as people spontaneously start interacting in a group without being formally introduced. Even topics that are taboo in the Western context are dealt with fairly easily, such as one's faith, one's job, salary, age, etc. However, discussing one's family with outsiders is one of the taboos in the Indian context.

However, group techniques remain unused due to the following problems inherent in India and similar traditional societies:

- It is hard to have long-term groups (more than 10 sessions).
- The concept of punctuality is an alien concept in traditional Indian society.
- The concept of an appointment is viewed in a very flexible manner by the patients.

Still, it is definitely possible to have very effective groups if we remain flexible in our expectations and are ready to operate within a very non-Western approach to the groups with regard to punctuality, regularity, etc.

The key notions operational are:

- Keep the groups open: Anyone can enter and leave as they wish.
- Keep the time flexible: Such as between 2–4 pm on the same day every week.
- Even if the group is expected to have 10–12 members, conduct the session if only five members come.
- Go back to the issues again and again when new members or missing members arrive.
- Remember the factor of multilingualism in India.
- Keep the groups homogenous with regard to problems, though not necessarily age, gender or social class.
- Take care that sensitive issues such as sexuality are discussed in groups homogeneous in age and gender.

Two kinds of groups that may be constituted are:

a. Parent Groups

- The groups may consist of parents with children with similar problems, like learning difficulties.
- Parents with psychotic children
- Parents of adolescents
- Parents with disabled children
- Parents with problems themselves such as marital difficulties, alcoholism, etc.

b. Children Groups

- Group work in small groups has been effective with children with hyperkinesis, specific learning disability, etc. The groups were found to promote self-understanding and reorganization of child-rearing practices among parents who attended the groups.

WORKING WITH PARENTS: AN EXAMPLE

Indiramma (2001) has reported her observations on group counselling of parents staying in the child and adolescent in-patient unit at NIMHANS, Bangalore. The data reflects the experience with

732 caretakers/guardians, in the age range of 20–51 years. The children consisted of a diagnostically heterogeneous group.

1. The group experience consisted of 80 sessions where the group used the sessions to serve the purpose of:

    - Sharing distress
    - Permitting emotional outbursts
    - Ventilation of emotions
    - Seeking clarifications
    - Supporting each other
    - Expressing satisfaction

2. Psycho-education was provided in the following areas:

    - Attention deficit hyperactivity disorder
    - Pervasive developmental disorder
    - Dissociative episodes
    - Epilepsy
    - Mental retardation
    - Psychoses
    - Emotion and conduct disorder
    - Learning disorder
    - Obsessive compulsive disorder
    - Substance abuse

    Psycho-education covers the causes, symptoms, medication, biological factors, changes in parental behaviour and school related issues.

3. The psycho-social aspects covered were child-rearing practices, importance of training, parental involvement in children's activities and behavioural management.

WORKING WITH CHILDREN

Rozario (1988) worked in small groups with 5–8 year-olds with specific learning difficulties instead of individual work and found significant improvements in reading, writing and mathematics skills in five such groups. In the learning disabled group, children drew strength and enjoyed increased self-esteem when they realized that they were not alone in facing these problems.

Oberoi (1993) used small groups of 3–4 hyperkinetic children involved in art work and cooperative play mainly to promote pro-social behaviour and set limits to aggressive and impulsive behaviour. On the other hand, the hyperactive children personally experienced the impulsive/aggressive behaviour as an unwanted experience, paving the way towards improved pro-social behaviour. Group work on study skills, too, is helpful for academic difficulties.

Life-skills education in groups is yet another example of group work. Life-skills education has been recommended by the WHO, UNESCO and UNICEF to promote child development and mental health among adolescents. A series of excellent manuals on life-skills and personal safety has been developed by Seshadri, Saksena and Saldanha (2008) and published by Macmillan India. These are for use with children from Classes III–IX. Colourful illustrations, simple text and graded activities called circle games are the strengths of these manuals. These can be used by teachers and parents for the children.

The life-skills covered are:

- Self-awareness
- Empathy
- Effective communication
- Interpersonal relationship
- Decision making
- Problem solving
- Creative thinking
- Critical thinking
- Coping with emotions
- Coping with stressors

The manuals are excellent, low-cost source material for urban school children with adequate academic skills.

SUMMARY

Working in groups is especially beneficial in developing countries where there is a scarcity of financial and manpower resources. Group counselling is not only economical in terms of the time and effort of the counsellor, the group takes over some of the counselling functions too. The 'peer counselling' aspect of the group is one of the main reasons for its efficacy. Group counselling can be carried out with parents and children alike. However the rigid Western framework of group counselling cannot be carried out in traditional societies like India. Greater flexibility and acceptance of cultural and family codes and mores becomes necessary.

SELF-EVALUATION

Short-answer Questions

1. What does group counselling promote?

2. What are the advantages of group counselling?

3. What are the disadvantages of group counselling?

4. What are the common problems encountered in parent groups?

5. What are the common problems encountered in children groups?

Multiple-choice Questions

1. Group counselling can be conducted in:

a. Open groups
b. Closed groups
c. Heterogeneous groups
d. Homogeneous groups
e. All the above

Answer: e

2. Functions of the group process:

a. Sharing distress
b. Ventilation of emotions
c. Seeking clarification
d. Supporting each other
e. All the above

Answer: e

3. Psycho education covers:

a. Causes
b. Symptoms
c. Medication
d. Nature of intervention
e. All the above

Answer: c

4. Working in groups in developing countries is to be encouraged in the light of:

a. Scarcity of trained manpower resources
b. Scarcity of financial resources
c. Time constraints
d. Homogenous groups

e. All the above

Answer: e

5. Problems faced in group counselling in Asian countries:

a. Only open groups operate in the natural setting
b. Group heterogeneity
c. Absenteeism and lack of punctuality
d. Harder to manage for inexperienced leaders
e. All the above

Answer: e

CHAPTER

22 Working in Schools

Working in schools is a vast and difficult exercise in India and other developing countries. Yet it needs to be attempted on a large scale for the following reasons.

Services to promote child development and mental health hardly exist across the developing nations as the child population in general is forgotten and marginalized, despite children forming half the national population. It thus becomes a major responsibility for all those interested in the welfare of children to intervene to promote child development. The task needs to be viewed in a holistic and integrated manner bridging the gaps between education, health and child development. All such innovative approaches should be objectively evaluated. It is widely acknowledged that a significant proportion of children from underprivileged backgrounds either drop out from school before they reach Class V or learn very little even if they continue. Therefore, work should be undertaken with primary school children.

This chapter focuses on efforts at developing strategies to promote child development both in the urban and rural areas.

URBAN EXPERIENCE IN INDIA

Several approaches have been used in Indian school settings in recent years. These include:

1. Creating awareness in schools through workshops/lectures in specific areas such as AIDS awareness, prevention of substance abuse, sexuality, etc. These may be considered as prevention programmes.
2. Specific attention to promoting study habits, personality development, and value education. These have generally been promoted by the administration rather than from the felt needs of children.
3. Specific areas where there is a felt need such as career counselling.
4. Many innovative approaches have been tried across the nation by NGOs such as Pratham, Akshara, and others to promote academic skills.

While all the above are necessary, promotion of healthy psycho-social development has been neglected.

IMPLICATIONS OF WORK DONE IN INDIA FOR DEVELOPING COUNTRIES AND IN THE GLOBAL CONTEXT

A Comprehensive School Mental Health Programme proposed by the WHO (Hendren et al., 1994) aims at:

1. Promoting psycho-social competence at the level of intervention integrated into school curriculum.
2. Mental health education as part of general health curriculum.
3. Psycho-social intervention for students needing additional help in school.
4. Professional treatment to be provided for students needing additional mental health intervention.

In regions where mental health has not received much attention, a mental health programme may initially focus on only one or two levels. However, to be maximally effective, an integrated programme is required at all four levels.

Much of the work described in the WHO document can be successfully adapted in India's elite schools. The programmes which directly intervene at various levels require greater manpower and financial resources. In addition, the document focuses on promoting psycho-social competence, mental health education and instruction, and the identification of and intervention in psycho-social and mental health problems.

The upcoming section focuses on psycho-social mental health problems, their identification and intervention.

IDENTIFICATION OF PSYCHO-SOCIAL PROBLEMS AND HIGH-RISK POPULATIONS

Risk-taking behaviour such as smoking, substance abuse, premature sexual activity and life-endangering adventures (such as reckless driving) may be an early indication that a young person is in danger of succumbing to more serious problems. Early intervention may prevent serious consequences. Psycho-social problems become evident through changes or deviations in emotions and/or behaviour. This may include aggressiveness, excessive shyness, the worsening of interpersonal relationships, poor school attendance, a decline in academic performance, widely fluctuating moods, changes in peer group, recourse to risk-taking behaviour, obsessive and compulsive behaviour, and unusually exaggerated or repressed feelings associated with physical illness. Learning problems can also lead to behavioural problems and failure in school, a very significant life stress.

Risk factors affecting a child can include developmental delay (late walking and talking), difficult temperament, history of physical or sexual abuse, chronic illness and disability, scholastic underachievement and being forced stay out of the home. It should also be recognized that children with visual and hearing problems, as well as those with specific learning problems (e.g. dyslexia) are at additional risk of mental health problems. Extra care needs to be taken by health professionals in screening for these disorders.

In the context of developing countries, perhaps the most common problems may be risk-taking behaviour such as drug and/or alcohol abuse, recklessness and gambling, conduct disorder, attentional and learning problems, emotional and somatic problems, and psychoses in children from psycho-socially deprived backgrounds. Child labourers and street children are particularly at risk, and require intervention at the community level.

An effective school mental health programme:

- Takes into account the relationship between the school and community environment, as well as any unique cultural values and identities;
- Identifies the socio-political conditions and processes likely to be associated with the establishment and survival of a comprehensive mental health programme in the school;
- Involves families and community members as active partners in planning, implementation and on-going evaluation;
- Utilizes the skills of school and community mental health professionals;
- Intervenes at multiple levels;
- Has a coordinating mechanism;
- Focuses on teacher and parent training; and
- Evaluates its effectiveness and utilizes this information in programme modification.

INTERVENTIONS IN SCHOOL SETTINGS

The studies reported in this chapter do not deal with schools where mental health services and remediation for scholastic problems are provided by school psychologists, counsellors and remedial teachers, as in Western countries. The present chapter will briefly focus on the work undertaken in school settings in India, before giving a description of the work carried out by the author and her colleagues since 1976.

Bombay Experience

In Bombay, Dhavale (1994) started a child mental health programme with the aim of early identification, treatment and assessment of causative contributors of mental health problems and screening of a large number of school children. Schools were taken as the bases of operations, and the programme catered to children from lower socio-economic strata who could not afford to seek help. Initially, groups of teachers and parents were met and the purpose of the project, the nature and management of child mental health problems were discussed. A team of psychiatric social workers, a clinical psychologist and a psychiatrist visited the schools for the assessment of the children who had been referred. Of 980 children, 73.06 per cent were identified as having problems such as enuresis, mental retardation, behavioural problems and hyperactivity. A number of recommendations were made to the education department, and initiatives such as starting special classes for mentally retarded children in specific localities were taken. The team found during the course of their work that the parents and teachers had no idea about mental health, and despite the orientation provided, they continued to refer children with physical problems.

In 1982, a school mental health clinic was set up in B.Y.L. Nair Children's Hospital to deal with child mental health problems in a more comprehensive manner and on a long-term basis. The clinic adopted a two-pronged approach consisting of direct assessment of children and an enrichment programme for high school students. In the course of 12 years, more than 15,000 children have been seen in the school mental health clinic. Nearly 70 per cent came with complaints of scholastic backwardness, and 50 per cent of these were found on evaluation to be mentally retarded. This necessitated screening of all the children in Class I.

The school mental health clinic also initiated an enrichment programme for one section of higher secondary students, i.e., for children with above-average intelligence, but who were academically backward. Various activities, projects, discussions, stimulation workshops and creativity camps were conducted. The programme was time-bound and lasted for three years. The evaluation showed that adolescents benefited significantly from the programme.

Bangalore Experience

A study (Kapur and Cariappa, 1979) of 42 teachers, assessing their perceptions of the behaviour problems of a primary school population of 1,522 children, revealed that 72 students were considered problem children. Frequent meetings of teachers and parents were suggested as the main method of solving several problems. The issues that emerged out of the study were: children from lower socio-economic strata, whose parents were less concerned about their children's education, had more problems in the classroom; children who were happy at home had fewer problems at school than those who were not.

A student enrichment programme (Parthasarathy, 1994), suitable for rural and tribal high school students was developed in rural Karnataka. The following inputs were offered in this programme:

- How to study effectively
- Causes of and remedies for failures in examinations
- Characteristics of efficient students
- Preparing for examinations
- Prevention of health problems
- Knowing about self and others
- Causes of interpersonal difficulties
- Future orientation
- Pupil-teacher expectations
- Principles of mental health

The programmes were classroom-oriented as well as group-oriented, conducted over 25 sessions, and were time- and personnel-intensive. Teacher involvement in such enrichment programmes was considered crucial by the mental health professionals who conducted the programme.

An important experiment was conducted in one of the schools catering to the slums of Shriramapuram. The school had 6,230 students and 138 teachers on its rolls, but no counsellors. It was housed in temporary structures, had overcrowded classrooms, and teaching aids were scarce. It typified the learning environment available to most school children in India.

Since the number of teachers was large, and the problems of normal and abnormal development varied across ages, the orientation courses were conducted separately for primary, middle-school and high-school teachers. In addition, an effort was made to ensure jargon-free lectures and discussions. This was facilitated by speaking in the local language. Earlier experience had revealed that experts tended to contradict themselves and there was a good deal of overlapping in what was being communicated. The team thus consisted of only two supervisors. The topics focused upon in the primary school were different from those of middle and high school.

The technique consisted of brief lectures with case illustrations, followed by a group discussion, which was considered the most important aspect of learning and was greatly encouraged by the supervisors. It was observed that instead of dwelling on elusive aspects of personality and motivation of the teachers, it was more practical to rely on concrete responses to observations and situations.

A group of 111 teachers participated in the orientation programme which was conducted in three batches. Participation was voluntary. Though the school had 138 teachers, nearly one-fourth of them chose not to participate.

When an orientation course of this kind for teachers is conducted in any school, one-fourth of the teachers may not attend at all, while of those who attend only two-thirds show improved performance. One-third would show no improvement, instead they may deteriorate. This is a pattern to be expected in most schools. It is the 66 per cent who improve who will be relied upon to identify and refer the children with problems; and the 10 per cent with top performance, if trained adequately, will be able to manage the children with problems. The expectation of mental health professionals and educationists that all teachers should be interested in mental health problems can prove to be counterproductive in the long run.

It must be made clear that for the orientation programme to succeed, the school and the visiting team must cooperate with each other and be accommodating. By yielding to inflexibility, the orientation programme may become totally marginalized and ineffective. These issues should be negotiated with both frankness and diplomacy to lead to a mutually beneficial endeavour instead of an one-sided affair. The above-mentioned problems indicate that sufficient ground work has to be done with the school management. The school authorities should feel that the programme is to their benefit, and it should be carried out in a reasonable manner within school hours, with teachers freed from their duties to attend 6–7 sessions. The content of the course should be explained and it should be highlighted that the programme would benefit the school.

In addition, we have always offered consultancy services during the period of the orientation course, once a week, over a period of 6–7 weeks, by asking authorities and teachers to refer children with problems and arrange for parents to meet the team. This not only helps the children, it also convinces the school authorities that the visiting team is sufficiently concerned to offer professional services. This also opens the door to future referrals. The visibility index of the team helps in setting up a liaison between schools and child guidance services, which would otherwise fail to be effective.

Delhi Experience

A study was conducted (Chowdhary et al., 1994) among 75 primary school-teachers of the perception of childhood psychiatric problems. Case vignettes of four disorders, i.e., hyperkinetic syndrome, over anxiety, somatoform and learning disorders were used. Teachers were able to identify hyperkinesis but not the others. They also had poor knowledge about their role in dealing with the problems. It was suggested that it was essential to enhance teachers' ability to identify and facilitate early intervention.

TEACHER RESISTANCE

When a group of teachers in any school are met for the first time, they often come with several apprehensions about the programme. The first and foremost apprehension is that a lot of extra work is going to be foisted on them, with the authorities colluding with the outside team. The second is that they would be required to attend the programme, whether they like it or not. It is a good practice to bring out these fears, anxieties and resentments into the open, freely and in the very first meeting with the teachers. The first session may be exclusively devoted to a free discussion about the issues the teachers are justifiably concerned over, such as being overburdened by extra duties. At this point some negotiation with the authorities too may be required. The timing of the sessions should be scheduled so as to be mutually convenient. Genuine appreciation should be shown where teachers are overworked and trying to do their best under very difficult circumstances. It must be made abundantly clear that they should attend the programme out of their own choice and not under pressure or compulsion.

Often, the first session starts with a sense of foreboding and pessimism. By using the group process skilfully, it is possible to get interested and optimistic teachers to be involved in the orientation programme. It is advisable to describe the content of the programme in brief, and leave the teachers to suggest in what ways it could benefit them. Unless there is a shift from a pessimistic to an optimistic response by the majority of the group, the programme is doomed to fail. An aggressive stance by the teachers should be countered by a non-confrontationist approach. It must be highlighted that 'caring for others' is a difficult job and that it has to be done voluntarily and not for any rewards, financial or otherwise. This process involves genuine respect for teachers, their integrity and concern, and this should be conveyed to them. The teachers must be portrayed as caring adults who will decide for themselves whether they will put in the little extra effort to help troubled children.

In addition, examples could be given of how overactive or scholastically backward children can be helped, and how it would make the management of the class easier for teachers. At the end of such, often stormy sessions, if the resistance does not melt away, one may have to abandon the programme. However, we have never had an encounter where teachers remained resistant. Thus, the first session of dealing effectively with teacher resistance is an important one. At the end of the session, the pre-assessment questionnaire may be given out, along with the explanation that it enables the team to tailor the programme to suit the teachers' needs. They must also be told that only group responses will be discussed and not individual ones. Some teachers who are very diffident may copy what their neighbour writes or request that the questionnaire be taken home and filled up. A very rigid stance about filling the questionnaire may be counterproductive. It is better to lose a questionnaire than a teacher!

PARENT RESISTANCE

As the goal of the programme is to reach out to children, the authorities and teachers should be requested to take parents into confidence, and information about consultancy services should be provided. In addition, parent–teacher meetings may be arranged and issues which surface during the orientation programme may be discussed. At schools catering to the upper strata of society, issues of over-expectation, overburdening through tuitions, absence of play and aspects of normal development could be discussed. With parents from poor socio-economic backgrounds, issues of absence of play, under-stimulation, child labour, alcoholism at home and their impact on children's emotional well-being and scholastic performance could be the focus. These should be tailored to suit the needs of the particular school and problems which occur in that community setting.

RURAL EXPERIENCE

The author carried out two programmes in the backward rural and tribal regions of Karnataka in Heggada Devana Kote (H.D. Kote) Taluk in Mysore District (Kapur, 2007)—one with rural school children and the other with tribal children. Both the programmes had two components—working with the children and with the teachers.

Universal Intervention with Children

The first programme consisted of universal intervention for the promotion of psycho-social development among 1,200 rural school children of Classes I–IX in a cluster of government schools. Another was a programme for 800 tribal children in nine impoverished residential schools run by the Social Welfare Board.

In both programmes, psychological assessment was carried out to assess the outcome before and after the intervention. The tests were used to assess attention, intelligence, memory (for only the tribal group), creativity, language and number skills. There was significant improvement as measured by tests in both the groups. The actual programme led to the creation of a video documentary and a set of four manuals*—three on child development and child mental health and one for preschool teachers.

The intervention was to promote the psycho-social development of children and included various activities to enhance the following areas of development:

- **Motor Development:** Activities for the promotion of gross and fine motor skills, eye-hand coordination and form perception through play.

* These are available at low cost at NIMHANS Publication Division, Bangalore in Kannada, Hindi and English.

- **Language Development:** Activities for the promotion of speech and language skills through word games, storytelling and enactment, story-building, singing, etc.
- **Development of Number Concepts:** Activities for the promotion of number recognition, identification, basic arithmetic concepts through games, board games, use of the abacus, etc.
- **Development of Intelligence:** Activities to promote attention, concentration, memory, problem-solving, analysis and synthesis, planning and problem-solving through puzzles, play, and games.
- **Development of Creativity:** Child-initiated art and craft work with inexpensive and locally available materials, and painting and drawing, both for the individual child and in groups.

In general, the approaches used for all the domains of psycho-social development were as listed below:

1. They were flexible.
2. They were continuously examined through observational methods, responses of the children, reactions of the teachers, and formal testing.
3. Changes and new activities were included as and when necessary.
4. Age-appropriate tasks were assigned, such as simple tasks for younger children and more varied and complex tasks for older children.
5. All tasks were carried out through play, games, art, craft, and drama and not through formal lessons.
6. Tasks were initiated and managed by the children while the team supported them as enthusiastic helpers.
7. Most of the materials used were natural, locally available and inexpensive. The sports equipment, games and stationery were donated to all the schools as the schools hardly had any play materials. The approximate cost of the material for each child worked out to Rs 100–120.
8. The most important aspect was that the children enjoyed the child-friendly activities and considered it 'fun time'.

The final aim was to promote their psycho-social development through the above-mentioned methods. The activities were carried out from Monday to Saturday for an hour a day. The teachers allotted the time either in the morning or evening at their convenience. It was ensured that our program in no way interfered with the regular classroom routine. The intervention was carried out for each of the classes in each school in a staggered manner. Each child was exposed to 20–25 sessions, sometimes even more. The field staff carried out the activities. Whenever possible, attempts were made to include the teacher, helper, a village elder or an older child.

Training of Teachers on Mental Health and Child Development

The training consisted of lectures, manuals, case histories, video documentation as well as demonstration of and discussion on the programmes conducted in the teachers' own school. Witnessing dramatic changes and improvement among the children seemed to have an impact on the teachers. The teachers were also involved in organizing camps for children with disabilities and mental health problems.

SUMMARY

In the Asian countries schools typically have poor infrastructure, manpower and financial resources. There are no school counsellors or resource rooms. Thus, it is essential that counselling components be introduced into the available school system. This could be done in different ways. One could work with an individual child or in groups. This could aim at promotion of psychosocial development and mental health of the children. One could in addition train the school teachers to sensitize them to aspects of normal development, enable them to identify mental health problems and to counsel the children in resolving scholastic and interpersonal problems in schools.

SELF-EVALUATION

Short-answer Questions

1. List the reasons explaining the need for school counselling.

2. Name some of the situations that require school counselling.

3. Who should be part of the school counselling team?

4. What domains of development can be targeted in the schools?

5. What are the mental health problems commonly encountered in the school setting?

Multiple-choice Questions

1. School counselling deals with:

a. Promotion of normal development
b. Mental health problems of children
c. Disabilities
d. Learning difficulties
e. All the above

Answer: e

2. School is a safety net for:

a. Disadvantaged children
b. Displaced children
c. Children at risk

d. With psychological disorders
e. All the above

Answer: e

3. The school programmes need to develop strategies appropriate to the:

a. Community setting
b. Socio cultural milieu
c. Age-gender context
d. Teachers
e. All the above

Answer: e

4. The context of school counselling includes:

a. Children
b. Family
c. Teachers
d. Community
e. All the above

Answer: e

5. School counselling promotes:

a. Psychosocial development
b. Mental health promotion
c. Scholastic achievement
d. Better relationships
e. All the above

Answer: e

PART

IV Matching Disorders and Counselling Techniques

CHAPTER

Counselling in General and a Case Illustration of Specific Developmental (Multiple) Delays

PROCESS OF COUNSELLING*

Counsellor Characteristics

1. A counsellor should care about the client.
2. She should be honest in her dealings with clients and informants.
3. She should try to consider everybody's viewpoints equally and impartially, without bias.
4. A certain formality in relationships should be maintained. For example, going to the cinema or to a restaurant with the client should be discouraged.
5. The counsellor should be a trustworthy person, who can keep confidential information to herself. For example, she cannot reveal the information that a child has stolen something from the school to the principal, without the child's permission. But she can persuade the child to own up to the wrongdoing and help the child resolve the situation. Confidentiality can be broken only in extremely serious circumstances, where there is danger of homicide or suicide, some similar possibility.

Steps to Counselling

Introduction and Explaining the Purpose of the Interview. It is necessary to explain to the client why he is being interviewed and how the counsellor is trying to help him. Starting the interview abruptly leaves the client confused and embarrassed. It is also absolutely essential to reassure the client that all information will be kept confidential and will not be divulged to anyone without his permission. The counsellor should be honest about the purpose of the interview. For example, she must not say, 'I can help you if you have any problems,' or, 'I am just being friendly; I am trying to help you with your studies.' It is better to say 'I have noticed that you look inattentive in class,' or 'Your father said you are not studying well.' A direct approach to the problem is the best one. If the counsellor is frank, the client in turn will respond in the same manner.

* The process has been jointly formulated by Illana Cariappa and Malavika Kapur of the National Institute of Mental Health and Neuro Sciences, Bangalore.

Facilitation of Removal of Blocks. Some clients are shy or reserved and may not talk freely. With such clients the counsellor has to make an extra effort by showing that she is interested in them and cares about them. With older children one talks with genuine interest about hobbies, favourite films, books, music or games. Younger children can be given some plain sheets of paper, colour pencils or crayons and asked to draw whatever they wish; this often elicits excellent cooperation. In addition, such drawings often give useful clues about their inner states of mind.

It is important that children should not be bullied or pressurized into giving information. An atmosphere has to be created where they will volunteer information. Always make it a point to talk about little things. The child may be a good singer, for example, and if you know of it, you could praise the child's talent. But there should be honest appreciation, no flattery.

Counsellors tend to become very anxious if the client becomes tongue-tied or tense. It is important that the counsellor relaxes and copes with the silence. She should ask a question and wait as long as necessary to get an answer.

Avoidance of Rambling Talk. Some clients tend to talk too much, without giving the counsellor a chance to conduct the interview. It may be necessary to first listen for about half an hour, without interrupting. After that, attempts should be made to make the client answer questions to the point. Often adolescents use this technique to get away from the interview situation. For example, if the client goes on talking about a film he has seen, in great detail; you may interrupt to say 'But I was asking you about how well you performed in your exams last month.' This approach will force the client to stop rambling about irrelevant issues. With some clients it may be necessary to use this technique often. As soon as the client realizes that you are aware of what he is trying to do, he will stop using this technique to avoid crucial issues.

Clarification of Problems. Sometimes the original version of the history (story) given by the client or those with him (informants) may not be very clear. One needs to clarify the situation. For example, a mother may say that the reason for the problem is that she does not keep well and that the boy's father comes home drunk every night. The counsellor has to ascertain what the actual problem is and how it relates to the given situation. The problem may be that the boy does not come home till late, or that he does not attend his classes regularly. If the mother expects the boy to give the drunken father his dinner and put him to bed, as she is too ill to cope with the task, it is not surprising that the boy stays out late. But if the boy misses school for the same reason, the problem is more serious. It is necessary to clearly state the problem for the sake of the informant, client and counsellor. Vague information does not help in resolving problems.

Picking up Cues. We tend to forget that we reveal a lot more about ourselves in our actions than by words. A counsellor should be observant about picking up such clues and hints given by the client. For example, the client may go on tapping the table or pressing his forehead or squinting his eyes, as if in pain; sit on the edge of the chair, as if ready to run away; may be dressed neatly in clean though old clothes or in dirty though expensive clothes. All these observations can reveal a great deal about the client.

Cross-checking Information. Quite often, information given by the client and other informants may need rechecking. For example, at the beginning of the interview the client (child) may have said that he had changed schools six months earlier, while at the end he may say that he had been staying home for a year before rejoining school. One should look for an accurate account of events. Inaccuracies may be due to forgetfulness or a deliberate attempt at deception. Thus, it is important to look for inconsistencies in the information given by different people. When versions vary, this gives important clues regarding the motives of the people providing the information.

Asking If There Are Any Doubts. As a last step, ask the client if there is anything he would like to discuss or if he has any doubts, as he may have some reservations regarding the interview, or some issues may not have been discussed openly.

Interviewing

Most initial interviews are carried out to collect information about the client. But it is important to remember that unless the client feels at ease with the counsellor, the information gathered may be minimal. All of us tend to reveal our innermost thoughts and feelings only to a person we can trust.

At the same time the counsellor should also feel comfortable with the client. If the counsellor gets irritated by him, the relationship between the two is bound to deteriorate into one of confrontation and annoyance. In an effective counselling situation, a warm, caring relationship is one of the most important aspects.

In addition to establishing trust, useful advice can be given at times. With some problems advice can be given straight away, while others may require further interviews and clarifications. For example, a client worried about masturbation may be reassured that it is not injurious to physical or mental health. However, if the problems are complex (e.g. marital disharmony between parents), additional interviews are required before any advice can be given.

Historical Information

- Name
- Age
- Sex
- Class

What are the complaints:

- According to the child?
- According to the parents?
- According to the teachers?
- According to other children?
- According to yourself?

Always get a descriptive account of disturbed as well as normal behaviour of the child (client).

- How long has the client been having the above problem?
- Were there any changes, events at home, school or in the neighbourhood at about the time the client started showing disturbed behaviour (e.g. change of school, birth of a brother or sister, failure in school, illness of parents, new or unreasonable teacher, and so on)?

However, you may find that some children have always had problems. In such cases you may have to make enquiries on adjustment problems at home and school. If the child is restless, distracted and aggressive, the following questions should be asked:

- Sleep pattern: As a baby, was he a good sleeper?
- Feeding pattern: As a baby, was he a fussy eater?

  As a baby, did he have difficulty in drinking milk?
  Was he a lonely child?
  Did he play by himself?
- Patterns of play: Did he cling to the mother?

  Did he play with younger children?
  Did he have one or two friends?
  Did he mix freely with others?
  Did he dominate the group?
- Punishment pattern: Has the child been punished at home or school and how (e.g. scolded, beaten, locked up)?

Observation of the Child

- How did the child behave when he approached you for the first time? For example, was he shy, fearful, anxious, angry, friendly, talkative, restless or fidgety? Did he take time to warm up or did he not talk at all? It is important that the child's behaviour and talk are described in detail. One need not use any technical words while doing so.
- How does the child behave with his parents?
- How does the child behave with his teachers?
- How does the child behave with other children?
- Is the child's behaviour in any way unusual (twitches the face, drums the table, etc.)?

This adds to your understanding of the child and the family.

Formulation

After you have described the sequence of events leading to the problem, and the actual behaviour (symptoms), you have to attempt to build links or connections between the history and the symptoms: e.g. the child is very aggressive in class, because he is being ill-treated at home by his parents who beat him for no reason at all; the child cannot cope with school work because of a change in the medium of instruction and so on. It is true that you cannot always have a complete answer. So you have to choose one or two alternative explanations as the possible causes of disturbance.

Strategies for Counselling

There are two possible ways of writing up a case. One is what you have actually done to resolve the problem; the other is what you propose to do in future, to solve the problem. An example of the former is that if you discover that a child sitting in the back row is inattentive in class because he is partially blind or deaf, you may move him to the front row and see if this helps the child to concentrate better. (This is what you actually do). Then you may propose to take or refer the child to an ENT surgeon or eye specialist. (This is a proposed arrangement.)

Quite often problems may not be as simple as the ones mentioned above. In a complex situation you may want to discuss the various possibilities before carrying out any action. For example, if an unmarried pregnant girl seeks help, the following courses of action may be suggested by the teachers:

- Call the parents.
- Meet the boy who was her partner.
- Arrange the marriage.
- Take her to a clinic.

In such a situation, discussion with a supervisor or a peer can be very helpful in determining the pros and cons of each of the above courses of action. Figure 23.1 outlines the various strategies.

Family	Child	School
	Attention deficit hyperkinesis autistic withdrawal	
Counselling	Attention enhancing Sensory motor stimuli	Remedial work
	Specific learning disorders	
Counselling	ADHD Autism } Remedial work	Remedial work
	Emotional disorder Conduct disorder	
Counselling	Play/Dyna. Psychotherapy	Remedial work

Figure 23.1 Holistic and eclectic psychosocial strategies for management

Case Illustration of a Child with Multiple Developmental Delays

Rekha, a four and a half year-old girl from a Hindu joint family of upper socio-economic status, was the second of two siblings.

She was brought in with the complaints that she was not mixing with others, was being aggressive, not sitting in one place, feeling afraid at night and speaking to inanimate objects from the age of three. Her personal history revealed a full-term normal birth; birth weight being 8.14 pounds. There were no pre- or peri-natal complications. She had delayed milestones in motor and language development. At the time of consultation her speech was characterized by poor articulation. In addition, there was uncoordinated gait with poor fine-motor skills.

Temperamentally, she was demanding, stubborn and overactive and lacked a rhythm in her schedules of sleep and appetite. She was pampered by all the members of the joint family. She often had temper tantrums. She was especially jealous of other young children in the family. On joining school at the age of three years, she was reported to have been restless and especially aggressive to other children in the class and hence could not be kept in school.

On assessment her IQ on the Binet-Kamat test was 100, and she had adequate form perception on Seguin Form Board. Her visuo-spatial skills were age-appropriate. Her social maturity quotient on Vineland Social Maturity Scale was average. On Children's Apperception Test (CAT) she gave stories which were surprisingly rich in fantasy.

Therapy consisted of the use of multiple techniques. Rapport was established with the child to enable the therapist to institute required management strategies. To increase her attention span, tasks such as beading, colouring and cutting paper, gradually extending to longer periods of time, were carried out. Her daily schedule was structured to include varied and interesting tasks. The parents were taught methods of consistent discipline and differential reinforcement techniques (verbal, 'time out', and not paying attention to unwanted behaviour such as talking to inanimate objects). Interaction with peers was encouraged in the ward setting. A series of graded exercises were planned for her writing difficulties. Tasks were assigned to increase her fine-motor skills and motor coordination (physiotherapy exercises, cycling, etc.). The family was encouraged to communicate with her at home and in school in the same language. The mother was instructed about speech exercises for the child's articulation problems. Rekha was also prescribed spectacles for the visual problem discovered during examination.

After 40 sessions, Rekha showed progress in almost all areas. Her mother took a great deal of interest in the programme once she perceived improvement by following the strategies adopted. At a six-month follow-up after strict maintenance of the schedule at home, Rekha's behaviour had improved markedly, and she could return to school and was reported to be normal in her social interaction and attentive to her academic work. The teacher had also evinced interest in helping the child in the school setting. It was indeed a heartening experience for the family, who had earlier been told by several specialists that Rekha was mentally retarded and nothing could be done to help her.

SPECIFIC DELAY IN MOTOR DEVELOPMENT

In children with language delay, hyperactivity and specific learning disabilities, minimal brain dysfunction or a certain degree of maturational lag have been hypothesized as causes. These may be manifested in neurological soft signs, electroencephalogram (EEG) abnormalities and so on. These children may be clumsy, with poor fine-motor coordination and gait disturbance. The presence of signs of immaturity of the nervous system has implications for intervention, which consists essentially of remediation to strengthen the areas of deficits by training in those skills. Principles of remediation are common to all the spheres of specific developmental delays, whether they overlap or not.

SELF-EVALUATION

Exercise

Look at the items in the Developmental Psychopathology Check List (DPCL) and note how many are present in the case that is illustrated.

(According to the DPCL [Kapur 1995])

The child .... aged .... years, boy/girl, studying in Class ...., medium of instruction ....

The child is 1st/2nd/3rd of siblings—comes from a joint/nuclear family.

Presents with complaints of .... of .... duration.

(i)

(ii)

(iii)

(iv)

(v)

	Score
A. Developmental history	
B. Developmental problems	
C. Psychopathology • Hyperkinesis • Conduct disorder • Learning/School disorder • Emotion disorder • *Obsessive compulsive • Physical symptoms • *Psychoses	
D. Family history Family interactions	

E. Temperament Easy – *Satvik* Difficult – *Rajasik* Slow to warm – *Tamasik*	
F. Support	

***To be referred to a specialist**

1. Please build a picture of the child that includes the complaints, duration of each of the complaints, developmental and family histories, temperament, stressors and environmental supports. Could you also speculate on what could have led the formation of the symptoms?

----

2. What techniques have been used?

(i)

(ii)

(iii)

(iv)

(v)

CHAPTER

24 Attention Deficit Disorders

HYPERKINETIC CONDUCT DISORDER: A CASE STUDY

John, a 10-year-old from a Christian nuclear family of middle socio-economic status, came to the clinic with complaints of over activity from the age of two years; stammering since the age of three; increased irritability and aggressive behaviour from the age of five; poor scholastic performance from the age of eight; and soiling pants from the age of nine years.

He was the only child, born after 10 years of marriage, and thus very precious. He had a full-term normal birth with no pre-, peri- or post-natal complications. His developmental milestones were normal except for the onset of stammering at the age of three years. Temperamentally, he was a child with high level of activity and low threshold of frustration tolerance. When psychologically assessed, he was found to have fluctuating attentional functions and very poor skills in reading, writing, arithmetic, though his IQ on the WISC (Wechsler Intelligence Scale for Children) was 91.

As a toddler, he was overactive, irritable and disruptive. But his parents were over-indulgent and yielded to all his demands because he was their only child. Gradually, when they discovered that he was not doing well at school, they became very punitive and insisted that he should study all the time. He was also prevented from playing with others and kept locked inside the house except when he had to go to school. Consequently, John became very aggressive, oppositional and indifferent to school work.

The management consisted of 30 sessions in out-patient and in-patient settings. With the child, attention-enhancing and remedial work for his specific learning deficits was carried out. Structuring of his daily schedule consisted of interesting remedial tasks, with a good deal of time for play and other ward activities, such as artwork and clay modelling, exercises, games, all of these being carried out in the company of other children. In the individual psychotherapeutic sessions, John expressed his distress about his poor academic performance and his fears that his parents may abandon him. He was able to verbalize much of his distress to the therapist.In addition, he was also told, using behavioural methods, about the need for reducing his disruptive and aggressive behaviour along with encopresis, the reinforcements being introduced with his concurrence. He was also referred to a speech pathologist for the problem of stammering.

To the parents, the chronology of John's symptoms and their linkage with his conduct and emotional problems were demonstrated to his parents. They were instructed about behavioural management which involved 'time out' for disruptive behaviour and maintaining 'Star Charts' with positive reinforcements for pro-social behaviour and for not soiling his pants. They were also told that John's attentional and learning problems were not deliberate, but inherent, and that he needed a special kind of help. They were counselled that expectations of high academic achievement and punishment at this stage would adversely affect John. The need to allow time for play, especially with other children, was emphasized. It was also suggested that marital problems between them may have led to inconsistency in handling John properly and to his inner distress.

At the end of 30 sessions, the child was totally free of his disruptive behaviour, and there was satisfactory progress in the area of attention, learning and speech problems.

GROUP WORK: MANAGEMENT OF HYPERKINETIC CONDUCT DISORDER IN A SMALL GROUP SETTING

The study by Oberoi and Kapur (1995) attempted to develop an intervention strategy for hyperkinetic conduct disorder and evaluation of its efficacy was conducted on 10 primary school children in a small group setting. The management was carried out over 15 sessions.

Developmental and Family History, School Performance and Temperament

Out of the 10, five children were delivered by caesarean section indicating the possibility of damage to the brain. Developmental problems in terms of clumsiness were recorded in three of them. Two had difficulties with articulation, another three were identified as having feeding problems, primary enuresis was present in two, whereas sleep-related disturbances were recorded for three of them.

Psychological disturbances such as crying easily, clinging to parents and shyness were recorded for two children. All of them were reported to be overactive with short attention spans, seven of them were distractible, and five were impulsive and stubborn. Disobedience was a complaint about three children. Seven of them were aggressive (on provocation) and three had temper tantrums and fought with peers. One child had a positive family history of mental illness; another one had a history of parental alcoholism and one child's father had been hyperactive in his childhood.

Six of the children had problems in their interactions with parents, parents of four were punitive, and two had parents who were over-expectant and over-indulgent. Inconsistent disciplining was present for eight of the children. Multiple parenting and sibling rivalry were present in two cases each. Serious parental disharmony was reported in the cases of two children.

Poor school performance was observed in four of them, with two each having reading and writing problems, and one having problems in arithmetic. Two had poor memory and were forgetful. Six of the 10 children had difficulty in getting along with their peers, whereas one child had problems with his teachers as well.

Seven of the parents reported their children to be temperamentally difficult to manage, with three of the children considered emotionally reactive, nine having high activity levels, three to be having poor appetite, two to be shy, and five regarded as aggressive by their parents. The development of sensitivity was lately emerging, in the case of seven children.

All the children on CBCL had high externalizing scores while one child also had high internalizing score.

The case descriptions of three children who formed the first group are illustrated below. The other seven children formed two more groups.

Case 1. V.K. was a 9-year-old boy, studying in Class III, from a middle-class family. His maternal grandfather (who was the child's main caretaker) reported him to be clumsy, inattentive, impulsive and stubborn from early infancy. The child would begin tasks, hurry through them and leave them half finished. Frequently he would mishandle and break things at home. For the past two years, on various occasions, he was talking back to his grandfather; hitting other children and getting into frequent fights.

His teacher found him to be a definitely bright student, who in the past had helped to carry her books. However, she reported him to be inattentive, easily distractible, fidgety and extremely restless. Often he would shout in class and disturb his peers. He was usually reprimanded for showing 'out of seat behaviour' (not being able to sit in one place) or for answering before his turn. His peers refused to play with him, and the senior school boys teased him.

Temperamentally, though affectionate and sensitive, V.K. had a low frustration tolerance and markedly increased activity level, which made him difficult to manage. He was an only child, born of a non-consanguineous union. The father, an electrical computer engineer, had died in 1991 after a prolonged illness. Since infancy, the child had been entrusted to the care of his maternal grandparents as his parents usually remained busy with their professions. The grandparents were over-involved and over-indulgent in their interaction with this child. The child showed dependence on his grandparents and would frequently ask questions about his father's death.

Behavioural observations during pre-intervention assessment revealed him to be restless and overactive. His responses on different tests were ill-planned and hurried, his manner of attempting the tasks was haphazard, and despite comprehending the test instructions correctly he made several errors. He also demonstrated a need for approval and reassurance from the examiner several times during the assessment period.

Case 2. S.S. was an 8-year-old boy, studying in Class III, from a lower-middle socio-economic background.

His parents reported that the child's problems had increased after his admission into school. The problems were: inability to pay attention or concentrate on his work; motoric over-activity like climbing chairs, tables and windows, jumping and running excessively; inability to sit quietly for a reasonable period of time; generally being destructive; being stubborn and crying easily.

According to the teacher, S.S., functioning at a below-average level, was a 'problem child'. He demonstrated little interest in studies and was unable to pay attention in class. He frequently disturbed other children. On several occasions, he would be beaten up by the teacher for disrupting the class discipline. The teacher felt that he had specific problems in reading and arithmetic.

His temperamental profile revealed him to be a sensitive and trusting child but one who was stubborn and aggressive (on provocation). The family history showed that he was the elder of two siblings, born of a non-consanguineous union. The father was a 40-year-old factory worker, educated up to Class X. His mother was a 32-year-old housewife. Parental disciplining was inconsistent, with the father being punitive and the mother feeling incompetent to handle him. His restlessness would become more obvious in the father's presence, which, in turn, further made the father angry and intolerant. The child feared his father as well as his class teacher.

During pre-intervention assessment, though initially restless, he would subsequently settle down and work on the tests in an orderly manner. However, after 15 minutes, he repeatedly expressed the desire to go back to the classroom and hence the assessment had to be continued the next day.

Case 3. S.K. was a 9-year-old boy, studying in Class III, from a middle-class family. His father reported that since infancy, the child had an unusually high activity level; he would be constantly breaking and throwing things, tearing paper, running and jumping around and was unable to complete any task. The child was impulsive, demanded money in excessive sums, threw frequent temper tantrums, got into fights and was non-compliant.

His teacher was exasperated. His impulsive, inattentive, aggressive and disruptive behaviour often brought him into conflict with school authorities. Branded as a 'trouble-maker' he was nicknamed 'loafer' and 'useless fellow' by his peers. In the previous school, due to the above-mentioned problems, he had been detained twice in Class II, and the parents had been asked by the principal to change the school. Temperamentally he was sensitive but a difficult child to manage and had an increased activity level.

Born of a non-consanguineous union, he was the elder of two siblings. In the presence of severe marital disharmony, disciplining at home was inconsistent. His father was over-indulgent; his mother was a suspicious woman and punitive towards the boy. Due to the child's problems, there were frequent quarrels between the parents. The child himself expressed anger towards people around him, was conscious of not being looked after and said that he 'hated the world'.

Behaviour observations during testing revealed him to be well-mannered and it was easy to develop a rapport with him. However, after the first five minutes, his restlessness became obvious. He responded to the test tasks in a hurried, ill-planned, haphazard and thoughtless manner.

Therapy Sessions for Group I

The three children (Cases 1, 2 and 3, i.e., V.K., S.S. and S.K.) formed the first group. The main characteristics of this group were:

- The boys were between the ages of 8 to 9 years.
- They were all students of Class III.
- They all had a core attentional deficit.
- They were motorically overactive.
- They had moderate to severe degree of behaviour problems and were aggressive.

- They had significant difficulties in interpersonal situations and often got into conflict with their environment, especially with parents, teachers and peers.
- They were rated by their teachers to be doing poorly (Cases 2 and 3).

Though the severity of problems varied across groups, attentional deficits, interactional difficulties and behavioural problems were present in all the three groups. As these were the target areas that intervention aimed to handle, an essentially uniform intervention programme was developed and implemented for all the groups.

Thus, the process of therapy as presented below, can be considered as a representative account of how intervention progressed in the other two groups as well. The qualitative differences between groups will be dealt with later.

Initial Phase: Sessions I to V. A brief, 30-minute introductory meeting was held, with the purpose of introducing the children to each other and to the therapist, and also to inform them about the broad outlines of the programme. The children were encouraged to talk about their likes and dislikes, following which a general outline of the programme was given. They were made to understand that each day all three of them and the therapist would involve themselves in a number of tasks and games. To complete these, it was essential to be attentive, friendly and cooperative. They were asked if they could think of any reason why they had been selected for the programmes. S.S. responded by saying that it was to play and to improve on their intelligence. None of the children could, however, understand that they were in anyway more problematic than their peers. This point was not stressed by the therapist at this stage. After playing snakes and ladders for 10 minutes, they were informed about the date and timings of the next sessions and were then sent back to their respective classrooms. All three children were observed to be distractible, restless and inattentive.

The major focus of sessions I to V was to help the children to understand and recognize the nature of their deficits and also to help them to make the association between their problematic behaviour and the negative consequences that they repeatedly experienced, both at school and at home. Such an understanding would convince them of the need for modifying their behaviour, and they would participate in the sessions with involvement and interest.

In the first session, the children and the therapist sat in a circle on the floor. All three children began complaining simultaneously about their reading test, about each other and how they were shouted at by the teacher. It was stressed that they should take turns to speak one at a time. V.K. hit S.K. This behaviour was discouraged immediately and they were reminded of the need to be cooperative and helpful. It was emphasized that during group sessions, complaining, abusing or hitting one another was to be avoided, but that apart from this they could feel free to communicate any of their problems as the group was a platform where they were to share their experiences, problems and difficulties. They were reassured that attempts would be made to find answers for these problems. A few other rules to be followed during the sessions were introduced. The agenda for the day's sessions was provided and the children were told that everyday tasks such as colouring, beading and scanning would be undertaken. After this the tasks were actually begun, with the therapist introducing and verbalizing aloud the strategies for planning and executing them.

In the colouring task, they drew lines all over the page without considering the boundaries of the sketched figures; on a wooden cube they could not even replicate simple sequential tapping; on visual scanning, the maximum numbers scanned were 12 in five minutes.

Before ending the session, the therapist briefly highlighted the need for cooperative work.

In the second session, the discussion revolved around why it was essential to follow certain norms and rules of behaviour, both at school and at home, and how disturbing, inattentive behaviour disrupted the total classroom functioning. The need for rules such as sitting in the seat, answering by turn, paying attention and not hitting or disturbing other classmates was explained.

The children were restless, unsettled, distractible and unable to participate much in group activities. No improvement on task performance was observed. To raise their interest, they were allowed to go out and play for 15 minutes. Following this, their participation in the scanning activity was again poor. The session concluded with each child summarizing the behaviour expected from him in the classroom.

In the third session, the therapist once again asked the children why they, amongst all their peers, had been chosen for the daily sessions. As the children did not respond, the therapist made an attempt to link up their behaviour to the negative consequences that they faced both at home and at school. It was explained how an improvement in behaviour was likely to facilitate their acceptance in both these situations. At that moment, S.S. said that his parents, especially his father, were punitive; and S.K. said that all his schoolmates hit him and teased him.

After providing the children a chance to ventilate freely, attempts were made to help them realize how they were partially responsible for the negative consequences that they experienced. After a detailed explanation, reassurance was provided that this state of affairs could definitely be modified if they too made consistent efforts.

The techniques of 'time out' and 'response cost', and their necessity in times of severe misconduct were explained to the group. They were clearly made to understand how and when these techniques would be used for their benefit, i.e., to help them gain control over their behaviour. They were asked for suggestions whether there were any other methods to deal with their misbehaviour, but none of them made any spontaneous contribution.

A motivational chart, stating problem behaviour in positive statements (e.g. did not disturb), was shown to the children and it was clearly explained which kind of behaviour would help them earn stars, both from the therapist as well as the teacher.

In the daily tasks, though still distractible, they showed more interest. They were able to colour together for 12 minutes and could undertake scanning for 10 minutes. Though they showed an interest in the cube task, they could not yet imitate the tapping sequences accurately.

In the fourth session, the issues raised the previous day were discussed further. The children were directly asked to find links between their disturbing behaviour and its consequences. S.K. immediately responded by saying that he was the naughtiest boy in class but felt angry as everyone called him 'bad'. The child was allowed to ventilate freely and each of his peers was asked to describe his positive qualities. Moreover he was made to understand that he was not the only one to face these difficulties but the other group members did too, and this was precisely the reason why they were attending the group sessions. This opportunity was also used to reassure the children that there were various ways in which they could overcome their problems, and learn to control themselves in difficult situations where they tended to become restless, inattentive and impulsive. V.K. said he was more talkative and 'played mischief' in class but that the previous day he had tried to be quiet and had earned two stars. This was reinforced, and the example set before the other children that they too could begin working in a similar manner. S.S. said that he also wanted to be attentive but could not. Once again the group was reassured that the purpose of these meetings was to help them achieve these skills. A qualitative difference was observed in their performance; in contrast to the earlier days they showed some interest in repeating the verbal self-instructions after the therapist before beginning the tasks. They also finished all tasks with less errors and better cooperation.

In the fifth session, it was observed that the children were restless, distractible and were talking out of turn. They were reminded of the group norms but for the first 15 minutes, no order could be maintained. During colouring, they were observed to be pushing each other and not sharing the colours. S.K. hit V.K. on the eye. 'Time out' was used, and later when S.K. was asked what he should have done instead, he voluntarily apologized to the other child. All were given feedback regarding their behaviour during the session. When this was being done, each child began shouting and complaining about the others. They were warned that if such behaviour continued, they would be sent back to their respective classes and the session would be discontinued. After this, though they were disturbed, they gradually settled down enough to attempt the attentional tasks. Before closing the session, the children were themselves asked the reason for the impulsivity and excitement. A few suggestions were volunteered by them, following which the therapist introduced certain self-control strategies that they could use at such times.

By the end of the first five sessions, one session with each child's teacher had also been held in which the teacher had been sensitized to the child's limitations; the use of positive instead of negative reinforcement was discussed and a motivational chart was handed over to the teacher, which she had to fill up and send home with the child so that parents could review and reinforce the child's positive efforts each day.

Likewise, one or two sessions had been held with each child's parents/caretakers. They were given detailed information regarding the nature of the child's problems. Parents were made to see how typical coercive interaction with children hindered progress, and how such exchanges become more frequent if the child was even partially successful at avoiding comments or undesirable situations.They were helped to realize why they often reacted to their child with increased control. Parents were asked to employ better methods of commenting upon, praising and noticing the child's positive behaviour, while ignoring his less acceptable behaviour.

Middle Phase: Sessions VI to X. The format followed in these sessions was similar to the one described for the first five sessions. The major emphasis of intervention in this phase was on strengthening the children's motivation to overcome problems of inattention and over-activity. This was done in several ways. First, the complexity level of the tasks was common for all the children, which meant the level matched the average capacity of the group. The fact that teachers and parents were reinforcing the children both at school and home further strengthened their motivation to continue approaching different situations and specific tasks positively. Instead of following the therapist's instructions blindly at this stage, they were encouraged to think for themselves the different strategies involving planning, and employ a systematic manner to approach tasks. Answering out of turn and complaining about each other (which frequently occurred) were discouraged. The various kinds of problem behaviour that had been reported earlier were taken up for discussion, and a more acceptable way of responding in specific situations was discussed. Though the participation of the children was minimal, when the therapist offered suggestions they showed an interest and made efforts to contribute to the discussions.

From the eighth session onwards, role-playing was introduced into the daily agenda. A few situations which all children found difficult to handle were chosen, and role-playing was attempted. However, the involvement of the children was minimal, as they hesitated to participate in this activity. Hence from the eleventh session onwards it was decided to discontinue its use, as the children's interest in this activity could not be generated.

Storytelling was introduced as a regular feature from the ninth session onwards. Initially brief and easy stories were chosen and general questions about these stories were asked. The children's attention was ill-sustained and they were unable to answer even simple questions following the completion of the stories.

However, improvements in other attentional tasks were gradually being observed. Almost everyday they were regularly and cooperatively completing the colouring exercise in 12–15 minutes, except in the seventh session when they tore the paper. On that day the positive reinforcements were withheld and the reason for this was clearly explained to them. Beading was progressing well and by the end of the tenth session, the children were, on an average, threading 46 beads each, within the standard time limit of 10 minutes. Likewise, improvements in scanning were evident. With verbal self-instruction, the children were making efforts to scan more systematically, doing up to 40 numbers in 7–10 minutes. Though the tapping task was still able to hold their interest, the improvement was minimal.

By this time, the children were relatively more settled and comfortable. As the sessions progressed, they were earning more stars, both from the therapist as well as from their teachers. Despite this, fluctuations in level of performance continued. There were times when they suddenly became excitable and impulsive, and sometimes even hit each other or entered into fights with their peers in school.

Regular contact with their teachers was maintained. The feedback that the teachers gave regarding the children's behaviour in the classroom each day was later given to the children during the sessions. In this way the programme's continuity and linkage extended from the classroom to the therapy sessions and in the home setting as well.

Final Phase: Sessions X to XV. During these sessions, the work initiated in the previous days was continued, with added emphasis on teaching the children to improve their attention by organizing and focusing it on every task that they attempted. They were encouraged to check and go over their work before finally handing it over to the therapist during the sessions, to the teacher in class, or to parents at home. To improve their organizational skills, they were asked to make lists of daily activities that they had to do, and to check every night the books they had to carry to school the next day. Various other simple activities which called for planning before their actual implementation were initiated. At first, parents were assigned the supervisory role, to help their children attain these skills resulting from cooperative play and team work.

Discussions during these sessions focused upon providing the children with the rationale behind cooperative play and team work, and explaining to them the benefits that resulted. The instances when they had worked cooperatively were highlighted, and these were contrasted with the negative consequences of fighting, hitting or beating. Their role as responsible students was stressed and they were entrusted daily with small tasks that required them to share their belongings (such as pencils, erasers, playthings, etc.) with their peers in school. Likewise, their role as an important growing member in the family was discussed with them.

By the time the intervention programme concluded, the children were regularly colouring complex pictures of landscapes, scenery, buildings, and models of their school. During the thirteenth session, they resorted to their haphazard manner of colouring. Feedback was given immediately, but that day it was not possible to alter their style of functioning. Otherwise, they regularly did the colouring exercise for 15 minutes everyday. The average number of beads threaded steadily increased to 67, and by the last session they were able to scan up to 80 numbers in 10 minutes (even though the size and boldness of the numbers had been reduced by this time).

On the cube, the replication of the more complex tappings was still not possible. But the children could reproduce simple tapping sequences correctly. Their efficiency on the storytelling task improved gradually as was evidenced by the fact that two out of three children were able to give most of the details of the stories.

While improvements were being observed, two of the children, S.K. and V.K., expressed feelings of low self-esteem during the eleventh session. V.K. said that everyone around him called him a naughty boy and the bus driver also threatened to beat and fine him. This meant that he actually was a 'bad child'. S.K., on the other hand, expressed his distress in the form of aggression, anger and hostility towards all adults and other children. During the sessions, attempts were made to elevate their self-esteem, but as the problems were serious they were taken up in individual sessions with both the children.

A finding worth mentioning here is that though individual differences in performance persisted all through the intervention programme, the children were actively making efforts to match their speed with that of the other group members. Moreover, the children were more settled and appeared happier because of the positive reinforcements and attention that was forthcoming from several adults around them.

Before concluding the programme, responsibility for continuing the attentional tasks at home was entrusted to the parents. The teachers were praised for their efforts and were asked to continue them in the future as well. The children were prepared for the termination of the programme and were promised that the therapist would occasionally keep in touch with them.

The above programme had focused on three targets: enhancement of attentional skills, pro-social behaviour and elimination of problematic behaviour. The termination of the intervention with the three groups coincided with the summer vacation. On assessment after the intervention the teacher ratings on Conner Rating Scale revealed a significant reduction in the mean scores from 18.2 to 7.5. Parents too reported a significant reduction in the extent of misbehaviour. On assessment of actual performance of these 10 children on psychological tests, the maturational age on a visuo-motor copying task improved significantly in all the groups, with the exception of one child. There was improvement in attentional functioning on a simple colour cancellation task. The methodical and sequential handling of complex cancellation tasks showed only a marginal improvement. This indicated that further training was required in stabilizing the gains on the attentional tasks. Their performance on a test of intelligence, which was average before the intervention, showed significant gains in terms of time taken. The group also showed significant reduction in impulsivity on a maze test.

After the summer vacation, the follow-up showed that nine children had maintained the improvement. The child who did not improve had been referred earlier to a child psychiatric clinic because of the severity of the problems.

WORKING WITH CHILDREN IN LARGE GROUPS

Twenty children were seen once a week over 3–4 months. Almost all the children had at least 10 sessions. The detailed picture of the hyperactivity at home, school and elsewhere was recorded. The children were tested before and after the intervention on attention, intelligence and level of hyperactivity and attention deficit. They were treated with the conventional package of activities for hyperactive children, as described in this chapter. In addition, certain diet and exercises from the ancient Indian tradition were included. These consisted of a diet suitable for the child's constitution, massage with medicated oil to head and body, certain asanas (yogic postures) and mudras (poses) recommended for children were also adopted. These were prescribed individually to the parents of the children to be carried out at home. Some exercises and activities were carried out for the entire group together, some in small groups and some were individual activities to be carried out in the clinic and at home. The children showed satisfactory improvement over 10 sessions, in the clinic, at home and in the school.

It must be noted that as the hyperactive and impulsive children lack pro-social behaviour, the group approach helps the counsellor to focus on the deficit social skills and work towards enhancing social skills in actual practice with the other children. Quite often hyperactive children do not realize the impact of their disruptive behaviour on others. When they themselves experience the impact of another's disruptive behaviour, they understand the need to control one's own impulsive behaviour. Immediate praise and approval of pro-social behaviour goes a long way in promoting the same.

INTERVENTIONS FOR HYPERKINETIC CHILDREN (FOR TEACHERS OR PARENTS)

1. Reduce distractions in study area (clear study table, no colourful posters on the walls).
2. Structure the task so that it is possible to proceed in a step-by-step manner.
3. Set short-term goals (answer one question or do two arithmetic sums).
4. Break long assignments into smaller parts so that child can see an end to the work.
5. Seat child near good role model or 'study buddy'.
6. Use some physical contact with the child, which may be a hand on the shoulder, or directing of arm and hand movements.

7. Avoid teaching at a frustration level. Teach at a tolerance level at which it is easy for the child to work and at a level that is challenging for the child.
8. Make sure the child completely understands what is being taught.
9. Teach when the child is well motivated and ready to work.
10. Shorten work/study periods to coincide with span of attention; use a timer.
11. Instruct child in self-monitoring.
12. Pair written instructions with oral instructions.
13. Cue child to stay on the task, i.e. provide signals.
14. Provide 'seat breaks', for example, to run errands, clean the blackboard, and collect books.
15. At times, allow the child to stand while working.
16. Use a multisensory teaching approach with specialized teaching materials.
17. Children get bored easily, so keep up their interest and motivation with adequate and immediate reinforcements.
18. Give frequent feedback of child's performance ('Good, keep it up.').
19. Be firm, do not allow the child to escape a task that you know he is capable of performing.
20. Be consistent. Do not alternate between giving in to the child and being firm about completing a goal.
21. Ignore minor impulsive behaviour.
22. Use time-out for misbehaviour.
23. Acknowledge positive behaviour.
24. Help the child organize his daily routine.
25. Look for signs of stress build-up and provide encouragement or reduce workload to alleviate pressure and avoid temper outbursts.

ATTENTION ENHANCING STRATEGIES

- Stringing beads: Big to small
- Matching, sorting
- Join-the-dot games
- Finger dexterity games
- Colouring within lines
- Painting within lines
- Mazes
- Cutting pictures and sticking them
- Jigsaw puzzles
- Scanning pictures, numbers
- Letter cancellation

- Hocus-focus (find differences)
- Reaction time apparatus to teach child to withhold responses
- Watching TV/listening to stories and narrating them.

FINGER/MOTOR CO-ORDINATION ACTIVITIES

- Plasticine/Clay play
- Scissor work: Scrapbook
- Hopping games
- Skipping
- Rangoli work
- Swimming
- Dancing
- Putting coins/buttons into slot
- Nuts and bolts
- Tapping board
- Finger puppets

SELF-EVALUATION

Exercise

Look at the items in the Developmental Psychopathology Check List (DPCL) and note how many are present in the case that is illustrated.

(According to the DPCL [Kapur 1995])

The child .... aged .... years, boy/girl, studying in Class ...., medium of instruction ....

The child is 1st/2nd/3rd of siblings—comes from a joint/nuclear family.

Presents with complaints of .... of .... duration.

(i)

(ii)

(iii)

(iv)

(v)

	Score
A. Developmental history	
B. Developmental problems	
C. Psychopathology • Hyperkinesis • Conduct disorder • Learning/School disorder • Emotion disorder • *Obsessive compulsive • Physical symptoms • *Psychoses	
D. Family history Family interactions	
E. Temperament	
F. Support	

***To be referred to a specialist**

1. Please build a picture of the child that includes the complaints, duration of each of the complaints, developmental and family histories, temperament, stressors and environmental supports. Could you also speculate on what could have led the formation of the symptoms?

----

2. What techniques have been used?

(i)

(ii)

(iii)

(iv)

(v)

CHAPTER

25 Internalizing Disorders

CASE ILLUSTRATION

Master NM was a 7-year-old boy from a lower socio-economic status (SES), semi-urban background. According to his parents, he was stubborn, got angry very easily, cried easily and was sensitive and shy since childhood. He was also reported to have poor memory and worrying about financial constraints in the family since the age of 2–3 years. The teacher reported that the child appeared fearful and tense in class and had minimal interaction with the classmates. He was also observed to be depressed and preoccupied in the classroom.

The family dolls used in the play therapy are described in Chapter 15 which is on play therapy. Illustration of the dolls are given in the inside cover.

If you want to be a good counsellor, you need to write down details of all the sessions as shown in this illustration by Shashi, Kapur and Subbakrishna (1999). This helps to monitor progress and plan future sessions.

Highlights of the Play Therapy Sessions

Session 1. The child initially appeared nervous and fearful but once he entered the playroom, he became very excited at the sight of the toys and dolls. He picked up the vehicle, pushed it to and fro, kept smiling and appeared happy. Later he picked up the little girl doll and fed her with the feeding bottle and made her sit on the cycle and said that he was taking her for a ride. He then picked up the toy telephone, dialled a number and said that he was calling up his friend Karthik to invite him for his sister's birthday, which he said was on the following day. Later he pulled the toy train and said that he was going to the Kolar Gold Fields (K.G.F.) to meet his sister and brother-in-law.

He picked up the grandmother doll, kissed her and said that she was going to the temple. Then he picked up the doctor doll and made him examine the baby doll and said that the baby had fever and the doctor was examining her. Later he played with the toy animals and arranged the kitchen set, saying he was cooking papad and rice for dinner.

Session 2. He initially identified grandmother as 'mother' and after sometime he identified her correctly. He said that his uncle was a policeman and that he was going to K.G.F. by train. As in Session 1, he said that the doctor was examining the baby because he had fever. He made the teacher hold the baby's hand and walk and called the baby the teacher's child. Later he played with the toy animals and picked up the gorilla and said that he was feeding it and liked it very much but in case it really appeared, he would run away.

He made all the children stand erect and said that they were playing and if the policemen happened to come, they would run away.

He reported that once his elder brother, elder sister and baby went to watch a drama. A policeman caught his brother as he was found to have consumed illicit liquor and put him behind bars. Then grandmother took him home and beat him badly. So brother ran away from home, ate at a hotel and slept somewhere. Then grandmother came in search of him, found him and took him back. At home, he did not answer to the grandmother about where he had been and then his sisters discussed grandmother beating the brother badly.

Session 3. He said that the mother cooked food, served them and took care of their needs. Once she happened to fall ill and the elder sister took care of her, giving her medicine on time, a bath, preparing food and feeding her. Her temperature shot up so the sister took her to the hospital and she recovered. Thereafter, the mother cooked food and took care of the children as before.

He said that while the mother slept, the elder sister disturbed her, so the mother got irritated and shooed her away. When the girl went out to play she accidentally put her hand into a snake hole and got bitten. On noticing, the family members took her to the hospital and she was fine. Later her mother asked why she had done so and she replied that it had happened without her knowledge.

He said the sister left home and went to her grandmother's house, where grandmother asked whether she wanted hot or cold water for a bath. She said she preferred cold water. She bathed and her hair grew long. She met an elephant on the way back home, who asked her to remove a thorn, which she did, and the elephant rewarded her with lot of sugarcane and she came home happy.

Session 4. He said that once his mother beat his little sister for refusing to eat food, so she got angry and went to the grandmother's house. (He then narrated the same story as in Session 3.) He further said that once someone kidnapped the baby. The mother went to the temple looking for her. There someone hit her on the head, and the grandmother found her there but some bad guys attacked her and a goddess appeared in disguise and saved them.

He said that once his parents quarrelled, so the baby and the little sister went with the mother whereas the elder sister and the father stayed alone. The mother along with other children went to the grandparents' house. The grandparents borrowed money from the moneylenders to bring them up. So the baby and the little sister started working hard and became rich. Then the elder sister and father were united with them.

Later the baby became greedy and a spendthrift, saying that it was his money and that he had the right to spend it, so the parents put him in a hostel. There the baby realized his mistake and came back home. But he again repeated the same behaviour, so the parents hit him on his head and he became mentally ill. He said the baby's name was Rajani and that on a full moon day Rajani would become very irritable. He was taken to the doctor, who advised that Rajani should not be allowed to go out on those days. Later, he became calm and quiet even on full moon days. He also mentioned that Rajani's father had met with an accident and eventually succumbed to his head injury. On his death bed, he requested Rajani to promise him that he would take care of his sisters. The father transferred the property to his name. After a few days the father expired. Later, the sister got married and went to her husband's house as she was scared of her brother's behaviour. After a few days Rajani completely recovered and became a police officer.

Session 5. He said that a snake had once appeared when the children were playing. They all screamed and people came out with sticks and killed it. Later, they kept milk for it as they believed it would come back to life after death.

He said that one day the brother told the villagers, as a joke, that a lion had come. And when all the villagers gathered he told them it was a lie. And once, when the lion really appeared and the brother screamed nobody came to his rescue, and the lion ate him up. So grandfather told the others that if they lied, the same thing would happen to them too.

Then he picked up the baby and said that the baby was pampered at home and did not go to school. Once, the teacher instructed him to bring his parents but he did not inform them. So the teacher came to his home and complained to the parents that he did not study and that he always made up excuses to return home. His mother grew angry and beat him badly. He then ran away from home but his brother found him and brought him back.

He said the baby imagined ghosts when anyone narrated ghost stories. As a result, he would refuse to go out in the dark and would be unable to concentrate on studies. Usually, the elder sister would scare him about ghosts by telling ghost stories and that she always picked up a fight with him for trivial reasons.

He said the baby was interested in outside eatables and the mother beat him for not studying and always eating. The baby was very sensitive to criticism, brooding if anyone spoke ill of him or beat him.

Session 6. He said that the mother once met with an accident while lighting the gas stove as her saree caught fire and then the father saved her. He then instructed the mother that he would cook henceforth. While cooking, his shirt caught fire but he did not tell anybody about it.

He said that the brother was scared of strangers as he had seen a stranger beating a boy. Once when the grandparents came home he refused to talk to them. He was taken to the doctor who said there was nothing wrong with him. But he remained totally housebound and aloof. At school, he imagined ghosts and fights between him and his sister and was also scared that his father might beat him. He would also worry about debts at home and whether they would be thrown out of the house for not paying the rent. To pay the rent, the father asked many people in vain for a loan before finally getting it, and now the creditors troubled them at home.

Once the grandmother suffered a head injury. While she was bleeding, the baby took her to the hospital but the elder brother was not at all concerned even though he noticed it. He sat at home and ate his food.

Once the mother and the co-sister had a fight, so the mother did not allow the younger brother to go downstairs to play with their children. Since the parents failed to pay the fees, the teacher sent the brother home. He sat at home for two months and got bored as he was not allowed to go out to play or to peep through the window and mother refused to get him chocolates. So he sat at home worrying about it.

Session 7. He said that the brother borrowed money from his friend and when questioned by the father he lied. So the father sent him out of the house and the uncle brought him back. But again the father hit him though the mother stopped him. Then the brother repented for his mistakes, by not sleeping for two days.

He said that one day, a lizard accidentally fell into the food while cooking and the mother served the food to the grandfather, baby and little sister without noticing it. They realized it when they started eating and rushed to check on the others but found them dead. The father and brother came home late from work and the mother informed them.

He said that the younger brother was stubborn by nature and acted impulsively. Once he inserted his fingers into an electric socket and though the sister complained to the mother she was scolded for complaining as the mother did not believe he could commit such an act. The brother always makes many demands as the grandmother gives him money quite often.

He said that the father remarried because the mother had expired, and that in actuality the father had killed her. He also said that the dead mother came back in the disguise of a crow and the brother kept food for the crow everyday. Then the grandfather also died and became a crow. The stepmother ill-treated the brother because he was clever compared to his other siblings. So the mother appeared as a ghost and gave him a lot of gold.

He said that the uncle and aunt demanded cash from their married son. The daughter-in-law, who was very greedy and quarrelsome, ill-treated the uncle and aunt by making them do all the household chores. At last she drove them out of the house. The uncle reminded the son that though he had brought him up now he did not even want to look after them. They left the house to stay in a temple, where they found a treasure and became rich. Their son became poor and repented for his mistakes and thereafter the whole family lived happily.

Session 8. He said that the parents were very rich but had lost their wealth by loaning money to everybody. As a result, the father took a loan to pay the fees but the mother used that money for cooking without his knowledge. The father and brother went in search of a job but they did not get one. Then the grandmother lent them money but the brother fell into bad company and misused that money. So the parents punished him and he apologized. With the money saved, the parents got the elder sister married. Once, the father sent the brother to bring the sister home. The brother killed her for the sake of property and came home, lying that she had refused to come. When the father learnt the truth, he beat the brother to death. After this incident, they invested all the hopes on the younger brother, who was brought up by the teacher as they were not financially stable enough to educate him. He pursued his education and became an officer but when his parents visited him, he refused to accept them. So the parents lived alone. Then the teacher explained the truth to the brother and he went back to them and lived happily.

Later, the child picked up the toy animals and played with them. He said that the goat took care of all the other animals and cooked food for everybody. It also protected the rest from the lion. The other animals realized that they were troubling the goat by making it do all the work and so they went away. Then the goat lived alone.

Session 9. The child said that once the grandfather had fever and the grandparents came to ask the parents for money, but the father saw them coming and asked the mother to tell them that he was not at home. So the grandmother lodged a police complaint for the missing father, saying she needed money as she had admitted the grandfather in the hospital. Then the grandparents got to know that the father had lied to them, so they committed suicide. The father was happy to be rid of people asking him for money. Later, the little girl suffered from fever and he was forced to borrow money, incurring a lot of debt. Now he repented for cheating the grandparents. Then he began consuming alcohol excessively and the mother stopped serving him food. When he began asking the neighbours for food they complained to the mother. She lodged a police complaint against the father and he was jailed. Now the neighbours began to look down on the family, so the mother requested the police to release the father but he was killed in the police encounter. Since there was no earning member, the little girl joined a dance troupe. A policeman felt sad and supported their family financially. Then the mother began coughing blood and was diagnosed with cancer. But she hid the news from her children and died. The policeman took care of the girl but later he died too, so the girl went to a forest and lived happily with the animals.

Towards the end of the session, the child complained to the therapist that there was nobody at home to teach him and help him with the homework. And he was scared to tell the parents if anyone beat him, as they would pick up a fight with them (as he was the only son). And so he would worry about it without telling them.

Session 10. The child said that once the father went through a difficult phase. He borrowed from the moneylenders without informing other family members. The moneylenders came to their home demanding their money. So the mother worked hard to repay the loan and instructed the father not to borrow again. But he continued to borrow money and even once demanded money in the presence of the grandparents. The mother told him that she had given the grandparents the money owed to them. The father then demanded money from the grandparents and took it, making the mother angry. She went with the grandparents to the village. The little girl stayed with the father but he neglected her. So the mother returned to take the girl away. The father locked up the mother and put the girl into the well, but someone noticed and saved her. Again, the father put her on the electric pole and told everybody that the mother was responsible for it. Now everybody scolded the mother. The girl escaped to a new place and became rich. The mother found her and lived with her. The father suffered from leprosy and repented for his mistakes. He was reunited with them and lived happily.

Towards the end of the session, the child reports that through the play sessions he had learnt not to worry, not to be afraid of ghosts or to believe in them. He said that now he talked to others and did not brood over anything.

Therapist's Observations

During the interview, the child appeared initially anxious and fearful. But once he came into the playroom, he appeared very cheerful and jumped with excitement at the sight of the toys. He was found to be very active in the playroom in the first session itself, and he also involved the therapist in the play. He spoke spontaneously and at times the therapist found it difficult to record it verbatim. Though there was an element of imagination and fantasy added to the stories, there was also an element of realism in every theme. The child would give elaborate descriptions of the stories and be completely engrossed in narrating them. After every session he was reluctant to leave the playroom. In fact, after every session, the therapist had to remind him that it was time to wind up. In one of the sessions, the child commented that he liked all the toys displayed and enjoyed playing with them.

During the sessions, the following observations were made:

Depicting Oneself. The child depicts himself as being pampered by the parents because he is the only son. If punished by teachers or beaten by anyone, he ponders over it by himself, trying to decide whether or not to inform his parents as they would fight with the person. He expresses a feeling of being cooped up, as the parents do not let him play with the neighbours and he feels lonely at home. At times he plays with his elder sister but she quarrels quite often and refuses to talk to him. The child is disturbed by her behaviour. He also depicts himself as being poor in studies and that there is nobody to help him in studies. The elder sister teaches him at times but he feels that she is very rude and harsh and beats him for trivial reasons. The child also feels depressed when the mother refuses to send him downstairs to play with the aunt's children due to quarrels between them. He also depicts himself as worrying about academic performance. He worries about debts at home and creditors who come to his home to trouble them. There is also the repeated theme of a child growing up and taking a responsible role and resolving the financial debts at home. The child also depicts himself as being stubborn and acting impulsively.

Fears. The child says he fears ghosts and that the elder sister would scare him with ghost stories. He would imagine ghosts in the dark and feel extremely scared. He would also imagine ghosts in the classroom and as a result would not be able to concentrate on studies. He is extremely scared of the dark and therefore is housebound at night. The child also says that he is scared of strangers for the fear of being kidnapped by them and being abandoned on the streets.

Aggression. There is anger towards the elder sister, as in one of the stories he says that she is bitten by a snake when she complains to the mother about him and is also sent out of the house. There is anger towards his cousin also, who is depicted as being mentally ill and disturbing the family members. He describes him as being dishonest, disobedient, selfish, indulging in drinking illicit liquor and being turned out of the house by his parents. He also murders his married elder sister for the sake of property and the father kills him when he finds out. Anger is also expressed towards the father, who spends extravagantly and then starts borrowing from moneylenders, causing the parents' separation. The father kills the mother and remarries, and the stepmother ill-treats the children. The father also troubles the little sister who lives with him and blames the mother for his actions. The child expresses a death wish for the mother. In one of the stories he says that she is afflicted with cancer and dies and in another story he says that she meets with a fire accident and is saved by the father. He also expresses a death wish for the grandmother. In one of the stories he says that she meets with an accident and succumbs to a head injury. In addition, the father refuses the grandparents monetary help, for which they commit suicide. There is anger towards the uncle and aunt as well, who are portrayed as greedy and who refuse to financially help the grandparents. The father is also portrayed as excessively consuming alcohol and complaining to neighbours that the mother does not take care of him.

Resolution. The child resolves the aggression towards the elder sister by saying she takes care of the needs of the children when the mother falls sick and takes good care of mother as well. A snake bites the sister and she is rushed to the hospital, where she recovers. He says that though the sister is sent out of the house, the mother goes in search of her and brings her back home. He resolves the anger towards the cousin brother by saying that a doctor treats him as he is mentally ill and then his condition improves. He also says that after the death of the father he takes good care of the siblings and becomes a police officer. Though the brother is turned out of the house for consuming illicit liquor, the mother goes in search of him and brings him back home. The brother also repents for his mistakes and feels guilty about his behaviour. Though the parents are separated, the children work hard, become rich and reunite and the father repents for taking alcohol and ill-treating the girl and the mother. The father is afflicted with leprosy; he repents for his mistakes, and they all reunite and lead a happy life. The uncle and aunt also repent for their behaviour towards the grandparents and become good.

HIGHLIGHTS OF THE COUNSELLING SESSION

Certain themes were checked with the parents. In one of the stories, the child had narrated that his brother was mentally ill and was very troublesome. The parents reported that the child's uncle's son was mentally ill, would become very irritable and behave harshly on certain occasions. On a few occasions he had also wandered away from his house as he had borrowed money from his friends. He had been treated at NIMHANS for epilepsy and psychiatric problems and mild improvement was seen. The parents were shocked to learn that the child was aware of these problems.

The parents also reported that his relationship with the elder sister was not cordial as she would often trouble the child, scare him about ghosts and disobey them. The parents reported that the child liked the second sister with whom he had a cordial relationship and who would help him with studies. They also reported that the child's uncle had remarried, as his first wife—who happened to be the child's aunt (i.e. mother's sister)—had expired. The uncle's second wife reportedly ill-treated the children and so the child's mother brought them up, causing them to incur heavy debts after the marriage of the child's cousin. At times—when they were unable to afford school fees or to celebrate festivals at home—they would discuss their debts in the child's presence. The parents also reported that they did not let the child play outside as they lived in a slum and the neighbourhood was not good, with frequent, unpredictable rioting. They said they could not afford private tuitions for the child and that the father coached the boy only during exams. The rest of the time the father was busy with his work.

In one of the stories, the boy depicted the father as consuming alcohol. When this was checked with the father, he admitted to occasionally doing so at home, as he got a free quota from the military canteen. Dependence on alcohol was not reported and he would not misbehave after having drinks. In one of the stories, the child reported that a lizard fell into the food and the mother served the food without noticing. When checked with the parents, they reported that it had happened in the neighbourhood. Strategies were laid down for each of the abovementioned problems.

DISCUSSION WITH THE SISTER

A separate counselling session was held with the elder sister. She was told that the child was affected by the ghost stories she narrated and also by her frequent fights over trivial matters. She was asked to advise the child whenever he went wrong and also to compromise with the child as he was disturbed by her behaviour. The sister was asked if it was possible for her to spend some time to teach the child. She said it would be possible only when she did not have exams, as private tuition would be beyond their reach. Regarding ghost stories, she reported that she did it for fun and did not realize the consequences of the same. She assured the counsellor that she would not repeat it in future.

DISCUSSION WITH THE TEACHER

A separate counselling session was held with the teacher. She was counselled about the effects of using punitive measures with the child, as he was anxious and fearful about the teacher. He was found to be on the last bench in class, so a change in his seating arrangement (i.e. to move him forward), was suggested.

DISCUSSION WITH THE PARENTS

It was checked with the parents whether any alternatives could be generated, as the child was feeling bored at home and cooped up. The father reported that he would get military quarters shortly and that they would let him play freely once they shifted. Further, every Sunday, he would take him to a ground to play. The father also assured that he would take extra care of the child's studies by making time for him in his schedule. Regarding taking alcohol, the father reported that he would stop gradually. He explained that as there had been no separate room at home, he had been drinking in the child's presence, not realizing that it affected him. The parents were also counselled about their over-involvement which was stunting his growth. They agreed to allow greater independence in certain things and reduce their over-involvement. The parents were told that they should entrust him with responsible jobs to the furthest extent possible and recognize that he was growing up.

They were also told to reason with the child when he talked about ghosts, and encourage him to go outside on his own.

DISCUSSION WITH THE CHILD

The child was counselled regarding being scared of ghosts. On being asked if he had seen a ghost and whether it existed in reality, he replied that he had watched it only on television, and heard stories from the sister; and that there was no reason to believe in ghosts, as things occurring on television did not exist in reality. The child was also counselled to freely express to his parents his worries about his academic performance and other things that bothered him.

OUTCOME

As the therapy progressed, the parents expressed their shock at the child's awareness of family matters. They even wondered whether it was astrology as the therapist knew every detail of their family matters. The parents were also in tears upon learning about all the things that bothered the child. They felt very guilty, as they had told the therapist in the initial sessions that the therapy would affect his studies and that they were not hopeful about the outcome of therapy.

The parents reported that the child had started doing things independently, did not believe in ghosts and would handle minor purchases on his own. His interactions with the family members and friends had improved. He was also reported to be less anxious. Quarrels between him and his sister had reduced and a cordial relationship was reported. The teachers also reported that the child's interaction with other classmates had increased, he appeared less anxious, less scared, was cheerful in class and attempted to answer questions raised in the class. At the end of the sessions, when the child was asked how he felt about play, he reported that he had learnt not to worry and not to believe in ghost stories. He also said that he now did things on his own, had seen so many toys for the first time and enjoyed playing with them.

SELF-EVALUATION

Exercise

Look at the items in the Developmental Psychopathology Check List (DPCL) and note how many are present in the case that is illustrated.

(According to the DPCL [Kapur 1995])

The child .... aged .... years, boy/girl, studying in Class ...., medium of instruction ....

The child is 1st/2nd/3rd of siblings—comes from a joint/nuclear family.

Presents with complaints of .... of .... duration.

(i)

(ii)

(iii)

(iv)

(v)

	Score
A. Developmental history	
B. Developmental problems	
C. Psychopathology • Hyperkinesis • Conduct disorder • Learning/School disorder • Emotion disorder • *Obsessive compulsive • Physical symptoms • *Psychoses	
D. Family history Family interactions	
E. Temperament	
F. Support	

***To be referred to a specialist**

1. Please build a picture of the child that includes the complaints, duration of each of the complaints, developmental and family histories, temperament, stressors and environmental supports. Could you also speculate on what could have led the formation of the symptoms?

----

2. What techniques have been used?

(i)

(ii)

(iii)

(iv)

(v)

CHAPTER

26 Externalizing Disorders

DISTURBANCE OF CONDUCT AND EMOTION: A CASE ILLUSTRATION

Ramu, a nine-year-old boy from a rural, nuclear family of middle socio-economic status, came with the following complaints: Going out of the house to the graveyard, being withdrawn, and frequent crying spells in the last 10 months following the sudden death of his father. Other complaints were: not obeying elders, beating other children, refusing to go to school and running away from school, being irritable and having temper tantrums.

The child was the last of nine siblings, a favourite of the dominant, upright father who was a goldsmith by profession. Ramu had been pampered by his father to the exclusion of all the other members of the family. Prior to the onset of the disturbance, the father died of cardiac arrest in a hospital. As Ramu was very attached to the father, the family did not tell him that his father was dead. Consequently, he did not participate in the last rites and the various rituals associated with the death. Nor was he told why everyone was upset or distraught. When he was eventually told that his father would never come back, he became withdrawn, lost his appetite and sleep, started going to the graveyard and refused to go to the school. Three months later, when the family tried to force him to go back to school, he started showing disruptive and aggressive behaviour. The sibling rivalry which had been present earlier became very intense. As no one could discipline him, they began to yield to all his unreasonable demands.

Ramu's IQ was 67 and his social maturity on the Vineland Social Maturity Scale was eight and a half years. He had significant problems in reading, writing and arithmetic. The Children's Apperception Test portrayed a feeling of being alone and deserted, but he was devoid of imagination.

Work with the Child

Ramu was admitted to an in-patient facility. On establishing a rapport with him, the therapist was able to get him to ventilate his distress at the loss of his father and the feeling that no one in the family loved him. He repeatedly referred to his father's death and it was seen that he needed to grieve sufficiently. The therapist accepted his anger against the rest of the family but explained to him that his mother and sibling did care about him in their own way, which he had not needed when his father was alive. His disruptive behaviour and the behavioural management were discussed with him, and a contract was drawn up between the mother and the child. He was also taught how to express his normal anxieties and fears to others.

Work with the Mother and Elder Brothers

Ramu's need to grieve and talk about the death of his father was emphasized. The degree of the loss felt by the child and the feeling of being excluded from the family was explained to them. In addition, behavioural management of 'time out' for temper tantrums, and appropriate reinforcements for disruptive or conforming behaviour, as well as the need for the passive mother to be assertive with him was suggested. They were told about the nature of his academic difficulties and asked not to pressurize him to study long hours and also to arrange for him to get extra help in school work when he went home. It was arranged that he went through some of the mourning rituals and visited the graveyard regularly. The mother had learnt to manage his disruptive behaviour as well as make him feel that they wanted him and cared for him. His performance at school was not seen as a priority at this juncture. The therapy consisted of 25 sessions in the in-patient setting and the child showed almost complete reduction of disruptive behaviour. Ramu displayed a normal mood on discharge and follow-up.

Working with the Family

Adverse family factors consisting of marital disharmony and mental illness in the parents, difficulty in relationships manifested in poor and inconsistent disciplining are some of the issues which may be dealt with by counselling the family. When these problems cannot be corrected or can be only partially modified, the child may be taught how to distance himself emotionally from these difficulties (or physically through placement in residential schools, homes of relatives who care for the child, etc.).

Parents could be taught the practice of 'time out' for disruptive behaviour and positive reinforcement, especially token economy, for eliciting socially acceptable behaviour. Setting limits for behaviour and structuring the daily schedule with the consent of the child is often helpful.Handling aggressive behaviour in the child through aggression on the part of the adults may be counterproductive in the long run as the child may imitate the aggressive treatment meted out to him. Encouraging the parents to praise the child for good behaviour and to enhance his self esteem is essential. Parents should exercise their minds to highlight positive points instead of being preoccupied with the negative attributes of the child.

Working with the Child

If the child has brain damage, mental retardation or severe hyperkinesis, the methods for behavioural management become restricted. In the case of severe disruptive behaviour, one may resort to drug management. Attention-enhancing training, remediation, activity planning and structuring of academic work often help a child with specific learning disability or scholastic problems to cope with academic problems. Lack of social skills often leads to conflicts with adults and peers, and this could be dealt with by role-play and modelling, active training and demonstration of the effects of pro-social behaviour. While dealing with conduct disturbances, one often comes across subjective distress, fear and anxiety. Emotional distress needs to be dealt with by psychotherapeutic efforts, beginning with establishing a rapport, followed by building a trusting relationship. Several of the supportive psychotherapeutic measures, of reassurance, suggestion, environmental manipulation at home and school can be used effectively.

The implications for intervention thus indicate a holistic approach to the issue, remedial approaches to help cognitive and perceptual-motor deficits, family therapy with parents, and individual psychotherapy. The presence of symptoms of emotional disturbance is often seen as a good prognostic indicator. Thus, exploration into subjective distress which is not apparent at the outset should be carried out in all cases of conduct disturbance.

SELF-EVALUATION

Exercise

Look at the items in the Developmental Psychopathology Check List (DPCL) and note how many are present in the case that is illustrated.

(According to the DPCL [Kapur 1995])

The child .... aged .... years, boy/girl, studying in Class ...., medium of instruction ....

The child is 1st/2nd/3rd of siblings—comes from a joint/nuclear family.

Presents with complaints of .... of .... duration.

(i)

(ii)

(iii)

(iv)

(v)

	Score
A. Developmental history	
B. Developmental problems	

C. Psychopathology • Hyperkinesis • Conduct disorder • Learning/School disorder • Emotion disorder • *Obsessive compulsive • Physical symptoms • *Psychoses	
D. Family history Family interactions	
E. Temperament	
F. Support	

***To be referred to a specialist**

1. Please build a picture of the child that includes the complaints, duration of each of the complaints, developmental and family histories, temperament, stressors and environmental supports. Could you also speculate on what could have led the formation of the symptoms?

----

2. What techniques have been used?

(i)

(ii)

(iii)

(iv)

(v)

CHAPTER

27 Learning Disorders

A CHILD WITH SCHOLASTIC PROBLEMS: A CASE ILLUSTRATION

Raja was an eight-year-old boy studying in the third standard. His class teacher referred him to the child guidance clinic because of his aggressive behaviour and poor scholastic performance from the time he joined school.

Family History

Raja was the third of four siblings. His father was 40 years old and had studied up to the eighth standard. He worked as a lorry-booking agent earning Rs 2,500 per month. He was alcohol-dependent. Raja's mother was a 32-year old housewife who had studied up to the fifth standard. The house atmosphere was not congenial. Raja's father often came home drunk and quarrelled with the mother. The children were frequently subjected to severe physical punishment.

Personal History

Raja's birth was a full-term normal delivery. His developmental milestones were normal. He started schooling at the age of five. However, from the very beginning he had problems with reading, writing and arithmetic. Temperamentally, he was found to be active, easily provoked and aggressive.

A psycho-educational assessment showed that he had an IQ of 101 on the Wechsler Intelligence Scale for Children. In arithmetic, he could do only simple and graded addition and simple subtraction. Language assessment showed that his reading and spelling were below first-standard levels. He took an unusually long time to write, and his writing was characterized by no spaces between words, missing letters, substituted letters, failure to use capital letters and omission of lines while copying.

Remedial work consisted of the following:

1. **Remediation in Arithmetic:** Instruction began with teaching him concepts at a concrete level using objects, then at a semi-concrete level using lines drawn on the blackboard, and finally at an abstract level without using any aids.

As Raja already knew simple and graded addition and simple subtraction, the remedial education started with graded subtraction. At the concrete level he was asked to group 16 beads and then take away 12 beads from the group. Once the child became familiar with the concept of subtraction at the concrete level, the concept was taught at a semi-concrete level using lines drawn on the blackboard. During the process, the concept of 'carry-over' was also taught. Once he was familiar with graded subtraction, multiplication was taught using beads, at a concrete level, and using lines at the semi-concrete level. Then, Raja was encouraged to do the problems without any aids. Similarly, division was also taught. These exercises were given to the mother and the child and over-learning was encouraged.

2. **Language-reading, Spelling and Writing:** The assessment indicated that Raja lacked two important skills required for reading: the ability to recognize simple common words, and a knowledge of phonics. A list was prepared of common words that appeared frequently in his textbooks. Everyday he was made to write two to three words on a flash card. He had to pronounce those words loudly and write them on the blackboard without looking at the card. He was encouraged to use these words in a sentence. At the end of the week, he was made to revise all the words learnt during the week was made. Phonic skill was taught using decoding units. There were 108 decoding units and each unit had a set of words. Each set was organized into four levels of increasing difficulty, A to D. The exercise for Raja started with level A from set 1, and then set 2 and so on. In addition to teaching sight words and training him in phonics, he was given daily drill exercises in reading, and the mother was asked to supervise the work at home.

   In order to teach spelling skills, a letter–sound combination was taught. A regular word from his textbook was given; he was asked to say it aloud and articulate it clearly, and put every sound down on the paper. Then, the correct spelling was shown to him. To teach the irregular sound words, he was asked to find a word he knew how to spell correctly that had the same characteristic as the word he was working on (example: to recall 'motion', he was asked to spell 'station'). He was also asked to pronounce every syllable in a word. Further, he was asked to memorize the irregular words.

   Behavioural charts were introduced to improve handwriting speed and to reduce errors in copying. Everyday, he was given a passage of 100 words to copy. Time taken and the number and type of errors were recorded in the chart. The format of daily assignment was as follows:

Date	Time Taken	No. of Errors	Type of Errors
06.08.92	15 minutes	8	Incorrect punctuation
		5	Incorrect capitalization
		5	Omission of letters

   At the end of the week, depending on the progress made, he was given verbal reinforcements. After two months of remedial teaching over 15 sessions, reassessment showed that Raja had improved a great deal in all the areas.

3. **Counselling the Parents:** The parents of the student were seen three times over a period of two months. They were also told about the nature of the specific disability which Raja had despite being of average intelligence. They were told how they were serving as bad models to

the child. They readily agreed to avoid situations that would provoke violence in the family. They decided to avoid fighting in the presence of the children. They were advised to create the right kind of atmosphere at home in the evening so that the children could sit and study. The eldest sibling was asked to help Raja to complete assignments given at school.

The parents were counselled on how to discipline the child. They were told not to pay attention to his unwanted behaviour and to show appreciation when he exhibited desirable behaviour. They were advised to avoid physical punishment and instead use other forms of negative reinforcement such as 'time out'.

A package of intervention described in this case study encourages the parents to help the child in the remediation programme on a daily basis. This is important because the therapist in the clinic often cannot have more than one session a week with the child. Most of the children who come with such complaints of scholastic backwardness show marked progress with 15 to 20 sessions over one academic year, given the right kind of assessment, diagnosis and remediation programme.

WORKING IN SMALL GROUPS

The study done by the author indicated that 25 children studying in the fourth standard at English-medium schools, identified by the teachers as poor readers, were weak in recognizing simple common words and they were unable to exploit the system of phonics. Therefore, a target was set for remedial education: (a) improving their basic sight words and (b) improving their phonic skills.

For the first target, the list of basic sight words given in their text book was used. These words were written on flash cards and everyday the students were familiarized with 4–5 words. They pronounced the words loudly and wrote these words on the blackboard without looking at the card. They were encouraged to use those words in a sentence and made to use the words at least once during the remedial education class. At the end of the week special attention was paid to revising all the words learnt during the week.

For teaching and improving phonic skills Rosner's (1985) decoding units were used. This list contains 108 decoding units and each unit has a set of words. Every set is organized into four levels of increasing difficulty. Each student was requested to start first with level A from set 1, then proceed to level A from set 2 and so on. He was then asked to proceed to level B as before and then to level C. The level at which a student can read all the words adequately was his level of reading. That level was kept as the starting point.

First the decoding unit was taught as '/a/n/means/an/'; when the student could pronounce the word, the first word from thc unit of that level was taken. The student was next told '/b/an/means/ban/'. The student repeated it. Then the next word in the unit was taught.

In addition to teaching them sight words and training in phonic skills they were also given daily reading practice for 10–15 minutes. Common errors included repeating words, spelling out words, omitting words, difficulty in pronouncing certain syllables, ignoring punctuation and mumbling. The mistakes were noted down and the children were told about the mistakes they had made at the end of the reading. The following day, they were reminded of the mistakes and advised to avoid such mistakes. If the mistakes were corrected or the errors reduced, they were given verbal reinforcements by the group.

At the end of 25 sessions, the reading performance of the group showed a significant improvement. The overall errors made in reading came down from 59 to 13 after the therapy sessions.

SPELLING

Spelling is the forming of words through traditional arrangements of letters. The ability to spell is essential because it allows one to read the written word correctly. Carpenter and Miller (1982) found that children who had trouble recognizing words in reading had poor spelling skills. Ekwall (1985) notes that phonetic spellers mispronounced phonetically irregular words. He suggests that a child, in order to spell, must be able to read the word, possess knowledge and skill in certain relationships of phonics and structural analysis, apply phonic generalizations, visualize the word and use motor ability to write the word. According to him, spelling problems may stem from problems in visual memory, auditory memory and auditory and visual discrimination.

Lovitt et al. (1969) used the study-test technique with fourth grade children and found significant improvements in the spelling skills. Bryant et al. (1981) used fixed and flow word lists wherein spelling words are presented and taught in fixed word lists. They reported improvements in the spelling performance of children using this method. Kauffman et al. (1978) tested the effectiveness of imitation methods in teaching spelling skills. In this method, the teacher provides an oral and written model of the spelling word and the child is required to imitate the model by spelling the model aloud and writing it. The child receives immediate feedback and praise for correct responses. Incorrect responses are followed by retraining. They found this method was particularly useful for words that did not follow regular phonetic rules—words for which the child should use visual memory.

The authors taught the students letter-sound combinations through phonics. The mismatches, or words with irregular spellings were taught using rote memory. The student was encouraged to use some senses other than just eyes and ears. The word to be learnt was shown to the student. He pronounced it loudly, pronouncing every letter. He wrote the word down in his notebook. Then he wrote the word five times with his eyes closed. Each day they were given drill exercises using the techniques mentioned above. They were given five words at the beginning of the session and asked to look at them carefully. Then they wrote the spelling of each word without looking at the list. If they made mistakes they were asked to look at it again, use the cues given as before and write the correct spelling. The post-therapy assessment indicated significant improvement. The average spelling score of the students went up from 6.00 to 8.76.

WRITING

Writing is a tool for communication and it is both a skill and a means of self-expression. The complex process of writing integrates visual, motor and conceptual abilities and it is a major means through which students demonstrate their knowledge of academic subjects. Classroom instruction in handwriting usually begins in kindergarten. After the third grade, emphasis is placed on writing as a form of meaningful self-expression. Mercer and Mercer (1985) list the following common errors among learning disabled children: slowness, incorrect directionality of letters, too much or too little slant, spacing difficulty, messiness, inability to stay on a horizontal line, illegible letters, too much or too little pencil pressure, and mirror writing.

Wiederholt et al. (1983) suggest that teachers in the primary grades should devote at least 10 minutes each day to teaching handwriting. They should demonstrate the correct way to form letters and supervise students' handwriting efforts carefully. Also, the teacher should help the student develop a positive attitude towards handwriting by encouraging progress and stressing the importance of the skill. Hofmeister (1981) lists six instructional errors to avoid: unsupervised handwriting practice, lack of immediate feedback on errors, lack of emphasis on student analysis of errors, failure to provide close range models of correct letter formation, repeated drill of both correct and incorrect letter production and misplaced emphasis on activities of limited value.

The author found the following type of errors in her study of 25 learning disabled children with writing disabilities: improper holding of pen, wrong positioning of the writing paper, illegibility of some letters, incorrect spacing, errors in punctuation, omission of words, adding words and overwriting. It was also found that many students were slow in writing and that their handwriting became illegible if they had to write faster.

The target set was to improve the speed of writing and to reduce the number of errors in writing. Behavioural charts were maintained to improve speed. Each day, they were given a passage of 100 words to copy. The time taken to copy the passage, number of errors and the type of errors were recorded on a chart as shown below. At the end of the week, a curve was drawn on the board to show the progress made by the student. Depending upon the progress made, the student was given verbal reinforcements by others in the group. Simultaneously, the student was also made aware of his errors in writing and advised to look at the previous days' writing and take a note of time taken, total number of mistakes and the type of errors.

There was an overall improvement in the speed of writing. The average time taken by the group came down from 20.20 minutes to 18.32 minutes. Similarly, the average number of errors made by the group came down from 10.48 to 7.16 after 25 sessions of therapy.

ARITHMETIC

Students with learning disabilities often find it difficult to master arithmetic skills and concepts. Arithmetic problems are common at all age levels. During the preschool and primary years they have difficulty in sorting objects by size, matching objects, understanding the language of arithmetic or grasping the concept of rational counting or one-to-one relationship. At the elementary school level, they have trouble with computational skills. In the middle and upper grades they have problems with fractions, decimals, and measurements. Also, many secondary students face problems in place values and basic facts like addition, subtraction, multiplication and division.

Ashlock (1982) found that the error patterns that were developed by children were the result of incomplete concept formation. Roberts (1968) identified four error categories with third grade students: wrong operation—the student subtracted when he should add; obvious computational errors—the student applied the correct operation but made errors in recalling a basic number fact; defective algorithm—the student added without regard for place value; and random response—there was no relationship between the problem-solving process and the problem.

Otto and Smith (1980) offer the following principles for remedial maths teaching: write specific objectives to deal with specific problems; arrange regular practice sessions; provide immediate and positive feedback during practice sessions; provide for concrete learning experiences; keep an accurate record of error levels and response rates; encourage children to set goals; ask questions; match the task activities to the child's levels of competence; and diagnose errors regularly.

The author taught the 25 learning disabled students over 25 sessions. The basic operations of addition, subtraction, multiplication and division were taught, first by using concrete operations, followed by semi-concrete operations, and then abstract operations. At the concrete level, sticks and beads were used to teach the concepts. At the semi-concrete level, beads and sticks were removed; instead lines were drawn on the blackboard or the notebook and the same procedure was followed. At the abstract level the students were encouraged to do the calculations mentally without using any aids. When they were learning multiplication, they were asked to learn the multiplication tables everyday. The average test score for the students went up from 22.4 to 24.8, and statistically this was a significant improvement.

BEHAVIOURAL PROBLEMS AND LEARNING DISABILITIES

It is generally believed that the prevalence rate of behavioural and emotional problems is higher among poor performers as compared to normal students. This view is supported by various studies. Krouse and Krouse (1981) reported that there was greater maladjustment, immaturity and inadequacy among under-achieving children than among students performing at their expected levels.

In the study with 25 learning disabled students, the author found that two students were disturbed as indicated by Rutter Proforma-B. The first student was found to exhibit aggressive behaviour, picking up fights with others at little provocation. His father was an alcoholic and a lorry driver by profession. His mother was an illiterate housewife. The house atmosphere was not congenial as there were frequent quarrels. The boy was seen over 10 therapy sessions. During the initial sessions he accused others of picking on him. He was made to role-play some of the incidents, which helped him realize his responsibility in those episodes and the bad outcome of his aggressive behaviour. He was made to reflect on what other alternate behaviour he could have adopted and the possible consequences of such alternate behaviour. Parents were counselled regarding the need to foster a congenial home atmosphere for the good of the child over three sessions. The teachers reported a 60 per cent improvement at the end of the second month.

The second student was a girl who was sensitive, shy and withdrawn. It was found that she had a lot of negative feelings about herself. She was given 10 sessions of rational emotive therapy which focused on building positive thinking. The mother and teachers were counselled regarding the need of positive reinforcements to build her self-image. At the end of 10 sessions both the teacher and the mother reported significant improvement.

A study conducted by Sadashivan (2009) compares two methods of intervention for specific reading disorder. Twenty children were selected in the age group of 10–13 years, with average to above average intelligence and without co-morbid psychiatric conditions of Specific Reading Disorder. The children with reading disorder (RD group) were randomly allotted to two groups of 10 children each. One group of 10 received phonological awareness intervention (PA group) while the other received neuro-psychological intervention (NP group). Both the RD groups (i.e. PA and NP groups) received 20 sessions of 40 minutes duration bi-weekly for each child after school hours. The PA group received inputs to enhance phonological awareness skills such as segmentation, is lation, deletion and tracking of speech sounds using games and visual material. The NP group on the other hand received inputs to enhance their attention, concentration, working memory, verbal learning strategies, planning and organization and memory skills. After intervention, both treatment groups showed significant improvement in their reading score which was maintained three months after the intervention. Cognitive changes and phonological processing skills showed different outcomes in response to intervention. While the PA group had improved attention, verbal and visual memory and visual perception, the NP group had enhanced verbal fluency, inhibition control, verbal learning and immediate visual memory. Phonological awareness at phoneme level improved significantly after PA intervention while the improvement for the NP group was at the syllable level. The improvements were maintained at a three-month follow-up for both groups with the PA group being significantly higher than the NP group on verbal working memory, and the NP group was significantly higher on verbal fluency three months after intervention. While both the methods are effective, they appear to enhance different skills. Perhaps if used together these might be even more effective.

Remedial education need not be carried on through long drawn out sessions. Many students can show significant improvement even with as many as 25 sessions. This remedial education can be carried out by teachers within the school set-up. Training teachers for remedial education has to include the following:

- Assessing the educational needs of the students
- The ability to design and implement suitable intervention programmes
- Developing the ability to work effectively and harmoniously with class teachers
- The remedial teacher has to be taught to help the students with behaviourial problems and counsel the parents and teachers as and when necessary

Learning disabled students need remedial education which has varied instructional objectives depending on the individual's needs, varied entry points into curriculum, varied pacing, active participation of the learner, use of varieties of instructional techniques and finally criterion-referenced evaluation of the learner.

SELF-EVALUATION

Exercise

Look at the items in the Developmental Psychopathology Check List (DPCL) and note how many are present in the case that is illustrated.

(According to the DPCL [Kapur 1995])

The child .... aged .... years, boy/girl, studying in Class ...., medium of instruction ....

The child is 1st/2nd/3rd of siblings—comes from a joint/nuclear family.

Presents with complaints of .... of .... duration.

(i)

(ii)

(iii)

(iv)

(v)

	Score
A. Developmental history	
B. Developmental problems	
C. Psychopathology • Hyperkinesis • Conduct disorder • Learning/School disorder • Emotion disorder • *Obsessive compulsive • Physical symptoms • *Psychoses	
D. Family history Family interactions	
E. Temperament	
F. Support	

***To be referred to a specialist**

1. Please build a picture of the child that includes the complaints, duration of each of the complaints, developmental and family histories, temperament, stressors and environmental supports. Could you also speculate on what could have led the formation of the symptoms?

----

2. What techniques have been used?

(i)

(ii)

(iii)

(iv)

(v)

CHAPTER

28 Therapies for Somatization and Chronic Physical Illness in Children

AN ADOLESCENT WITH HYSTERIA: A CASE ILLUSTRATION

Mohan was a 13-year-old boy from a rural Hindu family of consanguineous marriage and low socio-economic status. Despite being away on work most of the time, the father was a strict disciplinarian and leader in the family. The mother was quite indulgent and affectionate to all the children. Mohan was the eighth of nine siblings. He was brought in with the complaint that he had been unable to walk for the past three months due to a pain in his legs.

Mohan had a full-term normal birth, and his developmental milestones were normal. He started school at the age of six years and did well at studies. His parents had high ambitions for him and wanted him to be a doctor or an engineer.

Temperamentally sociable and friendly, he tended to sulk when his demands were not met. After his examinations, he suffered from malaria and was bed-ridden for a month. On recovery, he complained of weakness in his legs, and consequently the parents did not send him to school as the school was two miles away from home. Soon he complained of extreme weakness and pain in the legs and became bed-ridden. During this time, his mother took care of him by washing, bathing and dressing him. Family and friends attended to all his needs. He was also taken to several faith-healers in the village. On psychological assessment, his IQ was found to be average. On a projective test, he showed aggression towards his parents as they were punitive, though this information had not been elicited in the history taken earlier.

In the course of the individual psychotherapeutic sessions, Mohan ventilated his feelings about his home situation. He had felt very hurt as his father had refused to buy a bicycle for him or give him money for going to school by bus. He was also not allowed to wear long pants, while all his friends wore them and teased him for wearing short pants. The reason for both was the family's dire poverty. For Mohan, the 'primary' gain of the symptoms was in avoiding school. The 'secondary' gain was the affection and care showered on him by everyone when he was ill. The symptoms were modelled after the ones he had experienced during his fever.

The symptom removal was aimed at through suggestion and persuasion. Mohan was instructed to carry out a large number of physical exercises in a graded fashion. He was also encouraged to play with the other children and participate in all the ward activities. Within three days of being admitted to the ward, he was totally free from the symptoms. Considering that at the time of admission he was carried into the ward, this was nothing short of a miracle for Mohan's family.

During the next few sessions Mohan continued to talk about his difficulties at home. His parents, especially his father, were told the nature of the problem that caused Mohan's illness, and possible solutions were discussed in the presence of the child. The relationship between mental distress and bodily symptom was dealt with at length with Mohan and his family. At the end of 15 sessions, the parents had clearly understood the problem and decided that he would be sent to school by bus and, when possible, he would be given a pair of long pants. They also agreed that Mohan would learn to talk to his parents when he became distressed, and that they would listen and not brush him aside.

In this case, the aspects of 'primary' and 'secondary' gains, model, and illness behaviour are clearly demonstrated. Mohan did not have an immature personality. When faced with a developmental stressor of loss of status amongst his peer group, and having to conform and obey as he had done in the family context, the conversion modelled after his physical illness was apparently the best possible solution. His parents, being basically affectionate and caring, enabled him to become totally symptom-free and to go back to school.

INTERVENTION STRATEGIES

Exploration into the nature of stress in a case of hysteria is essential. Some stressors could be:

1. **Stressors unique to the child:** A child who was terrified of going to school because of poor performance and punitive teachers hears hallucinatory voices telling him not to go to school.
2. **Developmental stressors:** These could include birth of a sibling, joining school and attaining puberty.
3. **Stressors common to a subculture:** In the Indian setting, social expectations in a particular caste, class or religious group can create conflicts with new social values which in turn produce stress in the individual members. For example, the restrictive lifestyle of adolescent girls in Muslim or orthodox Brahmin families, or non-acceptance of the child's or peer group values by the family can be very stressful to the adolescent. It is important to go beyond primary and secondary gains to find the meaning, especially the symbolic meaning, which the child attempts to communicate. Symbolism does not necessarily mean psychoanalytic symbols. The symbolic act could be close to real feelings and emotions as in sobbing and rapid breathing (hyperventilation). Facial expression and distress manifested through body language can give clues to be explored further. Projective tests often unravel stressors not revealed to the conscious mind.

The following are some of the steps in multimodal therapy of hysterias:

1. Explore in detail the nature of symptoms and their relation to psychosocial stressors.
2. Attempt at linking this in a simple, understandable fashion and communicating it to the patient and his family and significant others. Family therapy is the technique of choice.

3. Provide a substitute solution to the problem, which is better than the one adopted by the patient, i.e., the hysterical symptom.
4. Discourage the use of drugs or a placebo, as this strengthens the belief of the patient and the family that the illness is physical.
5. Discourage actions which maintain the symptoms by the way of secondary gains (by the child and the family).
6. Play down the importance of symptoms but pay attention to the individual's psychological distress that the symptoms attempt to convey.
7. Demonstrate the importance of not paying attention to the symptom and consequent reduction of the same.
8. Culturally accepted solutions are as good as any: for example taking a vow or going to a healer can be simultaneously tried along with dynamically oriented psychotherapy. However, harmful practices such as branding the child with a hot instrument for treatment of 'fits' must be discouraged.
9. Instances of keeping the individual away from the environment which produced hysteria should be minimized; the exception being situations which clearly require removal of the child from the environment. In the long run, it is better for the child to learn to cope with difficulties than to expect changes to be brought about in his environment.

SELF-EVALUATION

Exercise

Look at the items in the Developmental Psychopathology Check List (DPCL) and note how many are present in the case that is illustrated.

(According to the DPCL [Kapur 1995])

The child .... aged .... years, boy/girl, studying in Class ...., medium of instruction ....

The child is 1st/2nd/3rd of siblings—comes from a joint/nuclear family.

Presents with complaints of .... of .... duration.

(i)

(ii)

(iii)

(iv)

(v)

	Score
A. Developmental history	
B. Developmental problems	
C. Psychopathology • Hyperkinesis • Conduct disorder • Learning/School disorder • Emotion disorder • *Obsessive compulsive • Physical symptoms • *Psychoses	
D. Family history Family interactions	
E. Temperament	
F. Support	

***To be referred to a specialist**

1. Please build a picture of the child that includes the complaints, duration of each of the complaints, developmental and family histories, temperament, stressors and environmental supports. Could you also speculate on what could have led the formation of the symptoms?

----

2. What techniques have been used?

(i)

(ii)

(iii)

(iv)

(v)

Children at Risk and Resilience in Childhood

All the chapters, including the present one, focus on children who have encountered various difficulties at home, school or in society. Whether or not a child can cope with these adversities also depends on the child's inherent attributes, such as temperament and intelligence. When we plan intervention we need to note that some children are competent survivors and emerge out of adversities as stronger individuals, while some others suffer from mental health problems.

The point being made here is that some children do not need intervention. However, it is necessary for the counsellors to know and identify those traits and external situations that make them invulnerable. Basically, the focus is on strengthening the child's inner resources to better cope with an adverse situation. Thus, we as counsellors have a great deal to learn from the 'resistant' children, or those who bounce back despite adversities.

Intervention for children-at-risk of all kinds consists of providing experiences that contribute to:

- Relief from stress and help to relax
- Releasing pent-up emotions
- Reliving trauma and making it easier to bear
- Promoting normal development

The impetus to the study of children who succeeded in life despite challenges came from the pioneering longitudinal study of high-risk children in the island of Kahui in 1955 by Emmy Werner (Werner, 1989; Werner and Smith, 1992), who reported that some children were resilient despite odds. Werner related it to the presence of a parent or mentor providing nurture, support and a role model to the children.

WHAT IS RESILIENCE?

Definitions of resilience vary, the briefest ones being 'bouncing back' or hardiness as a behaviour characteristic. Masten and Reed (2002) describe this personality trait as a class phenomenon in childhood, characterized by patterns of positive adaptation in the context of significant adversity or risk. Two judgments are embedded in this definition; one: doing fine with a set of expectations (competence), and the other: extenuating circumstances that pose a risk or threat to good outcomes. Both sets of factors appear contributory. There is consistent evidence to suggest that physical and mental health and well-being can be seriously harmed by the experience of poverty and other adverse situations and events (Duncan and Brooks-Gunn, 1997; McLyod, 1998).

Both animal and human studies demonstrate that the intra-uterine environment is also a crucial factor that can impact subsequent development. Talge et al. (2007) report that maternal stress during gestation, including smoking and the use of psychotropic medication increases the child's risk of cognitive delay and Attention Deficit Hyperactivity Disorder (ADHD).

Socioeconomic disadvantage, maternal hardship and family breakdown greatly increase the risk of developing adjustment problems, such as educational failure, behaviour problems, psychological distress and poor health later on.

On the other hand, there is evidence that some children do seem to be able to do well despite adversity (Luthar and Cicchetti, 2000; Luthar et al., 2000; Rutter, 1987). The observation of positive outcome in the face of adversity has led to a paradigm shift away from a pathogenic or deficit model based on expectations of strong unidirectional effect towards adjustment problems or ill-health instead of health and wellbeing (Antonovsky, 1979; Cicchetti and Garmezy, 1993; Huppert et al., 2005).

The above issue is of great relevance to developing countries like India, beleaguered by poverty and a host of other related disadvantages. Focusing on resilience permits us to examine the positive outcomes seen in developing nations.

WHAT CONTRIBUTES TO RESILIENCE?

The sources of resilience lie both within the individual and on proximal and distal environmental factors. Secure attachment with parents, supportive families and social networks contribute equally to resilience.

Within the Child

Good cognitive abilities, attentional and problem-solving skills are some factors within the cognitive domain. Easy temperament in infancy and childhood and an adaptable personality later are important. Other factors that build resilience are positive self-perception and self-efficacy, faith and sense of meaning in life, good self-organization of emotional arousal and impulses, talents valued by self and society, good sense of humour and general appeal or attractiveness to others.

Within the Family

A close relationship with care-giving adults, parenting high on warmth, structure, monitoring and expectations, positive family climate with low parental discord, an organized home environment, parental post-secondary education, and protective qualities, involvement with child's education, socio-economic advantages, outside-the-family relationships, close relationships with competent pro-social and supportive adults and a connection with rule-abiding peers are some of the important family variables.

Within the Community

Important contributors appear to be the presence of effective schools, ties to pro-social organizations, school, clubs, etc., neighbourhoods with high collective expectations, high level of cultural activity, good public health services and health connectivity.

Thus, resilience may be related to **individual** in-built invulnerability (physical and psychological well-being) or to **environmental** factors ranging from biological and psychological to socio-cultural factors embedded in the family and community settings.

INTERVENTION

Is intervention required? Is it feasible and possible? This is a question that has no easy answer. In this section we examine (*a*) the historical background dating back to myths and legends in the Indian context, and (*b*) indulge in a leap of faith to the contemporary levels of understanding resilience. In the scenario of Indian mythology, both gods and mothers have attempted to make their wards invulnerable. In the epic Mahabharata, Karna and Duryodhana had been blessed with strong protective invisible armours, yet remained vulnerable to risk at the very end. The demon Hiranyakashyapu was blessed with immortality as he could be killed neither by a man nor an animal, neither during the day nor the night. But Lord Vishnu himself as an avatar bearing the body of a man and lion killed him at twilight. It is interesting to note that in our myths such boons towards invulnerability have met with failures due to some loophole or oversight. Whether removing all the sources of distress can protect a child from sorrow is a question answered by the story of Gautama Buddha. Prince Siddhartha, who was brought up in the most congenial environment, renounced his very happy state at his first experience of misery. He then went on to become the enlightened one, undergoing all kinds of adversities. In short, a human being cannot be protected by removing adversities, but his or her resilience can be built and enhanced through personal efforts.

In the contemporary context, strategies for promoting resilience are seen as risk-focused, asset-focused and process-focused (Masten and Reed, 2002). Thus, intervention strategies need to be holistic. They must focus on the internal physical and psychological realms of the individual as well as proximal and distal environmental factors affecting physical, interpersonal and societal domains of individuals' feelings. Intervention and care can strengthen inner resources by recommending lifestyle changes and providing favourable proximal and distal variables.

RESILIENCE AND COMPETENCE FROM AN ASIAN PERSPECTIVE

While studying the positive psychological framework, attempts are made to study ancient Indian paediatric texts. The study of Ayurveda and the *Dharma Shastras* with regard to resilience and competence in childhood yields some interesting findings.

Triguna is the constitutional and inherited psychological predisposition present at birth. In Ayurveda, treatment treats as pivotal the *Triguna* and *Tridosha*—the psychological and physical predisposition of the individual that contributes to individual differences. The three *Guna* can be present in a person/child in varying proportions. *Satva*, *Rajas* and *Tamas* are the *Triguna* and *Vata*, *Pitta Skapha* (similar to humours in the ancient Greek system of medicine) are the *Tridosha*. While the *Tridosha* contribute to physical health or disease, *Rajas* and *Tamas* contribute to psychological problems; *Satva* is allotted a very unique position in the whole scheme—it is the very essence of resilience or invulnerability. *Satva* as a protective factor is an *a priori* hypothesis, and yet finds support in a wide range of empirical efforts of ascetics, yogis and other groups of people who aim to become *Satvik* through changes in their lifestyle.

Developmentally appropriate counselling techniques categorized under 'play' and 'art' are described in Chapters 15 and 16. These can be used for individual children and also with those at risk, such as physically, emotionally or sexually abused children. Group settings are described in Chapters 21 and 22 and can be used for children in orphanages, street children or those facing natural/man-made disasters.

Working with play and art appears to be the safest and most enjoyable media, as long as these do not use interpretive and authoritarian approaches.

A CHILD AT RISK: A CASE STUDY

Durga—a nine-year-old girl who was a victim of sexual abuse—was brought from the orphanage to the therapist. The details of the first two sessions are given here.

First Session

Durga came into the room quietly and showed no fear when the door was closed. She asked if she could touch the things lying in the room. When she was told everything was hers to play with, she went to the doll house and picked up the cradle with a baby. She kept on rocking it and repeating how beautiful it was. She then asked if she could have it. It was again explained that everything was for her and for other children to play with. She then wanted to know if the therapist could make a cradle. She was told that they may be able to get her one at a later date. From the cradle, she moved on to systematically explore all the dolls. Whenever she wanted to lift the costume, she would lift it saying, 'This is petticoat, knickers and dress.' She was enamoured by the costume and the jewellery. She pointed at the doll of a young girl and said the woman doll was the mother and proclaimed another as the mother's mother. When asked whether the grandmother liked the child, she said, 'earlier did so' but refused to elaborate. The village woman carrying an infant was appreciated. According to her, the infant in the cradle possibly belonged to another village woman. After going through all the dolls, she put each of them back exactly as she found them. Then she explored the kitchen utensils. She twice played a cooking and serving game, naming each utensil, cooking procedure and the dishes and pretended to cook elaborately. When the door was opened by another child, she went and closed it and turned and checked whether the therapist was attending to her. She also placed the infant and the woman together and put plates in front of them and fed them.

She also said, they would go and come back again. She briefly explored the other toys, puppets and sand box. Once again she picked the wooden rings of different colours and said they were children. Next to them she put larger rings as mothers and block as fathers, a unit of child, mother, father, and the rest as furniture. She was highly imaginative in ascribing names to chairs, benches, trees, etc.

She also brought the infant and baby girls to play on the swing and the slide. She started putting the girls into the cradle too. Finally she took the various vehicles and crashed them with the infant and the girls inside them. She dashed the scooter against their foot. But the girl was unhurt. She put all the wooden rings, blocks and vehicles back on the shelf again. On the top shelf she saw the gun and pretended to shoot the family and herself with it for about 30 seconds and she then put it away immediately. After one hour she was told that the time was up. However, she said she was not finished and played for another ten minutes. She was assured that she could play again next week and was given a crayon box and paper to take back to the orphanage.

Observations on Durga

1. She is very quiet and methodical in her approach to the objects in the play. She systematically picked up and looked at everything with keen interest and appreciation, punctuated by 'Very nice', '*Chennagide*' for everything.
2. Eye contact and smiling at the therapist increased as the session progressed and finally she thanked the therapist and shook hands as she left, but her hands were cold.
3. The main theme was family, daily cooking, eating and other routine chores. But the infant in the cradle and the two young girls remained the centre of all the narratives. Clothes and jewellery were highly appreciated too.
4. Mother, father and child are seen as units.
5. One instance of aggression took place where she pretended to shoot the family dolls and held the trigger against her own temple while making sounds of gunshots lasting 30 seconds in an otherwise contented and happy play session of 80 minutes.

Second Session

Durga came on time and was happy to meet the therapist. She had not brought the drawings she had made but she said that she had drawn homes and babies. The play themes were discrete as in the earlier session.

The first theme revolved around the cooking dishes and dolls. This time, the focus was on two little girls and not the baby in the cradle as before. She was again fascinated by the jewellery on the dolls, especially the bangles. The cooking was elaborate involving all the steps. The subsidiary themes were:

1. A policeman caught a run-away girl. She cried and her mother and grandmother came to claim her and took her home.
2. Father and mother fought viciously. Father snatched the *mangala sutra*, beating the mother and so on. The grandmother tried to pacify them.
3. The children (the two girls) ran away to their grandmother and stayed there. The children were fed and sent to school and then food was sent to school in a tiffin carrier.
4. While commenting about the dresses, Durga would specifically mention each item of the underclothes. At one instance, she straightened the blouses and *pallu* saying one should not expose one's body parts and looking at the therapist said, 'You also don't, do you?' She then said aloud, 'Because that makes men look at you!' in a very adult style of narration. In the previous session, she had simply tugged at the neckline of the girl doll, which had a wide necked dress.

The **second theme** was around the sand box.

1. She pretended to be digging, sighing tiredly as if she were a coolie.
2. She looked at the pelican toy and asked what it was. When told it was a *kokkare* (pelican), she included it in the game. She twisted its neck and said that some people kill the bird to eat it. Then she appeared to regret it and brought it to the therapist and said it has come to the hospital and the doctor to be treated. She used the diary and pen from the apron pocket for making medical notes and injections, cured the bird and sent it home.
3. The grateful pelican brought food in the tiffin carrier and later money for the doctor.
4. She wrote her name in the diary and said 'yes' when asked if she should like to go to school. She briefly played with the puppets. Then she brought the books out and said 'You be the mother—not the real one, but the pretend one—and tell me the stories'. Then she herself made up the stories. She was quite unhappy to leave the playroom when the hour was up. At that point, she picked up the pistol and pretended to shoot the therapist.

Observations Across Sessions

(i) The cradle was replaced by the girls.

(ii) The themes were often self-referential—runaway child with policeman, marital fights, immodest clothing of women who lure men were described.

(iii) She involved the therapist as a healer and mother into the themes as the sessions progressed.

CASE ILLUSTRATION[1]

First Session

Sumathi, an eight-year-old girl from an upper middle-class family, second of the siblings of extended family, and with multiple caretakers, came with the complaints of pulling her own hair and bedwetting for almost one year. While pregnant with Sumathi, the mother had breast cancer and the baby of 10 days was left with the paternal grandmother in another city. She was very attached to the grandmother and stayed with her till she was six years old. She was brought to the parents' home where she joined Class I. The teachers found her very quiet, withdrawn and not interested in studies. She also found English difficult as her mother tongue was Kannada. Her teacher used to threaten her a lot.

Further interviewing revealed that she felt very alienated in her parents' house. Her elder brother, who was 13, used to tease her constantly. Her habit of pulling her own hair had made her nearly bald. This in turn caused everyone to tease her as they could not see why she should be doing it. The first task was to explain to the family that the child pulled her hair due to distress and anxiety as she was away from the only person she was emotionally bonded to.

The child was provided 15 sessions of play, artwork and story-writing as she showed interest in all the three activities.

Second Session

She took out all the dolls and chairs. She arranged the chairs in four rows. The teacher doll was made to stand with a pencil as stick. The policeman came and pulled the teacher, and dragged her away. The teacher's hands were tied. The child then put all the dolls and toys away.

(Note: The child expresses her conflict with the teacher and plays out so that the teacher is punished.)

In her artwork and play session she introduced Pinky, the doll. In this third session, she arranged the chairs. She prepared food for a celebration, with Pinky by her side. People present included grandparents, uncle, aunt, friends and Pinky but not the mother. She was very happy after the play session.

The child's writing, play and artwork found expression of her problems. As the sessions progressed over three months her hair-pulling had stopped and her hair was growing back. Earlier she used to tie a scarf on her head but now she could wear her little hairclips and ribbons, special gifts from the counsellor as a reward.

In addition, a 'star chart' was introduced for her bedwetting. Gradually assessment and remediation for learning difficulties were introduced.

---

1. The photographs of the family dolls and Sumathi's play are given on the inside cover.

SIBLINGS EXPOSED TO SEXUAL ABUSE: A CASE ILLUSTRATION[2]

Savithri was a six-year-old from a wealthy family studying in Class I at a private school. She was brought in with complaints of lack of interest in school and lagging behind in class, day-dreaming and disturbing other children in the class for the past year. She had changed school—the nursery teacher used to beat her a lot. She had a nine-year-old sister who had also become dull, threw tantrums and refused to draw though she used to be good at it.

Savithri had normal developmental milestones. She was a fussy feeder till the age of five years. She did not score above the cut-off score in the DPCL. She complained of punitive teachers. During the play and artwork she revealed sexual abuse by a boy-servant and the maid-servant. Whenever she complained to the parents about it, they paid no attention. Finally, suspecting something amiss, the maternal uncle brought her to the clinic.

During her play session, she called the servant boy 'bad' and made herself ugly though she was cute and revealed the details of his touching her genitals and all over her body. She also revealed that the maid-servant forced her to suck the maid's breasts. She was threatened with a beating if she complained to any one. In further session it was revealed that both the siblings were abused a great deal—the mother was busy with the new baby leaving the children in the charge of the servants. Both the girls were at the superior level of intellectual functioning. In the play both sisters together beat up and tortured the servant doll (female) and told her to go away and never come back (photographs drawn in black crayon). Extreme hostility and aggression was shown towards the servants both in the play and art sessions. The older girl's pencil drawing of chewing nails appear to suggest a great deal of anger, frustration and sarcasm.

During the counselling play and art sessions, both the girls expressed a great deal of anger. The uncle played a significant role in taking on the role of protector of the children (included in the family picture by the elder sister). The servants were sacked and both the children recovered fairly soon after that. Poor performance at school had been a mere symptom of distress. As the situation at home improved dramatically, the school problems disappeared.

Problems with domestic help are a typically Asian, upper-class phenomenon where children are tended to mostly by servants. 'Upstairs–downstairs' is a common phenomenon in wealthy homes. However the days of the old trustworthy family retainer hardly exist anymore, substituted by a transient population living in slums.

SUMMARY

Children are at risk of developing psychological problems for no fault of their own. Often, adverse factors in the environment are to blame. In such cases children do need help through counselling and protection from an uncongenial environment. Though it is impossible to remove all the stressors, counselling can help build the child's resilience.

---

2 The art work and writing of both the girls is included in the inside cover.

CHAPTER

30 Special Issues of Counselling/ Therapies in the Asian Context

INTRODUCTION

Aggression in child development is an important area of concern. A large number of books and articles on violence and aggression term it 'aggression in children' or 'violence in children'. In the Asian context it needs to be broadened to include 'aggression or violence against children'.

Aggression as a response to violence in the family or school bears close examination. The cycle of violence perpetuated by an abused child is a well-known phenomenon. But there are numerous children who suffer abuse without retaliating, taking revenge or reliving it vicariously. We need to pay attention to those who suffer in silence, resulting in stress-related mental health symptoms or compromised psycho-social development.

In authoritarian, hierarchical and traditional countries like India, violence against children needs to be examined and counselling services provided. Such violence may occur deliberately or inadvertently, directly or indirectly in a manifest or latent manner. But the effects may be equally devastating. Some of the examples that follow highlight these points:

AGGRESSION IN THE COMMUNITY

Man-made disasters like wars and riots, and natural disasters like earthquakes, floods or cyclones will first impact the family and consequently children in the family. It is, however, believed that for children below the age of eight years, the family can act as a protective shield. But the family should itself be healthy and resilient so as to offer such protection.

AGGRESSION IN THE FAMILY

There could be an uncongenial family environment as in the case of extreme poverty, alcoholism or mental illness in the parents where the harmful effects may or may not be deliberately caused. Within each family there are interpersonal problems such as marital, family or sibling discord which may not be construed as harmful to the child, but which do adversely affect the child's mental health.

These can be divided into manifest and latent such as:

- Parental aggression (physical and verbal).
- Parental illness such as depression, mental illness, alcohol/drug abuse, serious chronic illness that may have a devastating impact on young children. These could also include physical and sexual abuse such as child labour, incest, prostitution and pornography.

AGGRESSION IN SCHOOLS

An uncongenial school environment can hamper the child's normal development and cause mental health problems. The treatment or supportive measures are of paramount importance in counselling children. This section covers aggression against children caused in schools and homes.

Aggression by the Teachers

Asha, a five-year-old, stopped going to school. She had initially gone quite happily to the school where her mother was a teacher. School refusal started when she was punished by the teachers for not answering questions and sometimes not completing the homework. When the mother was asked why she had permitted her colleague to beat her child she guilelessly replied that all children are beaten at school but none of them refuse to attend school. It appeared that the mother, too, tended to align with the school system. As advocates of the child, we asked the mother to transfer the child to a school where the teachers were reputed to be kind. Promptly, the child went to the new school and settled down. Newspaper reports in the country carry numerous stories where children have been punished so severely that they have been maimed, blinded and even died under the severe punishment meted out to them in the schools. A statement by Anagol (2003) that the only teaching aid used by teachers in India is a stick reflects the stark reality of the Indian education system.

The only solution to the aggression faced by children at school is to withdraw the child. Though corporal punishment is legally banned in India, it is widely practised. Thus, what we need is some kind of movement promoting the rights of the children.

Aggression by Peers

Aggression by peers or bullying is on the rise, especially in urban India. This can only be resolved through group counselling in the school setting and by taking strict action against the perpetrators.

The World Health Organization describes four kinds of violence in schools:

- Aggression against school property
- Aggression against other children
- Aggression against teachers
- Aggression by teachers against children

A rise in the first three types of aggression has been noted in the Western world. In India and probably in all Asian countries the fourth type—namely aggression by teachers against children—remains a major cause for concern as the families too appear to condone it, believing that it is in the child's best interest. An authoritarian approach to education and child-rearing is a fairly common phenomenon in Asian countries. This could be one of the reasons why behaviour methods have been assimilated more quickly on Indian soil than other dynamic and child-centred methods.

Thus, in the context of counselling a great deal of preparatory work has to be done with parents and teachers to demonstrate the ineffectiveness of aggressive methods in dealing with children. It must be emphasized that positive approaches seem to yield positive results.

The Burden of High Academic Expectations

Both parents and teachers place a high premium on academic achievement. This is more so in small families with one or two children. Poor or rich alike, parents want their children to excel in academics. As a fallout of this, the following things have happened:

- Long school hours with heavy syllabus lead to one-way instruction by the teacher and encourage rote-learning by pupils.
- The heavy burden of long hours of 'tuitions' to help the child with school responsibilities. In reality, these tuitions too are an extended version of the overcrowded class following the same kind of approach as in the schools.
- Homework: All schools and each teacher assign homework separately for his/her subject, which adds up to several hours each day. Often, as the child is reluctant to do it, the mother spends equally long hours forcing the child to complete it. At times in her desperation, she may complete the task herself. Not doing homework is treated as a crime and children get severely punished for non-compliance.
- No time remains for play, with six hours of schooling, two or more hours of tuitions and homework, leaving no time for hobbies or play.
- Consequently the child sneaks or openly watches television; most of the programmes watched are developmentally inappropriate.

MEDIA

Visual Media and Violence *Among* and *Against* Children

Films play the role of the most potent instruments of transmission of culture to children, intentional or not, beneficial or not. Films have an unavoidable and arresting presence, reflecting and shaping social identities and behaviours. However, films need to be developmentally appropriate, that is matching the child's understanding at the cognitive, language, emotional, social and moral levels at each phase of his/her development. So the themes, languages, constructs and actions might be differently understood by the child when she/he is two as opposed to three, five, six or 10 years old. When dealing with films, the parents/children had to go and see the movies in a cinema hall. A major transition occurred with the advent of television, making films accessible at home.

The focus here is on visual media such as cinema, TV, video, cable and satellite TV and their effects on children. The beneficial effects in terms of education are indisputable, but that is not the point of discussion here. Since the advent of visual media, there have been several field and laboratory studies of their short term and long-term adverse effects.

Early reports of television viewing in children and its relationship to physical and verbal aggression came from Joy et al. (1986), in a study of a small Canadian town which they called 'Notel' before and after the introduction of the TV, and two control towns that already had TV. A cohort of 45 first and second graders was observed prospectively for two years on objectively measured acts of physical aggression such as hitting, biting, etc. Rates did not change in the control groups, but in Notel, it increased by 160 per cent. Eron and Huesmann (1984) followed up a cohort of 875 children in a semi-rural US county and reported that TV viewing at eight years predicted serious crime acts by the age of 30, particularly in boys (Columbia Cohort Study).

In a retrospective control study Kruttschnitt et al. (1986) compared 100 male felons and 65 men without any history of offence, matched on age, race, track of residence, and, after controlling for school performance, exposure to parental violence, baseline criminality, and childhood exposure to TV violence, approached statistical significance ($P < 0.10$). Most of the Canadian and US studies of the effect of prolonged childhood exposure to TV (two years or more) show positive relationship contributing a later physical aggression, though all of them do not reach a statistically significant level (Centerwall, 1989). A South African study by Conradie et al. (1987) of 2,200 white children followed up for five years, two years before and three years after the introduction of TV, reported significant increase in physical and verbal aggression.

These studies appear to suggest that the viewing of violence on screen by children has an adverse effect in terms of facilitating subsequent aggressive behaviour. However, those in the media industry ask an ingenious question: Would you become a serial murderer after seeing a movie on the theme? Some even talk of its cathartic value. Some believe that the statistical significance of probably two per cent is not something to be concerned about, and that there are other more important contributors such as poverty, family violence, etc. Therefore, a definite suggestion predisposing personality traits and vulnerability makes some children more vulnerable than most. This controversy reflects a basic differences predilection for environmentalistic or genetic contributors.

Thus there are several nuanced positions one can take:

(a) Only vulnerable children with non-supportive families and low socio-economic status who extensively view TV violence are likely to end up as criminals, while for the majority it is an innocuous or even an educative medium. However, the research trends have changed a good deal in the recent years. While the US National Commission on the Causes and Prevention of Violence in 1969 said that TV was not a principal cause but a contributing factor along with low income, unstable homes, the 1982 update has supported a closer positive relationship.
(b) Aggression is a learnt behaviour: Longitudinal studies by Milavsky et al. in 1982 suggested a small effect along with other predictors as environment on personality. British and Finnish

studies tend to support the environmental vantage viewpoint. Experimental studies showed that violence is learnt in different ways through the visual media:

- Imitation
- Activating latent tendencies for aggression
- Desensitization to sympathy for the victim
- Acceptance of violence as normal way to conflict resolution

There has been a spate of reports of young offenders, specially the sensational case of torture and murder of the two-year-old James Bugler by two 10-year-old boys in the UK, where TV/video were seen as major contributors as these children did not come from disturbed families. British TV violence and crime rates among adolescents are less than US television violence and crime rates. Many of the retrospective studies suggest stronger links than earlier suspected. Eron and Huesmann (1984) linked violent crime, wife and child abuse across all socio-economic strata and IQ. Bailey (1993) reported that the viewing of violent and pornographic videos was a significant causal factor for subsequent acts.

(c) In a dynamic approach to the understanding of aggression, Centerwall (1994) highlighted the role of TV in the development of the superego, replacing the family as the sole influencing agent before the advent of TV.

(d) The developmentalists highlighted stages of moral development where from 1–4 years of age there is self-centred morality, at 5 years a more acceptable morality, from 5–7 years a preoccupation with justice, and from 8–14 years concern that people should think well of them. Thus what the child views and understands depends on his/her stage of development. What it means to the programmer may be understood quite differently by the child at different stages of development.

(e) The context of entertainment as projected by the industry:

- It is all fun and a way to while away time.
- The child receives distorted images which he/she has not had personal experience of. This is especially dangerous when love, sex, and violence are equated.
- Brutality is portrayed to escalate the appeal to the jaded viewer.
- Victims are portrayed as sub-human and thus, are not to be pitied.
- Victims deserve violent treatment. For example, in the James Bugler case, the perpetrators Robert and John explained that James had to be hit 30 times because he kept getting up!

The industry spends billions on advertising as they know about the impact of visual media. The protagonists of uncensored programmes fail to recognize the differing levels and stages of maturity and stability, the level of imagination children are capable of, and, worse, the use of desensitizing and flooding techniques by systematic repetition, thus reducing the original accompanying emotion.

A child attains normal development in different domains such as physical, cognitive, language, emotional, social, moral and sexual development. These occur in a specific unique fashion, in infancy, childhood (early, middle and late) and adolescence (early and late). Any event is seen, unde stood and responded to differently by children at different stages. On the other hand, most TV programmes are created by adults who presume to know the developmental levels of the children. The child goes through four stages of cognitive development and can understand the events limited by his understanding at that particular stage. It is thus essential that meanings of events as meant to be conveyed are explained to the child or he might completely misunderstand the message.

The experience with children brought in for child guidance in India often reflects that indiscriminate TV viewing, regardless of the child's age, has serious repercussions. These may manifest as poor interaction with the caretakers, and continuously looking at a TV in a four-month-old or a fearful reaction to a violent scene, in a case where the mother usually had her nine-month-old on her lap while viewing TV. Long-term social and emotional deprivation, coupled with long hours of TV viewing, has been seen in children presenting autistic symptoms. Short-term manifestations such as aggression, whining, temper tantrums and fear reaction soon after TV viewing hours have also been noted.

THE INDIAN SCENARIO

1. Adults and children share TV viewing and very few programmes are suitable for young children.
2. Adults and children alike view TV into the late hours, thus depriving children of much-needed sleep.
3. Descriptive accounts have been found of reduced interest in school work both in cities and rural areas.
4. Especially since the advent of video, cable and satellite technology, there is an unlimited supply of unsuitable material in one's own home.
5. TV is often used as a babysitter.
6. TV viewing, rather than play, is encouraged. Unlike TV, play promotes the overall development of children.

It is impossible to allow this situation to continue. But what are the problems in containing this? Newson (1994) has aptly stated that even the liberated generation have been naive in permitting the present practices to go unquestioned.

Some case illustrations from developmental perspective seen in the clinics:

1. A boy was born into a joint family. The grandparents viewed TV all day and late into the night, keeping their precious grandchild in their laps so that they did not have to give up watching television. At the age of four months, the baby was noticed to stretch his neck, look around and focus on the TV. He failed to make eye contact with his mother, instead locating the TV and watching the flashing lights and listening to the noises. Within 3–4 weeks of the family being told not to watch TV and attend to him instead, the strange behaviour disappeared.
2. A case of autism: A four-year-old girl was brought to the a clinic with classic picture of infantile autism. The history revealed that she was the only child of a young couple settled in the Middle East. When she was born, the mother had no domestic help or social support as they had recently moved from India. The mother spent the entire day busy with household chores and the father spent long hours at the office. When the child started walking, the mother did not want her to get dirty or fall down. She made the child sit on the bed and kept the TV on

constantly. By the time the child was two, she had no companion except the TV. At the age of one and a half, she started showing repetitive movements, an odd use of words and had become emotionally withdrawn. The mother was helped to understand the need to bond with the child and provide the child with all-round stimulation through play with the mother and other children.

3. A child aged eight years, studying in Class II, came with the complaints of disobedient and aggressive behaviour. The parents were manipulated into allowing the TV to be kept on, thanks to the child's severe temper tantrums. The day he was brought to the clinic, he had beaten up his parents and had broken things around the house because there was a major electrical breakdown at home. The parents were told about the need to set limits, not yield to the temper tantrums and asked to disconnect the TV. Although they were apprehensive, they were reassured and asked to follow the instructions at least for a week. There was a marked improvement in his behaviour a week later. He was rewarded with short spells of developmentally appropriate programmes for half an hour to one hour a day.
4. There were many cases of young hyperactive children who demanded long TV viewing hours. Inattentive and disruptive behaviour along with fights with siblings showed an increase even after an hour's programme with violent content.

SUMMARY

There are many factors contributing to violence among children. These could be violence in schools and violence in the community emerging out of individual and social causes. These in turn create a cycle of violence among and against children. However, there are child policies and laws in place to counter the above to the greatest extent possible. There are organizations working towards the amelioration of family and social pathologies. But there is nothing in place to protect our children from the ubiquitous visual media.

Uncongenial environments and stressors posed by the family, school and the community may have a serious impact on children, not only by compromising normal development but also by possibly causing mental health problems.

Whether these are deliberate or not, their impact can be devastating to children. In fact, while obvious problems such as the impact of violence can be resolved, the unperceived ones such as violence in the school setting and in the visual media are equally important and cannot be overlooked.

Appendix

DEVELOPMENTAL PSYCHOPATHOLOGY CHECK LIST (DPCL)

The study of child psychopathology from a developmental perspective should ideally include the nature of specific items suitable for the setting, age and gender differences, developmental history and temperament along with psychosocial correlates such as family interaction, stressors and social supports. There is a need in the developing countries to have a screening tool that is comprehensive and developmental in perspective. The test needs little training and can be used with equal ease with the literate and illiterate population as it is orally administered to adults. It also can form the basis for developing strategies for the management of the child. In short DPCL is designed to bridge the gap between assessment and clinical practice. Those of you who use this in your work, may share the data with the author if you wish.

1. **Item Selection:** The DPCL has 124 items and six subsections. Items were selected based on the research findings of Oommen (1990), Daniel (1989), Uma (1988), John (1980), Vythilingam (1991) and Reddy (1991) that led to the inclusion of hyperkinesis, emotion and conduct disorders, hysteria, learning disorders, autism and psychoses respectively. A 100 children attending the Child Guidance Centre at NIMHANS were administered the DPCL by four investigators and suitable items were selected.
2. **Sample Selection and Preliminary Standardization:** 221 children below the age of 16 and without mental retardation were selected.
   - 25 cases were seen by two independent raters as a reliability exercise (Interclass Correlation Coefficient [ICC]) via analysis and the variance was 0.96 (significant at 0.001 level).
   - 45 cases were assessed both on CBCL (Achenbach and Edelbrock, 1983) and DCPL for validation purposes.

   The results showed significant positive correlation between Emotion Disorder of DPCL and Internalizing Disorder of CBCL. Hyperkinesis and Conduct Disorder of DPCL and Externalizing Disorder of CBCL had significant positive correlation. On cluster analysis seven clusters emerged. These were emotion disorder, hyperkinesis, psychoses, learning disorder, hysteria, conduct disorder and autism (for further details: Hirisave, Oommen and Kapur, 2006).

   Note: Of all the clusters, the clusters on psychosis and autism need to be evaluated by mental health experts, hence the cases need to be referred.

DEVELOPMENTAL PSYCHOPATHOLOGY CHECK LIST (DPCL) FOR CHILDREN

Malavika Kapur

A.	Developmental History	No (Absent)	Yes (Present)
1.	Did the mother, before, during or just after child birth, suffer from any problems like illness or difficult labour?	0	1
2.	Did the child have any serious illness soon after birth? (If yes, specify).	0	1
3.	Has the child had epilepsy, suffered a head injury, infection or any other serious illness? (If yes, specify).	0	1
4.	Has the child had any problems in seeing? (If yes, describe).	0	1
5.	Has the child had any problems in hearing? (If yes, describe).	0	1
6.	Between the ages of 1 and 3, could the child walk, climb, throw a ball? (If not, mark as present).	0	1
7.	By the age of 3, could the child cut paper, thread beads? (If not, mark as present).	0	1
8.	Between the ages of 1 and 3, could the child speak in small sentences? (If not, mark as present).	0	1
9.	Between the age of 1 and 3 years, could the child show appropriate emotional expression in relation to parents and others and did he/she enjoy playing with other children? (If not, mark as present).	0	1
10.	Between the age of 3 and 5 years, could the child feed, wash and dress him/herself? (If not, mark as present).	0	1
B.	**Developmental Problems** **Currently or in the past, has there been a problem:**		
11.	Of dropping things, falling or tripping frequently.	0	1
12.	For brief periods when the child cried continuously to the extent of holding breath, becoming stiff, and turning blue in the face.	0	1
13.	Of making odd or funny, repeated movements of the face, body, arms and legs.	0	1
14.	In pronouncing words clearly (e.g. 'labbit' for 'rabbit').	0	1
15.	In speaking, like stammering or stuttering.	0	1
16.	Not talking at all and remaining mute, despite knowing how to speak, in some situations and to some people.	0	1
17.	Repeating the words spoken by others exactly in the manner it was heard, without appearing to understand the meaning.	0	1
18.	Appearing to understand what is being said but seemingly not being able to answer.	0	1
19.	Of not being able to understand what is being spoken.	0	1
20.	Appearing to understand and know how to speak, but speaking in a manner which other people find difficult to understand, and refusing to use gestures to convey his/her needs.	0	1
21.	Not being able to relate to people.	0	1
22.	Not being able to play with other children.	0	1

23.	Feeding such as overeating, under-eating, food fads or fussy eating habits, and eating non-edible things such as mud (if present, specify).	0	1
24.	Wetting clothes or bed from a very early age.	0	1
25.	Resuming wetting of the clothes or bed, after being dry earlier on.	0	1
26.	Of soiling of the clothes with stools, or has constipation (if present, specify).	0	1
27.	Sleeping such as sleepwalking, sleep talking, teeth grinding, nightmares, etc. (If present, specify).	0	1
28.	Masturbating or any other sexual problem (which is indulged in public).	0	1
C.	**Psychopathology (The items below are marked as being present only when they occur often or most of the time but not when they occur occasionally) Does the child have the problems of:**	**0**	**1**
29.	Poor attention.	0	1
30.	Distractibility (if the child is doing a task and someone enters the room, or he hears a sound, does he easily get distracted by this?).	0	1
31.	Inability to sit in a place, and always moving around.	0	1
32.	Acting without thinking, like not looking out for the traffic while crossing the road.	0	1
33.	Stubbornness.	0	1
34.	Disobedience.	0	1
35.	Often interrupting others playing, talking, being disruptive while playing, or breaking / throwing things frequently.	0	1
36.	Quarrelsomeness and fighting.	0	1
37.	Aggression as seen by hitting, biting and pinching others (with/without provocation).	0	1
38.	Getting very angry, crying a lot, rolling on the ground and continuing to be so for a long time, when his/her demands are not met.	0	1
39.	Going to school and coming back on time, but actually does not attend the school.	0	1
40.	Indulging in lying and cheating.	0	1
41.	Refusing to go to school and staying back home for a duration of weeks or months.	0	1
42.	Poor school performance.	0	1
43.	Difficulty in reading.	0	1
44.	Difficulty in writing.	0	1
45.	Difficulty in arithmetic.	0	1
46.	Forgetfulness or poor memory.	0	1
47.	Daydreaming.	0	1
48.	Being very quiet and reserved (withdrawn).	0	1
49.	Talking very little even with family members.	0	1
50.	Worrying.	0	1
51.	Anxiousness and nervousness.	0	1
52.	Shyness and timidity.	0	1
53.	Is fearful of animals/people/situations.	0	1

54.	Clinging.	0	1
55.	Crying easily.	0	1
56.	Going on doing a particular thing over and over again, such as washing hands, or repeatedly saying certain numbers, or expressing that certain thoughts come to his/her mind repeatedly to the extent that it interferes with his/her daily activities.	0	1
57.	Complaining of dizziness or giddiness.	0	1
58.	Complaining of aches and pains.	0	1
59.	Complaining of always feeling tired.	0	1
60.	Complaining of stomach ache.	0	1
61.	Fainting spells.	0	1
62.	Attacks of jerky movements and unconsciousness (fits or convulsions to be differentiated from epilepsy by a clinician).	0	1
63.	Complaining of pulling sensation of the limbs.	0	1
64.	Chronic physical illness (specify, if present).	0	1
65.	Physical handicaps (specify, if present).	0	1
	(The items 66 to 67 are to be marked as present if it has occurred more than once in the past or present) Currently or in the past, has there been a problem:		
66.	Of hearing voices and seeing things when no one was around.	0	1
67.	Of maintaining postures, being stiff, over long periods of time (if present, describe).	0	1
68.	Of saying that he/she was a great person, or a bad person, or that he/she was being harmed by other people without a real basis for such beliefs.	0	1
69.	Of talking and laughing to self.	0	1
70.	Of very poor appetite, sometimes leading to loss of weight.	0	1
71.	Of poor sleep/disturbed sleep.	0	1
72.	Of wetting and soiling during illness and being unaware of it.	0	1
73.	Of loss of interest in play and daily activities.	0	1
74.	Of moving and responding unusually slowly.	0	1
75.	Of being depressed, sad and dull.	0	1
76.	Of talking much more or faster than he/she normally used to.	0	1
77.	Of being irritable.	0	1
78.	Of being unusually cheerful and happy (others, if any).	0	1
D.	**Psychosocial Factors** **Family History of:**		
79.	Anyone with mental illness.	0	1
80.	Anyone drinking alcohol excessively.	0	1
81.	Anyone with epilepsy.	0	1
82.	Anyone with problems in reading, writing or arithmetic.	0	1
83.	Anyone suffering from bed wetting.	0	1
84.	Anyone having speech problems.	0	1
85.	Anyone being very dull or mentally retarded.	0	1

E.	Interaction in the Family and Stressors		
86.	Have there been any precipitating events at the time of onset of the problems? Specify if present. Is there any evidence of:	0	1
87.	Problems with parents (if present, describe).	0	1
88.	Sibling rivalry (jealous of brothers and sisters).	0	1
89.	Marital disharmony (parents fight a lot).	0	1
90.	Punitiveness (parents frequently resort to hitting, beating or punishing the child).	0	1
91.	Over expectations (the parents expect from the child beyond his abilities, especially in school performance).	0	1
92.	Over involvement (the parents are involved with all the child's activities to the extent that he/she does not do anything on his/her own).	0	1
93.	Overindulgence (the parents meet all the demands of the child, whether reasonable or not).	0	1
94.	Indifference (the parents are not bothered about the child's physical or psychological needs).	0	1
95.	Inconsistent disciplining (the parents do not agree about the way the child is to be disciplined).	0	1
96.	Multiple caretaking (the child has been brought up by a number of adults in the family).	0	1
97.	Single parent (the child has been cared for by a single parent).	0	1
98.	Any change of school, medium or specific subjects or teachers, leading to unhappiness in the child.	0	1
99.	The child complaining of problems with teachers.	0	1
100.	The child having problems in playing, mixing or socializing with other children.	0	1
101.	The child having problems such as poverty and other stressors, not covered in the above section (if present, specify).	0	1
	Temperament Profile		

F.	**Descriptions of some aspects of the child's nature or temperament are given, and each description has three options to choose from. Encircle the options which fit the child best. If the description is not applicable, it may be mentioned, especially for younger children.**				
		S	**R**	**T**	**Not Applicable**
a.	**Psychosocial**				
102.	Easy to manage	Mostly	Not at all	Somewhat	
103.	Independent (can manage himself/ herself)	Mostly	Somewhat	Not at all	
104.	Dependable	Mostly	Somewhat	Not at all	
105.	Sensitive (to others needs, emotions)	Mostly	Somewhat	Not at all	
106.	Sensitive (only about oneself)	Somewhat	Mostly	Not at all	
107.	Trusting	Mostly	Somewhat	Not at all	
108.	Trustworthy	Mostly	Somewhat	Not at all	
109.	Moral (discriminates between good and bad. Knows it is bad to hit others, steal, etc.)	Mostly	Somewhat	Not at all	

b.	Bio-social				
110.	Sleep	Moderate	Too little	Too much	
111.	Appetite	Moderate	Too little	Too much	
112.	Activity	Moderate	Too little	Too much	
113.	Emotionality	Cheerful	Angry/ Tense	Dull (Non-reactive	
114.	Persistence	Good	Variable	Too little	
115.	Sociability with family members	Adequate	Mostly	Not at all	
116.	Sociability with others outside	Adequate	Mostly	Not at all	
117.	Aggression (verbal)	Not at all	Mostly	Somewhat	
118.	Aggression (physical)	Not at all	Mostly	Somewhat	
	TOTAL	S =	R =	T =	NA =

Note: Each column total shows a predominance of *satvik*, *rajasik* or *tamasik* temperaments in comparison to each other. The total consists of encircled options under each category. *Satvik* is a more desirable temperament than *rajasik* or *tamasik*.

I.	Helpful Factors for Management		
119.	Does the child have any helpful person at home/outside: Somebody with whom the child is attached to, who helps the child, takes him/her out, buys the child gifts? (If yes, describe).		
120.	Does the child have friends in the neighbourhood or school? (If yes, describe).		
121.	Does the child have interest in drawing, painting, games, music, etc.? (If yes, describe).		
122.	Does the child have any special talents? (If yes, describe).		
123.	Is the child good at sports? (if yes, describe), and		
124.	Is the child creative, can put together commonplace objects in a new fashion, or make objects with hands? (If yes, describe).		

119-124: High score indicates more helpful factors.

Other Observations, if any:

Summary		
A.	Development history	1 – 10
B.	Development problems including autism	10 – 28
C.	Psychopathology	
	(i) Hyperkinesis (ADHD)	29 – 31
	(ii) Conduct disorder	32 – 40
	(iii) Learning problems	41 – 46
	(iv) Emotion disorder	47 – 55
	(v) Obsessive-compulsive neurosis	56

Contd.

Summary		
	(vi) Somatic symptoms (including hysteria)	57 – 65
	(vii) Psychoses (mania, depression and schizophrenia)	66 – 78
D.	Psychosocial stressors	79 – 101
E.	Temperamental profile	102 – 118
F.	Helpful for management	119 – 124

Note: The details of scoring and standardization, and the translated versions in Kannada, Tamil, Telugu, Malayalam, Marathi, Hindi and Gujarati are available with the author and may be provided to the users on nominal payment.

Record Sheet

Developmental Psychopathology Check List for Children

Malavika Kapur

Sl. No.: Date:

Name of the Child:

Age: Sex: Class:

Mother Tongue: Languages Spoken:

Medium of Instruction: Handedness:

Details Regarding the Family: Age: Education: Occupation:

Child Lives With: ☐ Father ☐ Mother Others.....................

Number of siblings and the order of birth:

Person giving the details:

How has he/she known the child?

Presenting complaints: Duration:

1. ....
2. ....
3. ....
4. ....
5. ....

Consanguinity: If present, specify:	Urban	Rural	

A.	Developmental History	No	Yes/Present	
1.	Pre-peri-postnatal problems of mother	0	1	
2.	Postnatal problems of child	0	1	
3.	Epilepsy, head injury, infections	0	1	
4.	Poor vision	0	1	
5.	Poor hearing	0	1	
6.	Gross–motor	0	1	

7.	Fine–motor	0	1	
8.	Speech/language	0	1	
9.	Emotional–social	0	1	
10.	Self help	0	1	
B.	**Developmental Problems**			
11.	Clumsiness	0	1	
12.	Breath holding	0	1	
13.	Tics, mannerisms	0	1	
14.	Speech/articulation	0	1	
15.	Stuttering/stammering	0	1	
16.	Elective mutism	0	1	
17.	Echolalia	0	1	
18.	Language (expressive)	0	1	
19.	Language (receptive)	0	1	
20.	Language (deviant)	0	1	
21.	Inability to relate to people	0	1	
22.	Inability to play with children	0	1	
23.	Feeding problems	0	1	
24.	Enuresis (primary)	0	1	
25.	Enuresis (secondary)	0	1	
26.	Encopresis	0	1	
27.	Sleeping	0	1	
28.	Sexual problems	0	1	
C.	**Psychopathology**			
29.	Poor attention	0	1	
30.	Distractible	0	1	
31.	Restless/Overactive	0	1	
32.	Impulsive	0	1	Attention Deficit Hyperactivity
33.	Stubborn	0	1	
34.	Disobedient	0	1	
35.	Disruptive	0	1	
36.	Quarrelsome	0	1	
37.	Aggressive	0	1	
38.	Temper tantrums	0	1	
39.	Truancy	0	1	
40.	Lying and stealing	0	1	Conduct
41.	School refusal	0	1	

42.	Poor school performance	0	1	
43.	Reading difficulty	0	1	
44.	Writing difficulty	0	1	
45.	Arithmetic difficulty	0	1	
46.	Forgetfulness, poor memory	0	1	Learning difficulties
47.	Daydreaming	0	1	
48.	Withdrawn	0	1	
49.	Talks little	0	1	
50.	Worrying	0	1	
51.	Anxious	0	1	
52.	Shyness/timidity	0	1	
53.	Fearful	0	1	
54.	Clinging	0	1	
55.	Cries easily	0	1	Emotion
56.	OCD	0	1	OCD
57.	Dizziness	0	1	
58.	Aches and pains	0	1	
59.	Tiredness	0	1	
60.	Stomach ache	0	1	
61.	Fainting spells	0	1	
62.	Fits	0	1	
63.	Pulling sensation	0	1	
64.	Chronic physical illness	0	1	
65.	Physical handicaps	0	1	
66.	Hallucinations	0	1	
67.	Catatonic feature	0	1	
68.	Delusions	0	1	
69.	Talking/laughing to self	0	1	
70.	Poor appetite	0	1	
71.	Poor sleep	0	1	
72.	Incontinence	0	1	
73.	Loss of interest	0	1	
74.	Psychomotor retardation	0	1	
75.	Depression	0	1	
76.	Pressure of ideas	0	1	
77.	Irritable	0	1	
78.	Elated	0	1	Psychoses

D.	**Psychosocial Factors** Family History			
79.	Mental illness	0	1	
80.	Alcoholism	0	1	
81.	Epilepsy	0	1	
82.	Learning problems	0	1	
83.	Bed wetting	0	1	
84.	Speech problems	0	1	
85.	Mental retardation	0	1	
86.	Precipitating factor	0	1	
87.	Problems with parents	0	1	
88.	Sibling rivalry	0	1	
89.	Marital disharmony	0	1	
90.	Punitiveness	0	1	
91.	Over expectation	0	1	
92.	Over involvement	0	1	
93.	Overindulgence	0	1	
94.	Indifference	0	1	
95.	Inconsistent disciplining	0	1	
96.	Multiple caretaking	0	1	
97.	Single parent	0	1	
98.	Change in school/medium/subjects	0	1	
99.	Problem with teachers	0	1	
100.	Problem with peers	0	1	
101.	Poverty	0	1	

E.	**Temperamental Dimensions**	**S**	**R**	**T**	**NA**
102.	Management				
103.	Independence				
104.	Dependability				
105.	Sensitivity (others)				
106.	Sensitivity (self)				
107.	Trusting				
108.	Trustworthy				
109.	Moral				
110.	Sleep pattern				
111.	Appetite				
112.	Activity				

113.	Emotionality				
114.	Persistence				
115.	Sociability (family)				
116.	Sociability (others)				
117.	Aggressive (verbal)				
118.	Aggressive (physical)				
F.	**Helpful Factors**				
119.	Helpful person	0	1		
120.	Friends	0	1		
121.	Interests	0	1		
122.	Talents	0	1		
123.	Sports	0	1		
124.	Creativity	0	1		

Sl. No.	Summary	Total Score				Cut Off	Obtained Score
1.	Dev. History	10				3	–
2.	Dev. Problems / Disorders	18				5	–
3.	ADHD	4				2	–
4.	CD	8				4	–
5.	LD	6				3	–
6.	ED	9				3	–
7.	OCD	1				1	–
8.	Somatic Symptom	9				3	–
9.	Psychotic Symptom	13				3	–
10.	Family History	7				–	–
11.	Stressors	16				–	–
12.	Temperament	S	R	T	NA	–	–

Achenbach, T.M. (1966). The classification of children's psychiatric symptoms: A factor analytic study. *Psychological Monographs, 80*, 1–37.

Achenbach, T.M. (1991). *Manual for the youth self-report and 1991 profile.* Burlington, VT: University of Vermont, Department of Psychiatry.

Achenbach, T.M., & Edelbrock, C.S. (1978). The classification of child psychopathology: a review and analysis of empirical efforts. *Psychological Bulletin, 85(6)*, 1275–1301.

Achenbach, T.M., & Edelbrock, C.S. (1981). *Behavioral problems and competencies reported by parents of normal and disturbed children aged four through sixteen.* Chicago, IL: Society for Research in Child Development.

Achenbach, T.M., & Edelbrock, C.S. (1983). *Manual for child behaviour check list and revised child behaviour profile.* Burlington, VT: Queen City Printers.

Adams, P.L. (1973). *Obsessive children: A socio-psychiatric study.* New York: Brunner/Mazel.

Agarwal, G., Saksena, N.K., & Singh, S.B. (1978). Child rearing attitudes of mothers of emotionally disturbed and maladjusted children. *Indian Journal of Clinical Psychology, 5*, 111–16.

Ainsworth, M.D.S. (1973). The development of infant-mother attachment. In B.M .Caldwell & H.N.Riccuti (Eds.), *Review of child development.* Chicago, IL: University of Chicago Press.

Anagol, J. (2003). *Compulsory primary education: Opportunities and challenges.* Book 2. Pune: Indian School of Political Economy.

Anita, Gaur D.R., Vohra, A.K., Subash, S., & Khurana, H. (2003). Prevalence of psychiatric morbidity among 6–14 year old children. *Indian Journal of Community Medicine, 28(3)*.

Anniah, S. (1981). Phenomenology and syndromes in a child clinic. M.D. Dissertation, Bangalore University, NIMHANS, Bangalore.

Anthony, E.J. (1970). The behaviour disorders of childhood. In P.H. Mussen (Ed.), *Carmichael's Manual of Child Pathology.* New York: Wiley.

Antonovsky, A. (1979). *Health, stress and coping.* San Francisco, CA: Jossey-Bass.

Arulmani, G. (1991). Patterns of coping with psychosocial stressors amongst Indian adolescents. M.Phil. Dissertation. Bangalore University, NIMHANS, Bangalore.

Ashlock, R.B. (1982). *Error patterns in computation: A semi-programmed approach* (3rd ed.). Columbus, OH: Charles E. Merril.

Axline, V.M. (1947). *Play therapy.* Boston, MA: Houghton Mifflin.

Azrin, N.H., & Foxx, R.M. (1974). *Toilet training in less than a day.* New York: Simon & Schuster.

Azrin, N.H., & Nunn, R.G. (1977). *Habit control in a day.* New York: Simon & Schuster.

Bakwin, H., & Bakwin, R.M. (1972). *Behaviour disorders in children* (4th ed.). Philadelphia, PA: Saunders.

Balan, V. (1970). A study of some aetiological factors of behaviour problems in children. M.D. Thesis. Bangalore University, NIMHANS, Bangalore.

Baldev, K., Jain, C.K. & Manchanda, S.S. (1972). Behaviour disorders of childhood and adolescence. *Indian Journal of Psychiatry, 14*, 213–21.

Banerjee, T. (1997). Psychiatric morbidity among rural primary school children in West Bengal. *Indian Journal of Psychiatry, 39*, 130–135.

Banerjee, T., Mukherjee, S. P., Nandi, D.N., Banerjee, G., Mukherjee, A., Sen, B., Sarkar, G., & Boral, G.C. (1986). Psychiatric morbidity in an urbanized tribal (Santhal) community: A field survey. *Indian Journal of Psychiatry, 28*, 243–248.

Bapna, G. & Ramanujam, B.K. (1976). Clinical study of learning inhibition. *Indian Journal of Psychiatry, 18(1)*, 14–19.

Barker, P. (1976). *Basic Child Psychiatry* (2nd ed.). London: Crosby Lockwood Staples.

Bartak, L., Rutter, M., & Cox, A. (1975). A comparative study of infantile autism and specific developmental language disorder: I. The children. *British Journal of Psychiatry, 126*, 127–45.

Bassa, D.M. (1962). An analysis of cases attending child psychotherapy centres. *Indian Journal of Psychiatry, 4(3)*, 139–44.

Beery, K.E., & Buktenica, N.A. (1967). *Developmental test of visual-motor integration.* New York: Modern Curriculum Press.

Benton, A.L. (1955). *Benton visual retention test.* New York, NY: Psychological Corporation.

Berger, M. (1985). Psychological assessment and testing. In M. Rutter and L. Herson (Eds.), *Child and adolescent psychiatry: Modern approaches.* London: Blackwell Scientific Publications.

Bernstern, M. (1990). *Collapse at the foundation: A study of literacy among third standard students in western Maharashtra—an interim report.* Pune: Ashoka Foundation.

Bettelheim, B. (1967). *The empty fortress: Infantile autism and the birth of the self.* New York, NY: Free Press.

Bhakkoo, O.N., Kaur, S., Narang, A. and Verma, S.K. (1977). A longitudinal study of variations in development quotients (DQ) in the first 30 months of life. *Indian Journal of Clinical Psychology, 4*, 59–68.

Bharath Raj, J. (1977). *Manual of developmental screening test.* Mysore: Padmashree Publishers.

Bhargava, S., Garg, O.P., Singhi, S., Singhi, P., & Lall, K.B. (1988). Prevalence of behaviour problems in Ajmer school children. *Indian Journal of Pediatrics, 55*, 408–415.

Bhatia, M.S., Bhasin, S.K., Choudhary, S., & Sidana, A. (2000). Behaviour disorders among children attending a nursery school. *Journal of Mental Health and Human Behaviour, 5*, 7–11.

Bhola, P., & Kapur, M. (2000). Prevalence of emotional disturbance in Indian adolescent girls. *Indian Journal of Clinical Psychology, 27*, 217–222.

Bhola, P., Hirisave, U., & Kapur, M. (1997). Self perception and learning environment in children with scholastic skill disorders. In R. Hegde, S. Malhotra & L.P. Shah (Eds.), *Research endeavours in child and adolescent psychiatry in India.* Goa: Indian Association for Child and Adolescent Mental Health.

Binderglas, P.M. (1975). The enuretic child. *The Journal of Family Practice*, October, 375–80.

Bird, R.H., Canino, G., Rubio-St. Pee, M., Gould, M.S., Ribera, J., Sesman, M., Woodbury, M., Huertas-Goldman, S., Pagan, A., Sanchez-Lacay, A. & Moscoso, M. (1988). Estimates of the prevalence of childhood maladjustment in a community survey in Puerto Rico. *Archives of General Psychiatry, 45*, 1120–26.

Block, J.H., Block, J. & Morrison, A. (1981). Parental agreement disagreement on child rearing orientation and gender related personality correlates in children. *Child Development, 52*, 965–74.

Boszormenyi-Nagy, I. & Sprat, G.M. (1973). *Invisible loyalties.* New York: Harper & Row.

Bowlby, J. (1949). The study of reduction of group tensions in the family. *Human Relations, 2*, 123–28.

Bowlby, J. (1980). *Attachment and loss* (Vol.3). New York: Basic Books.

Brazelton, T.B. (196). A child-oriented approach to toilet training. *Paediatrics*, 29, 121–28.

Brigance, H.A. (1977). *Inventory of basic skills.* North Billerica, M.A. : Curriculum Associates Inc.

Bryant, N.D., Drabin, I.R. & Gettinger, M. (1981). Effects of varying unit size on spelling achievement in learning disabled children. *Journal of Learning Disabilities, 14*, 200–203.

Buck, C.W. & Laughton, K.B. (1959). Family patterns of illness: The effect of psychoneuroses in the parent upon the illness of the child. *Acta Psychiatrica Neurologica Scandinavica, 34*, 165–75.

Buss, A.H. & Plomin, R. (1984). *Temperament: Early developing personality traits.* Hillsdale, N.J.: Erlbaum.

Cantwell, D.P. (1978). Hyperactivity and antisocial behaviour. *Journal of American Academy of Child Psychiatry, 37*, 1171–75.

Cantwell, D.P., Baker, L., & Rutter, M. (1978). Family factors. In M. Rutter & E. Shopler (Eds.), *Autism—A reappraisal of concepts and treatment* (pp. 269–96). New York: Plenum Press.

Carpenter, D., & Miller, L. J. (1982). Spelling ability of reading disabled LD students and able readers. *Learning Disability Quarterly, 5(1)*, 65–70.

Cattell, R. B. (1936). *A guide to mental testing for psychological clinics, schools, and industrial psychologists.* London: University of London Press.

Centerwall, B.S. (1989). Exposure to television as a cause of violence. In G. Comstock (Ed.), *Public communication and behaviour* (Vol. 2). Orlando, FL: Academic Press.

Centerwall, B.S. (1994). Television and the development of the superego: Pathways to violence. In C. Chiland & G.T. Young (Eds.), *Children and violence: The child in the family* (Vol. 2). Newvale, NJ: Jason Aronson Inc.

Chacko, R. (1964). Psychiatric problems in children. *Indian Journal of Psychiatry*, 6, 147–52.

Chandani, J., Kapur, M., & Hirisave, U. (1999). Artwork of Indian children with mental health problems. *Behavioural Medicine, 2(2)*, 1–20.

Chandrashekar, C.R., Channabasavanna, S.M. & Reddy, M.V. (1980). Hysterical possession syndrome. *Indian Journal of Psychological Medicine, 3*, 35–40.

Chaudhury, S., Prasad, P.L., Zacharias, R., Madhusudan, T. & Saini, R. (2007). Psychiatric morbidity pattern in a child guidance clinic. *Medical Journal Armed Forces India, 63*, 144–146.

Chess, S. (1973). Marked anxiety in children. *American Journal of Psychotherapy, 17(3)*, 390–95.

Chawla, P., & Sahasi, G. (1989). Conduct disorder in primary school children. *Indian Journal of Clinical Psychology, 16*, 108–111.

Cicchetti, D., & Garmezy, N. (1993). Prospects & promises in the study of resilience. *Development and Psychopathology, 5*, 497–500.

Cicchetti, D. and Hesse, P. (1983). Affect and intellect: Piaget's contribution to the study of infant emotional development. In R. Plutchik and H. Kellerman (Eds.), *Emotion: Research and theory*, Vol.2. New York: Academic Press.

Cohen, M.W. (1975). Enuresis. *Pediatric Clinics of North America, 22*, 545–60.

Conger, J.J., & Miller, W.C. (1966). *Personality, Social Class and Delinquency*. New York: Wiley.

Connell, H.M., Irvine, L. & Rodney, J. (1982). The prevalence of psychiatric disorder in rural school children. *Australian and New Zealand Journal of Psychiatry*, 16, 43–46.

Conners, C.K. (1973). Rating scales for use in drug studies with children. *Psycho-Pharmacology Bulletin*, Special Issue on Children.

Conners, C.K. (1970). Symptom patterns in hyperkinetic, neurotic and normal children. *Child Development*, 41, 667–82.

Conradie, D.P., Heineke, M. & Botha, M.P. (1987). *The effect of television violence on television-naive pupils: A follow-up study over five years.* Pretoria: Human Sciences.

Cooper, S., & Wannerman, L. (1977). *Children in treatment: A primer for beginning psychotherapists.* New York: Brunner/Mazel.

Cravioto, J., & DeLicardie, E.R. (1973). Environmental and learning deprivation in children with learning disabilities. In Hallahan. P.P. & Cruickshank. W.M. (Eds.), *Psycho-educational foundations of learning disabilities.* Englewood Cliffs, NJ: Prentice Hall.

Crowther, J.H., Bond, L.A., & Rolf, J.E. (1981). The incidence, prevalence and severity of behaviour disorders among preschool-aged children in day care. *Journal of Abnormal Child Psychology, 9*, 23–42.

Cullen, K.T., & Boundy, C.A.P. (1966). Factors relating to behaviour disorders in children. *Australian Paediatric Journal, 2*, 70–80.

Cunningham, J., Westerman, H.H., & Fischoff, J. (1956). A follow-up study of patients seen in a psychiatric clinic for children. *American Journal of Orthopsychiatry, 26*, 602–12.

Dalal, M. (1989). Prevalence and pattern of psychological disturbance in school-going adolescent girls. M.Phil. Dissertation. Bangalore University, NIMHANS, Bangalore.

Dalal, M., Kapur, M., & Kaliaperumal, V.G. (1990). Prevalence and Pattern of Psychological Disturbance in School Going Adolescent Girls. *Indian Journal of Clinical Psychology, 17*, 83–88.

Daniel, E. (1989). A study of disorders of conduct and emotion. Doctoral Thesis. Bangalore University, NIMHANS, Bangalore.

Dash, S., Das, T., Swain, S.P., Mohapatra, P.K., Sengupta, J., & Kar, G.C. (2000, January). Trend of psychiatric morbidity in school children in Cuttack city. Paper presented at the 52nd Annual National Conference of the Indian Psychiatric Society, Cochin, India.

De Almeida-Filho, N. (1984). Family variables and child mental disorders in a third world urban area (Bahia, Brazil). *Social Psychiatry*, 19, 23–30.

Deivasigamani, T.R. (1990). Psychiatric morbidity in primary school children: An epidemiological study. *Indian Journal of Psychiatry, 32*, 3, 235–240.

Delacato, C. (1969) *Neurological organisation and reading.* Springfield, IL: Charles C. Thomas Co.

DeMyer, M.K., Barton, S., Alpern, G.D., Kimberlin, C., Allen, J., Yang, E., & Steele, R. (1974). The measured intelligence of autistic children: A follow-up study. *Journal of Autism and Childhood Schizophrenia, 4*, 42–60.

DeMyer, M.K., Hingtgen, J.N., & Jackson, R.K. (1981). Infantile autism reviewed: A decade of research. *Schizophrenia Bulletin*, 7, 388–451.

DeMyer, M.K., Pontius, W., Norton, J.A., Barton, S., Allen, J., & Steele, R. (1972). Parental practices and innate activity in autistic and brain damaged infants. *Journal of Autism and Childhood Schizophrenia, 2*, 49–66.

De Souza, A., Kapoor, H., Jagtap, J., & Sen, M. (2007). Prevalence and factors affecting enuresis amongst primary school children. *Indian Journal of Urology, 23(4)*, 354–57.

Dhavale, H.S. (1994). Initiating school mental health. Health for the millions. Special issue, *Mental Health, I. 20, 4*, 17–18.

Doll, E.A. (1965). *Vineland social maturity scale: Manual of direction* (rev. ed.). Minneapolis, MN: Educational Test Bureau (Currently American Guidance Service).

Dube, K.C. (1971). A study of prevalence and biosocial variables on mental illness in a rural and an urban community in Uttar Pradesh. *Acta Psychiatrica Scandinavica, 46*, 327– 359.

Dubey, D.R. (1976). Organic factors in hyperkinesis: A critical evaluation. *American Journal of Orthopsychiatry, 46*, 353–66.

Duncan, G.J., & Brooks-Gunn, Jeanne. (1997). *Consequences of growing up poor.* New York: Russel Sage Foundation Press.

Eggers, C. (1978). Course and prognosis of childhood schizophrenia. *Journal of Autism and Childhood Schizophrenia, 8*, 21–36.

Eggers, C. (1986). Conversion hysteria in childhood and adolescence. Proceedings of the 11th International Congress on New Approaches to Infant, Child, Adolescent and Family Mental Health, Paris.

Elnager, M.N., Maitra, P., & Rao, M.N. (1971). Mental health in an Indian rural community. *British Journal of Psychiatry, 118*, 499–503.

Ekwall, E.E. (1985). *Locating and correcting reading difficulties.* Columbus, OH: Charles E. Merrill.

Erikson, E.H. (1963). *Childhood and society.* New York: Norton.

Eron, L.D., & Huesmann, L.R. (1984). The control of aggressive behaviour by changes in attitudes, values and conditions of learnings. In R.J. Blanplank & D.C. Blanchand (Eds.), *Advances in Studies of Aggression* (pp. 139–71). Orlando, FL: Academic Press.

Fennuci, J. (1978). Genetic consideration in dyslexia. In H. Myklebust (Ed.), *Progress in Learning Disabilities* (Vol. 4). New York: Grune & Stratton.

Fernald, G. (1943). *Remedial Techniques in Basic School Subjects.* New York: McGraw Hill.

Florence, R. (1983). A study of certain psychosocial factors in disturbed children. M.Phil. Dissertation. Bangalore University, NIMHANS, Bangalore.

Freud, A. (1946). *The psychoanalytic study of the child.* London: Imago.

Freud, A. (1966). *Normality and pathology in childhood: Assessments of development.* London: Penguin.

Friedman, S.B. (1973). Conversion symptom in adolescents. *Pediatric Clinics of North America, 20*, 873–82.

Frostig, M., & Horne, D. (1964). *The Frostig program for the development of visual perception.* Chicago, IL: Follett.

Gada, M. (1987). A study of prevalence and pattern of attention deficit disorder in primary school children. *Indian Journal of Psychiatry, 29*, 113–118.

Gadow, K.D., Torgesen, J.K., & Dahlem, W.E. (1985). Learning disabilities. In M. Herson, V.B. Hasselt & J.L. Matson (Eds.), *Behaviour therapy for the developmentally and physically disabled: A handbook.* New York: Academic Press.

Garber, J. (1984). Classification of childhood psychopathology: A developmental perspective. *Child Development, 55*, 30–48.

Garner, D.M., Olmstead, M.P., Bohr, Y., & Garfinkel, P.E. (1982). The eating attitudes test: Psychometric properties and clinical correlates. *Psychological Medicine, 12*, 871–878.

Geetha, P.R. (1976). A comparative study of family interaction in childhood hysteria. D.P.M. dissertation. Bangalore: NIMHANS Publications.

Geetha, P.R., Shetty, G. & Venkataramaiah, V. (1980). A comparative study of family interaction in childhood anxiety and normal children. *Indian Journal of Psychological Medicine, 3*, 5–13.

Gesell, A., & Amatruda, C.S. (1947). *Developmental diagnosis* (2nd Ed.). New York: Hoeber-Harpe.

Getman, G.N. (1962). *How to develop your child's intelligence.* LuVerne, MN: Author.

Giel, R., De Arango, M.V., Climent, C.E., Harding, T.W., Ibrahim, H.H.A., Ladrido-Ignacio, L., Srinivasa Murthy, R., Salazar, M.C., Wig, N.N., & Younis, Y.O.A. (1981). Childhood mental disorders in primary health care: Results of observations in four developing countries. A report from the WHO collaborative study on strategies for extending mental health care. *Pediatrics, 68(5)*, 677–83.

Gillberg, C., Steffenburg, S., & Schaumann, H. (1991). Is autism more common now than ten years ago? *British Journal of Psychiatry, 158*, 403–409.

Gilpin, D.C. (1981). Hysterical disorders observed in a university child guidance clinic. In E.J. Anthony & D.C. Gilpin (Eds.), *Three further clinical faces of childhood.* New York: Spectrum.

Girimaji, S.G.(2001). Working with families: A focus on maladaptive rearing practices. In M. Kapur (Ed.) *Psychological therapies with children and adolescents.* Bangalore: NIMHANS Publications, No.45, 27–32.

Glueck, S., & Glueck, E. (1968). *Delinquents and non-delinquents in perspective.* Cambridge, MA: Harvard University Press.

Goldstein, G. and Hersen, M. (Eds.) (1987). *Handbook of psychological assessment.* New York: Pergamon Press.

Goodman, W.K., Rasmussen, S.A., Price, L.H., Riddle, M.A., Rapoport, J.L. (1986). Children's Yale-Brown obsessive-compulsive scale (CY-BOCS). New Haven, CT: Yale University Press.

Goodyer, I. (1981). Hysterical conversion reactions in childhood. *Journal of Child Psychology and Psychiatry, 22*, 179–88.

Gopala Rao, D. (1970). Study of some factors related to scholastic achievement. *Indian Journal of Psychology, 45*, 99–120.

Gowrie Devi, M. (1983). A study of the families of children with conduct disorder. M.D. Thesis. Bangalore University, Bangalore.

Graham, P.J. (1985). Psychosomatic relationships. In M. Rutter & L. Hersov (Eds.), *Child and adolescent psychiatry: Modern approaches.* London: Blackwell Scientific Publications.

Graham, P.J., Rutter, M. & George, S. (1973). Temperamental characteristics as predictors of behaviour disorders in children. *American Journal of Orthopsychiatry, 43*, 328–39.

Graziano, A.M., De Giovanni, I.S., & Garcia, K.A. (1979). Behavioural treatment of children's fears: A review. *Psychological Bulletin, 86*, 804–30.

Greenspan, S., Lourie, R.S., & Nover, R.A. (1979). A developmental structuralist approach to the classification of psychopathology of infancy and early childhood. In J. Noshpitz (Ed.), Handbook of Child Psychiatry. New York: Basic Books Inc.

Grossman, H.S. (1978). 'Foreword'. In S.G. Sapir and B. Wilson, *A professional's guide to working with the learning disabled child.* New York: Brunner/Mazel.

Gupta, I., Verma, M., Singh, T., & Gupta, V. (2001). Prevalence of behavioural problems in school going children. *Indian Journal of Pediatrics, 68*, 323–326.

Hackett, R., Hackett, L., Bhakta, P., & Gowers, S. (1999). The prevalence and associations of psychiatric disorder in children in Kerala, South India. *Journal of Child Psychiatry and Psychology, 40*, 801–807.

Hallahan, D.P., Kauffman, J.M., & Lloyd, J.W. (1985). *Introduction to learning disabilities.* Englewood Cliffs, NJ: Prentice Hall.

Haney, W. (1981). On the scientific basis of ability testing. *American Psychologist, 36*, 1021–34.

Hayden, T.L. (1980). Classification of elective mutism. *Journal of the American Academy of Child Psychiatry, 19*, 118–33.

Heilman, K.M. (1978). Language and brain: Relationship of localization of language functions to the acquisition and loss of various aspects of language. In J. Chall & P. Mirsky (Eds.), *Education and brain.* Chicago, IL: University of Chicago Press.

Hendren, R., Birrel, R., Weisen, & Orley, J. (1994). Mental health programmes in schools. Division of Mental Health, World Health Organization, Geneva, WHO/MNH/PSF/93.3, First Revision.

Hermelin, B. (1978). Images and language. In M. Rutter & E. Schopler (Eds.), *Autism: A reappraisal of concepts and treatment.* New York: Plenum.

Hermelin, B., & O'Connor, N. (1970). *Psychological experiments with autistic children.* Oxford: Pergamon Press.

Henn, F., Bordwell, R., & Jenkins, R.L. (1980). Juvenile delinquents revisited. *Archives of General Psychiatry, 37*, 1160–1163.

Herjanic, B., & Reich, W. (1982). Development of a structured interview for children: Agreement between child and parent on individual symptoms. *Journal of Abnormal Child Psychology, 10*, 307–324.

Hersov, L.A. (1960). Persistent non-attendance at school. *Journal of Child Psychology and Psychiatry, 1*, 130–136.

Hersov, L.A. (1977). School refusal. In M. Rutter & L.A. Hersov (Eds.), *Child psychiatry: Modern approaches.* Oxford: Blackwell Scientific Publications.

Hess, R.D., & Camara, K.A. (1979). Post-divorce family relationships as mediating factors in consequences of divorce for children. *Journal of Social Issues, 35*, 79–96.

Hetherington, E.M., & Martin, B. (1979). Family interaction. In H.C. Quay & J.S. Werry (Eds.), *Psychopathological Disorders of Childhood* (2nd Ed.). New York: Wiley.

Hewitt, L.E. & Jenkins, R.L. (1946). *Fundamental patterns of maladjustments: The dynamics of their origins.* Springfield, IL: D.H. Green.

Hirisave, U, Oommen, A & Kapur, M. (2002). *Psychological assessment of children in clinical setting* (2nd ed.). Bangalore: NIMHANS Publications, No.48.

Hoch, E.M. (1967). *Indian children on a psychiatrist's playground.* New Delhi: Indian Council of Medical Research.

Hoch, E.M. (1970). A longitudinal study of emotional, educational and social development of a small group of school children. Manuscript. New Delhi: National Council of Educational Research and Training.

Hoch, E.M. (1980). Research on cultural patterns and psychological development: A report. ICMR Task Force Study on Psychological Problems of Children, New Delhi: ICMR.

Hoch, E.M. (1993). Prevention and treatment intervention in the family. In Kapur, M., Kellam S.G., Tarter, R.E., & Wilson, R (Eds.) *Indo-US Symposium on Child Mental Health.* Bangalore: NIMHANS Publications.

Hofmeister, A.M. (1981). *Handwriting resource book: Manuscript cursive.* Allen, TX: DLM Teaching Resources.

Hollingsworth, C.E., Tanguay, P.E., Grossman, L., & Pabst, P. (1980). Long term outcome of obsessive compulsive disorder in childhood. *Journal of the American Academy of Child Psychiatry, 19*, 134–44.

Huppert, F.A., Baylis, N., & Keverne, B. (2005). *The science of wellbeing.* Oxford: Oxford University Press.

Hussaini, B.A. (1975). Changes in child rearing attitudes of mothers of emotionally disturbed children. *Indian Journal of Psychology, 50*, 232–42.

Indian Council of Medical Research (1984). *Collaborative study on patterns of child and adolescent psychiatric disorders.* New Delhi: Author.

Indian Council of Medical Research (2001). *Epidemiological study of child and adolescent psychiatric disorders in urban and rural areas.* New Delhi: Author.

Indiramma, V.(2001). Group counseling for the parents of children with psychological problems. In M. Kapur (Ed.) *Psychological therapies with children and adolescents.* Bangalore: NIMHANS Publications, No. 45, 33–45.

International Classification of Diseases, 10 (1992). *Classification of mental behaviour disorders.* World Health Organisation, Geneva: Oxford University Press.

Jagdish, H.N. (1990). *Single versus thrice weekly electroconvulsive therapy in the acute treatment of endogenous depression.* M.D. thesis. Bangalore University, NIMHANS.

Jiloha, R.C., & Murthy, R.S. (1981). An epidemiological study of psychiatric problems in primary school children. *Child Psychiatry Quarterly, 14(4)*, 1–12.

John, P. (1980). Psychiatric morbidity in children. M.D. thesis. Bangalore University, NIMHANS, Bangalore.

Johnson, J., & Myklebust, H. (1967). *Learning disabilities: Educational principles and practices.* New York: Grune & Stratton.

Jones, M.B., Offord, D.R., & Abrams, N. (1980). Brothers, sisters and antisocial behaviour. *British Journal of Psychiatry, 136*, 139–45.

Jonsell, R. (1982). Psychosocial risk factors in children. In E.J. Anthony & C. Koupernik (Eds.), *Child and his family* (Vol. 7). New York: John Wiley & Sons.

Joy, L.A., Kimball, M.M., & Zabrack, M.L. (1986). Television and children's aggressive behaviour. In T.M. Williams (Ed.), *Impact of television: A national experiment in three communities* (pp. 303–60). Orlando, FL: Academic Press.

Judd, L.L. (1965). Obsessive compulsive neurosis in children. *Archives of General Psychiatry, 12*, 136–43.

Kakar, S. (1970). Popularity, intelligence, economic status and academic achievement. *Indian Journal of Psychiatry, 45*, 233–37.

Kamat, V.V. (1940). *Measuring intelligence of Indian children.* London: Oxford University Press.

Kanner, L. (1957). *Child psychiatry.* Springfield, IL: Charles C. Thomas.

Kapoor, S.D. (1972). *Speed and accuracy test (SAT, LCT, MFT).* New Delhi: Psycho Centre.

Kapur, M. (1985). The pattern of psychiatric disturbance amongst residential school children: A preliminary report. *NIMHANS Journal, 3(1)*, 31–35.

Kapur, M. (1986). Beyond infant autism and childhood psychoses. Paper presented at the 11th International Congress on New Approaches to Infant, Child, Adolescent and Family Mental Health, Paris.

Kapur, M. (1993). Promotive and intervention strategies in the community. In M. Kapur, S.G. Kellam, R.E. Tater & R. Wilson (Eds.), *Indo-US Symposium on Child Mental Health.* Bangalore: NIMHANS Publications.

Kapur, M. (1995). *Mental health of Indian children.* New Delhi: Sage Publications.

Kapur, M. (2007). *Learning from children what to teach them.* New Delhi: Sage Publications.

Kapur, M., Barnabas, I.P., Reddy, M.V., Rozario, J. & Uma, H. (1994). Development of a check list for assessment of childhood psychopathology in the Indian setting. *Indian Journal of Clinical Psychology, 2(1)*, 40–52.

Kapur, M., & Cariappa, I. (1979a). An orientation course for school teachers on emotional problems of school children. *Indian Journal of Clinical Psychology, 6*, 75–80.

Kapur, M., & Cariappa, I. (1979b). Training in counselling for school teachers. *International Journal for the Advancement of Counselling, 2*, 109–15.

Kapur, R.L., Kapur, M., & Carstairs, G.M. (1974). Indian psychiatric survey schedule. *Social Psychiatry, 9*, 71–76.

Kauffman, J.M. (1985). *Characteristics of children's behaviour disorders* (3rd Ed.). Columbus, OH: Charles E. Merrill.

Kauffman, J.M., Hallahan, D.P., Haas, K., Brame, T. & Boren, R. (1978). Imitating children's errors to improve their spelling performance. *Journal of Learning Disabilities, 11*, 217–22.

Kaufman, A. (1979). *Intelligence testing with Tire WISC.* New York: John Wiley & Sons Inc.

Kaufman, J., Birmaher, B., Brent, D., Rao, U., Flynn, C., Moreci, P., et al. (1997). Schedule for Affective Disorders and Schizophrenia for School-Age Children—Present and Life time Version (K-SADS-PL): Initial reliability and validity data. *Journal of the American Academy of Child Adolescent Psychiatry, 36*, 980–988.

Kazdin, A.E. (1990). Learning theory and behavioural approaches. In M. Lewis (Ed.) *Child and adolescent psychiatry: A comprehensive textbook.* Baltimore, MD: Lippincott Williams & Wilkins, 87–99.

Kellam, S.G., Brach, J.D., Agrawal, K.C., & Emsinger, H.E. (1975). *Mental health and going to school: The Woodlawn program of assessment, early intervention and evaluation.* Chicago, IL: University of Chicago Press.

Kennedy, W.A. (1965). School phobia: Rapid treatment of fifty cases. *Journal of Abnormal Psychology, 70*, 285–89.

Kephart, N.C. (1971). *The slow learner in the classroom* (2nd Ed.). Columbus, OH: Merrill Publishing Company.

Kessler, J.W. (1972). Neurosis in childhood. In B.B. Wolman (Ed.). *Manual of child psychopathology.* New York: McGraw Hill.

Khanna, S., & Srinath, S. (1988). Childhood obsessive compulsive disorder. *Psychopathology, 21*, 254–58.

King, M.B., & Bhugra, D. (1989). Eating disorders: Lessons from a cross-cultural study. *Psychological Medicine, 19*, 955–958.

Kinsbourne, M., & Hiscock, M. (1978). Cerebral lateralization and cognitive development. In J. Chall & A. Mirsky (Eds.), *Education and the brain.* Chicago, IL: University of Chicago Press.

Kishore, A.N.R. (1988). Primary nocturnal enuresis: A study of possible aetiologic correlates. M.D. Thesis. Bangalore University, NIMHANS, Bangalore.

Klein, M. (1937). *The Psychoanalysis of children* (2nd Ed.). London: Hogarth Press.

Kolvin, I. (1971). Psychoses in childhood – A comparative study. In M. Rutter (Ed.), *Infantile autism: Concepts, characteristics and treatment.* Edinburgh: Churchill Livingstone.

Kolvin, I., Ounsted, C., & Roth, A. (1971). Cerebral dysfunction and childhood psychoses. *British Journal of Psychiatry, 118*, 407–14.

Kolvin, I., Wolff, S., Barber, L.M., Tweddle, E.G., Garside, R., Scott, D. McI., & Chambers, S. (1975). Dimensions of behaviour in infant school children. *British Journal of Psychiatry, 126*, 114–26.

Koocher, G., & Broskowski, A. (1977). Issues in the evaluation of mental health services for children. *Professional Psychology, 8*, 583–92.

Koot, H.M., & Verhulst, F.C. (1992). Prediction of children's referral to mental health and special education services from earlier adjustment. *Journal of Child Psychology and Psychiatry, 33(4)*, 717–29.

Koppitz, E.M. (1975). *The Bender Gestalt test for young children*, Vol. II. New York: Grune & Stratton.

Kovacs, M. (1987). Depression in childhood. In S.M. Channabasavanna & A.S. Shah (Eds.), *Affective disorders.* Bangalore: NIMHANS Publications.

Krouse, J.H., & Krouse, H.J. (1981). Toward multimodel theory of under achievement. *Educational Psychologist, 16*, 151–64.

Kruttschnitt, C., Heath, L., & Ward, D. (1986). Family violence, television viewing habits and other adolescent experiences related to violent criminal behaviour. *Criminology, 24(2)*, 235–67.

Kumar, K., Srinath, S., & Khanna, S. (1999, November). Prevalence of comorbidity in subclinical obsessive compulsive disorder in an urban adolescent population. Paper presented at the 5th Biennial Conference of the Indian Association for Child and Adolescent Mental Health, Bangalore, India.

Kurup, S. (1980). An epidemiological study of psychiatric morbidity in rural children. M.D. Thesis, Bangalore University, Bangalore, India.

Kushwaha, K.P., Singh, Y.D., Rathi, A.K., Singh, K.P., & Rastogi, C.K. (1992). Prevalence and abuse of psychoactive substances in children and adolescents. *Indian Journal of Pediatrics, 59*, 261–268.

Lahey, B.B., Vosk, B.N., & Habif, V.L. (1981). Behavioural assessment of learning disabled children: A rationale and strategy. *Behavioural Assessment, 3*, 3–14.

Laitman, R.J. (1981). A family therapy perspective on hysterical dynamics in childhood. In E.J. Anthony & D.C. Gilpin (Eds.), *Three further clinical faces of childhood.* New York: Spectrum.

Lal, N., & Sethi, B.B. (1977). Estimate of mental ill health in children in an urban community. *Indian Journal of Pediatrics, 4*, 55 – 64.

Lall, A.., Hirisave, U., Kapur, M. and Subbakrishna, D.K. (1997). Perceived peer relations, social competence in children with specific disorders of scholastic skills. *NIMHANS Journal, 15(2)*, 133–37.

Lapouse, R., & Monk, M.A. (1958). An epidemiological study of behaviour characteristics in children. *American Journal of Public Health, 48*, 1134–44.

Levine, M.D. (1975). Children with encopresis: A descriptive analysis. *Paediatrics, 56*, 412–16.

Levy, D.M. (1939). Release therapy. *American Journal of Orthopsychiatry, 9*, 713–39.

Linely, A., Joseph, S., & Hoboken, N.J. (Eds.) (2000). *Positive psychology in practice.* Hoboken, NJ: John Wiley & Sons.

Linschid, T.R. (1983). Eating problems in children. In C.E. Walker & M.C. Roberts (Eds.), *Handbook of clinical child psychology.* Hoboken, NJ: John Wiley & Sons.

Lotter, V. (1966). Epidemiology of autistic conditions in young children: I. Prevalence. *Social Psychiatry, 1*, 24–37.

Lowenfeld, V., & Brittain, W.L. (1987). *Creative and mental growth* (8th Ed.). New York: Macmillan.

Lovitt, T.C., Guppy, T.E. & Blattner, I.E. (1969). The use of free-time contingency with fourth graders to increase spelling accuracy. *Behaviour Research and Therapy, 7*, 151–56.

Ludlow, C. (1980). Children's language disorders: Recent research advances. *Annals of Neurology, 7*, 497–507.

Luthar, S.S., & Cicchetti, D. (2000). The construct of resilience: Implications for intervention and future policies. *Development and Psychopathology, 12(4)*, 857–85.

Luthar, S.S., Cicchetti, D., & Becker, B. (2000). The construct of resilience: A critical evaluation and guidelines for future work. *Child Development, 71(3)*, 543–562.

Lyon, G.R. (1985). Identification and remediation of learning disability subtypes: Preliminary findings. *Learning Disabilities Focus, 1*, 21–25.

Machover, K. (1951). Drawing of the human figure: A method of personality and other devices in understanding dynamics of human behaviour investigation. In H.H. Anderson & G.C. Anderson (Eds.), *Projective Techniques.* New York: Prentice Hall.

Mahat, P. (2008). *A study of the prevalence and pattern of psychological disturbances in school children and adolescents in Nepal.* Kathmandu: Tribhuvan University.

Mahler, M.S. (1968). On human symbiosis and vicissitudes of individuation. New York: International Universities.

Makita, K. (1966). The age of onset of childhood schizophrenia. *Folia Psyhchiatrica at Neurologica Japonica, 20*, 111–21.

Malhotra, S., & Malhotra, A. (1988). *Manual for Malhotra's temperament schedule.* Agra: National Psychological Corporation.

Malhotra, S., Varma, V.K., Verma, S.K., & Malhotra, A. (1986). Childhood psychopathology measurement schedule: Development and standardization. *Indian Journal of Psychiatry, 30(4)*, 325–31.

Malhotra, S., Kohli, A., & Arun, P. (2002). Prevalence of psychiatric disorders in school children in Chandigarh, India. *Indian Journal of Medical Research, 116*, 21–28.

Malin, A.J. (1970). *Vineland social maturity scale.* Lucknow: Indian Psychological Corporation.

Malin, A.J. (1971). Malin's intelligence scale for Indian children. *Indian Journal of Mental Retardation, 4(1)*, 15–25.

Manchanda, M., & Manchanda, R. (1978). Neurosis in children: Epidemiological aspects. *Indian Journal of Psychiatry, 20*, 161–65.

Mann, A.V., & Liberman, I.Y. (1984). Phonological awareness and verbal short-term memory. *Journal of Learning Disabilities, 17*, 592–99.

Mann, L. (1979). *On the Trail of Progress.* New York: Grune & Stratton.

Masten, A.S., & Reed, M.G.J. (2002). Resilience in Development. In S.R. Snyder & S.J. Lopez (Eds.), *The handbook of positive psychology* (pp. 74–88). Oxford: Oxford University Press.

Masterson, J.F. (1967). The symptomatic adolescent five years later: He did not grow out of it. *American Journal of Psychiatry, 123*, 1338–45.

Matsuura, M., Okubo, Y., Kato, M., Kojima, T., Takahashi, R., Asai, K., Asai, T., Endo, T., Yamada, S., Nakane, A., Kimura, K. & Suzuki, M. (1989). An epidemiological investigation of emotional and behavioural problems in primary school children in Japan. *Social Psychiatric Epidemiology, 24*, 17–22.

Matus, I. (1981). Assessing the nature and clinical significance of psychological contributions to childhood asthma. *American Journal of Orthopsychiatry, 51*, 327–41.

McCord, W., McCord, J., & Howard, A. (1961). Familial correlates of aggression in non-delinquent male children. *Journal of Abnormal and Social Psychology, 62*, 79–83.

McFarlane, J.D., Allen, L., & Honzig, P. (1954). *A developmental study of problems of normal children between 21 months and 14 years.* Berkeley, CA: University of California Press.

McGee, R., Silva, P.A., & Williams, S.M. (1984). Behaviour problems in a population of seven year old children: Prevalence, stability and types of disorder. *Journal of Child Psychology and Psychiatry, 23*, 251–59.

McGuire, J., & Richman, N. (1986). Screening for behaviour problems in nurseries: The validity and reliability of the preschool behaviour checklist. *Journal of Child Psychology and Psychiatry, 27*, 7–32.

McLyod, V.C. (1998). Socioeconomic disadvantage and child development. *American Psychologist, 53(2)*, 185–204.

McKendry, J.B. & Stewart, D.A.. (1974). Enuresis. *Pediatric Clinics of North America, 21*, 1019–20.

Mehta, M., Pandav, C.S., & Pande, P. (1991). Mental health problems in rural primary school children. *Indian Journal of Social Psychiatry, 7*, 32–39.

Mehta, P., Joseph, A., & Verghese, A. (1985). An epidemiological study of psychiatric disorder in a rural area in Tamil Nadu. *Indian Journal of Psychiatry, 27*, 153–158.

Mercer, C.D., & Mercer, A.R. (1985). *Teaching students with learning problems.* London: Merrill Publishing Co.

Milavsky, J.R., Kessler R.C., Stipp, H. & Rubens, W. (1982). *Television and aggression: A panel study.* Orlando, FL: Academic Press.

Miller, L.C. (1967). Dimensions of psychopathology in middle childhood. *Psychological Reports, 21*, 897–903.

Miller, L.C. (1983). Fears and anxiety in children. In C.E. Walker & M.C. Roberts (Eds.), *Personality processes.* New York: Wiley.

Miller, L.C., Barrett, C.L., & Hampe, E. (1974). Phobias of childhood in a prescientific era. In A. Davids (Ed.), *Child personality and psychopathology: Current topics* (Vol. 1). New York: Wiley.

Minuchin, S., Baker L., Rosman, B.L., Leibman, R., Milman, L., & Todd, C. (1975). A conceptual model of psychosomatic illness in children. *Archives of General Psychiatry, 32*, 1031–38.

Mishra, M.N. (1979). Psychological characteristics of cases attending CGC. *Indian Journal of Psychiatry, 4*, 169–76.

Mishra, A., & Sharma, A.K. (2001). A clinico-social study of psychiatric morbidity in 12 to 18 years school going girls in urban Delhi. *Indian Journal of Community Medicine, 26*, 71–75.

Mistry, V., & Mohite, P. (1984). Learning disabilities in primary grades. Project Report. Baroda: Department of Child Development, M.S. University.

Mohan, D., Thomas, M.G., & Prabhu, G.G. (1978). Prevalence of drug abuse in high school population. *Indian Journal of Psychiatry, 20*, 20–24.

Mulligan, G., Douglas, J.W.B., Hammond, W.A., & Tizard, J. (1963). Delinquency and symptoms of maladjustment: The findings of a longitudinal study. *Proceedings of the Royal Society of Medicine, 56*, 1083–86.

Mukherjee. S., Uma, H., Kapur, M. and Subbakrishna, D.K. (1995). Anxiety, self-esteem with specific disorders of scholastic skills. *NIMHANS Journal, 13(2)*, 117–21.

Muralidharan, R. (1983). *Personal-Social development of Indian children: Developmental norms of Indian children.* New Delhi: National Council of Educational Research and Training.

Murthy, R.S., Ghose, A., & Varma, V.K. (1974). Behaviour disorders of childhood and adolescence. *Indian Journal of Psychiatry, 16*, 229–37.

Muste, M.J., & Sharp, D.F. (1947). Some influential factors in the determination of aggressive behaviour in preschool children. *Child Development, 18*, 11–28.

Myklebust, H. (1981). Pupil rating scale—revised. New York: Grune & Stratton.

Nandi, D.N., Ajmany, S., Ganguly, H., Banerjee, G., Boral, G.C., Ghosh, A., & Sarkar, S. (1975). Psychiatric disorder in a rural community in West Bengal: An epidemiological study. *Indian Journal of Psychiatry, 17*, 87–89.

Nandi, D.N., Banerjee, G., Mukherjee, S.P, Sarkar, S., Boral, G.C., Mukherjee, A., & Mishra, D.C. (1986). A study of psychiatric morbidity of a rural community at an interval of 10 years. *Indian Journal of Psychiatry, 28*, 179–194.

Nandi, D.N., Banerjee, G., Mukherjee, S.P, Ghosh, A., Nandi, P.S., & Nandi, S. (2000). Psychiatric morbidity of a rural Indian community: Changes over a 20 year interval. *British Journal of Psychiatry, 176*, 351–356.

National Advisory Committee on Handicapped Children. (1968). *First annual report of the US office of education.* Washington D.C.:U.S. Department of Health, Education and Welfare, 1968.

National Council of Educational Research and Training (1988). *Integrated education for the disabled children.* New Delhi: Author.

National Institute of Mental Health (1992). *Diagnostic interview schedule for children.* Rockville, MD: Author.

Naumberg, M. (1966). *Dynamically oriented art therapy: Its principles and practice.* New York: Grune & Stratton.

Newson, E. (1994). Video violence and protection of children. *The Psychologist, 7(6)*, 272–74.

Ninan, T.P., & Kapur, M. (1989). A study of hysteria in early adolescence. *NIMHANS Journal, 1*, 43–47.

Oberoi, H.V. (1993). Intervention with six to nine years old hyperkinetic boys in the school setting. M. Phil. Dissertation. Bangalore University, NIMHANS, Bangalore.

Oberoi, H.V., & Kapur, M. (1995). Intervention with hyperkinetic boys in the school setting. *NIMHANS Journal, 13*, 123-131.

Offord, D.R., Boyle, M.H., Szatmari, P., Rae Grant, N., Links, P.S., Cadman, D.T., Byles, J.A., Crawford, J.W., Blum, H.M., Byrne, C., Thomas, H., & Woodword, G.A. (1987). Ontario child health study. *Archives of General Psychiatry, 44*, 832–36.

Oommen, A. (1990). A study of the hyperkinetic syndrome of childhood. Doctoral Thesis. Bangalore University, NIMHANS, Bangalore.

Ornitz, E.M., & Ritvo, E.R. (1976). The syndrome of autism: A critical review. *American Journal of Psychiatry, 133*, 609–21.

Otto, W., & Smith, R.J. (1980). *Corrective and remedial teaching* (3rd Ed.). Boston, MA: Houghton Mifflin.

Ounsted, C. (1970). A biological approach to autistic and hyperkinetic syndromes. In J. Apley (Ed.), *Modern trends in paediatrics.* London: Butterworths.

Parthasarathy, R. (1994). Promotion of mental health through schools. Health for the millions. Special issue, *Mental Health I 20*, 12–13.

Parvathavardhini. (1983). Psychosocial problems amongst rural children: An epidemiological study. M.Phil. Dissertation, Bangalore University, NIMHANS, Bangalore.

Peterson, D.H. (1961). Behaviour problems of middle childhood. *Journal of Consulting Psychology, 25*, 205–09.

Phatak, P. (1970). Motor and mental development of Indian children from 1 month to 30 months. Longitudinal growth of Indian children – Final report. Baroda: Department of Child Development, M.S. University.

Phatak, P. (1989). Revision and extension of Phatak DAP Scale for Indian children of age groups 2½ to 16½ years. *Psychological Studies, 29(1)*.

Pollak, J.M. (1979). Obsessive compulsive personality: A review. *Psychological Bulletin, 86*, 225–41.

Porter, B., & O'Leary, K.D. (1980). Marital discord and childhood behaviour problems. *Journal of Abnormal Child Psychology, 8*, 287–96.

Porter, R.B., & Cattell, R.B. (1963). *The children's personality questionnaire.* Champaign, IL: Institute for Personality and Ability Testing.

Prabha Chandra, S. (1987). Neuro-developmental and behavioural aspects of children with specific speech and language delay. M.D. Dissertation. Bangalore University, NIMHANS, Bangalore.

Prabhu, G.G. (1987). Child and adolescent mental health research in India: An overview. *NIMHANS Journal, 5*, 79–89.

Prakash, S. (1987). Childhood depression in a rapidly developing society: Some developmental issues and therapeutic considerations. In S.M. Channabasavanna & A.S. Shah (Eds.), *Affective disorders.* Bangalore: NIMHANS Publications.

Prashantham, B.J., Russel, S., Swamidhas, P., & Sudhakar, R. (2007). The prevalance of post-traumatic stress disorder among children and adolescents affected by tsunami disaster in Tamil Nadu. *Journal of Emergency Nursing, 5*, 3–7.

Premarajan, K.C., Danabalan, M., Chandrashekar, R., & Srinivasa, D.K. (1993). Prevalence of Psychiatry Morbidity in an Urban Community of Pondicherry. *Indian Journal of Psychiatry, 35*, 99–102.

Pritchard, M., & Graham, P. (1966). An investigation of a group of patients who have attended the children and adult departments of the same psychiatric hospital. *British Journal of Psychiatry, 112*, 603–12.

Proctor, J.T. (1958). Hysteria in childhood. *American Journal of Orthopsychiatry, 28*, 394–407.

Quay, H.C. (1964). Dimensions of personality in delinquent boys, as inferred from the factor analysis of case history data. *Child Development, 35*, 479–84.

Rae, W.A. (1977). Childhood conversion reactions: A review of incidence in paediatric settings. *Journal of Clinical Child Psychology, 6*, 69–72.

Raman, U., & Kapur, M. (1999). A study of play therapy in emotionally disturbed children. *NIMHANS Journal, 17*, 93–98.

Raman, V., Kumariah, U., Srinath, S., Uma, H., & Subbakrishna D.K.(2001). Behavioural and play intervention in children with emotion disorder. In Kapur, M. (Ed.) *Psychological therapies with children and adolescents.* Bangalore, NIMHANS publication No. 45, 77–86.

Rangaswamy, K., & Kamakshi, G. (1983). Life events in hysterical adolescents. *Child Psychiatry Quarterly, 16(1)*, 26–33.

Rao, P.N. (1978). Psychiatric morbidity in adolescence: An epidemiological survey of prevalence in high school adolescents. M.D. Thesis, Bangalore University, Bangalore, India.

Rao, S.G., Srinath, S., & Sharma, S. (1986). A study of 110 cases of unsocialized conduct disorder. Paper presented at the Annual Indian Psychiatric Society Conference, Jaipur.

Raven, J.C. (1965). *The coloured progressive matrices.* London: H.K. Lewis & Co.

Reddy, J.Y.C. (1991). A study of phenomenology and classification of psychoses of childhood and adolescent onset. M.D. Thesis. Bangalore University, NIMHANS, Bangalore.

Reed, G. (1963). Elective mutism in children: A reappraisal. *Journal of Child Psychiatry, 4*, 99–107.

Reich, W., Shayka, J.J., & Taibleson, C.H. (1991). *Diagnostic interview for children and adolescents (DICA-R).* Unpublished manuscript, Division of Child Psychiatry, Washington University.

Richman, N., & Graham, J.J. (1971). A behavioural screening questionnaire for use with 8 year old children: Preliminary findings. *Journal of Child Psychology and Psychiatry, 12*, 5–33.

Ritvo, E.R., & Freeman, B.J. (1977) National society for autistic children. Definition of the syndrome of autism. *Journal of Paediatric Psychology, 2(4)*, 146–48.

Roberts, G.H. (1968). The future strategies of third grade arithmetic pupils. *The Arithmetic Teacher, 15*, 442–446.

Robins, E, & O'Neal, P. (1953) Clinical features of hysteria in children. *The Nervous Child, 10*, 246–71.

Robins, L.N. (1966). *Deviant children grow up*. Baltimore, MD: Williams & Wilkins.

Robins, L.N. (1974). Antisocial behaviour disturbance in childhood: Prevalence prognosis and prospects. In E.J. Anthony & C. Koupernik (Eds.), *The child in his family: Children at psychiatric risk*. New York: Wiley.

Robins, L.N. (1978). Sturdy childhood predictors of adult antisocial behaviour: Replications from longitudinal studies. *Psychological Medicine, 8*, 611–22.

Robins, L.N., & Lewis, R.G. (1966). The role of the antisocial family in school completion and delinquency: A three generation study. *Social Quarterly, 7*, 500–14.

Rock, N.L. (1971). Conversion reactions in childhood: A clinical study on childhood neuroses. *Journal of the American Academy of Child Psychiatry, 10*, 65–93.

Rosner, J. (1985). *Helping children overcome learning difficulties*. New York: Walker & Company.

Ross, A.O. (1980). *Psychological disorders of children*. New York: McGraw-Hill.

Rozario, J. (1988). An epidemiological survey of prevalence and pattern of psychological disturbance of school-going early adolescents. M. Phil. Dissertation. Bangalore University, NIMHANS, Bangalore.

Rozario, J. (1991). Intervention strategies for scholastic backwardness. Doctoral Thesis. Bangalore University, NIMHANS, Bangalore.

Rozario, J., Kapur, M., & Kaliaperumal, D. (1990). An epidemiological survey of prevalence and pattern of psychological disturbance of school-going early adolescents. *Journal of Personality and Clinical Studies, 6*, 165–169.

Ruckmini, S. (1994). Psychological disturbance in 5 to 12 year old school children in a rural area. M. Phil. Dissertation, Bangalore University, Bangalore, India.

Rutter, M. (1967). A children's behaviour questionnaire for completion by teachers: Preliminary findings. *Journal of Child Psychology and Psychiatry, 8*, 1–26.

Rutter, M. (1978) Diagnosis and definition. In M. Rutter & E. Schopler (Eds.) *Autism: A reappraisal of concepts and treatment.* New York: Plenum.

Rutter, M. (1987). Psychosocial resilience and protective mechanisms. *American Journal of Orthopsychiatry, 57*, 316–31.

Rutter, M., & Garmezy, N. (1983). Developmental psychopathology. In P.H. Mussen (Ed.), *Handbook of child psychology: Social development* (Vol. 4). New York: John Wiley & Sons.

Rutter, M., & Giller, H. (1983). *Juvenile delinquency: Trends and perspectives*. Harmondsworth: Penguin.

Rutter, M. & Gould, M. (1985). Classification. In M. Rutter & L. Hers (Eds.), *Child and adolescent psychiatry: Modern approaches* (2nd Ed.). London: Blackwell Scientific Publications.

Rutter, M., & Lockyer, L. (1967) A five to fifteen year follow up study of infantile psychosis. Description of sample. *British Journal of Psychiatry, 113*, 1169–82.

Rutter, M., Cox, A., Tupling, C., Berger, M., & Yule, W. (1975). Attainment and adjustment in two geographical areas in the prevalence of psychiatric disorders. *British Journal of Psychiatry, 126*, 29–37.

Rutter, M., Maugham, B., Mortimer, P., & Ouston, S. (1979). *Fifteen thousand hours: Secondary schools and their effects on children.* London: Open Books.

Rutter, M., Shaffer, D., & Shepherd, M. (1975). *A multiaxial classification of child psychiatric disorders*. Geneva: World Health Organization.

Rutter, M., Tizard, J., & Whitmore, K. (Eds.). (1970). *Education, health and behaviour*. London: Longman.

Sachdeva, J.S., Singh, S., Sidhu, B.S., Goyal, R.K.D., & Singh, J. (1986). An epidemiological study of psychiatric disorders in rural Faridkot (Punjab). *Indian Journal of Psychiatry, 28*, 317–323.

Sachdeva, K. (1974). Aetiology of poor scholastic performance. *Growing Minds, 3*, 15–20.

Sadashivan, A. (2009). Comparing the efficacy of phonological awareness intervention with neuropsychological intervention in children with specific reading disorder. Doctoral thesis, University of New Zealand.

Sanua, V.D. (1986) The organic aetiology of infantile autism, a critical review of the literature. *International Journal of Neurosciences, 30*, 195–225.

Sarkar, A. (1990). Prevalence and pattern of psychological disturbance in eight to eleven year old shool-going children. M. Phil Dissertation. Bangalore University, NIMHANS, Bangalore.

Sarkar, A.B., Kapur, M., & Kaliaperumal, V.G. (1995). The Prevalence and Pattern of Psychological Disturbance in School Going Middle Childhood Children. *NIMHANS Journal, 13*, 33–41.

Sarkhel, S., Sinha, V.K., Arora, M., & DeSarkar, P. (2006). Prevalence of conduct disorder in school children of Kanke. *Indian Journal of Psychiatry, 48(3)*, 159–64.

Sattler, J.M. (1982). *Assessment of children's intelligence and special abilities* (2nd Ed.). Boston, MA: Allyn & Bacon.

Schaefer, C.E., & Connor, C.J. (1983). *Handbook of play therapy*. New York: John Wiley & Sons.

Sekar, K., Eswari, S.C., Indiramma, V., Shariff, I.A., & Murthy, N.S.N. (1983). The use of Rutter's scale by teachers in screening maladjusted children. *NIMHANS Journal, 1*, 105–110.

Sekar, K., Shariff, I.A., Eswari, S.C., & Muralidhran, D. (1983). Correlates of maladjusted behaviour of children in different schools. *Indian Journal of Psychological Medicine, 6*, 27–32.

Seltzer, W.J. (1985). Conversion disorder in childhood and adolescence: A familiar cultural approach, Part I. *Family System Medicine, 3(3)*, 261–80.

Sen, B., Nandi, D.N., Mukherjee, S.P, Mishra, D.C., Banerjee, G., & Sarkar, S. (1984). Psychiatric morbidity in an urban slum dwelling community. *Indian Journal of Psychiatry, 26*, 185–193.

Servan-Schreiber, D., Le Lin, B., & Birmaher, B. (1998). Prevalence of post-traumatic stress disorder and major depressive disorder in Tibetan refugee children. *Journal of the American Academy of Child and Adolescent Psychiatry, 37*, 874–879.

Seshadri, S., Saksena, S., & Saldanha, S. (2008). *On track: Classes 3–9*. Chennai: Macmillan.

Sethi, B.B., Gupta, S.C., & Kumar, R. (1967). 300 urban families: A psychiatric survey. *Indian Journal of Psychiatry, 9*, 280–302.

Sethi, B.B., Gupta, S.C., Kumar, R., & Kumar, P. (1972). A psychiatric survey of 500 rural families. *Indian Journal of Psychiatry, 14*, 183–196.

Singh, A.J., Shukla, J.D., Verma, B.L., Kumar, A., & Srivastava, R.N. (1983). An epidemiological study in childhood psychiatric disorders. *Indian Pediatrics, 20*, 167–172.

Singh, S., & Kamal Preet (1981). Drug abuse among school and college students in Punjab. *Child Psychiatry Quarterly, 14*, 5–11.

Sinha, U. K., & Kapur, M. (1999). Psychotherapy with emotionally disturbed adolescent boys: Outcome and process study. *NIMHANS Journal, 17*, 113–130.

Shah, A.V., Goswami, U.A., Manar, R.C., Hajariwala, D.C., & Sinha, B.K. (1980). Prevalence of psychiatric disorders in Ahmedabad: An epidemiological study. *Indian Journal of Psychiatry, 22*, 384–389.

Shapiro, C.T., & Jegede, R.O. (1973). School phobia: A Babel of tongues. *Journal of Autism and Schizophrenia, 3*, 168–86.

Sharma, S.N., Bhat, V.K., & Sengupta, J. (1980). Neurotic disorders in children—A psychosocial study. *Indian Journal of Psychiatry, 22(4)*, 362–65.

Shashi, K., Kapur, M., & Subbakrishna, D. (1999). Evaluation of play therapy in emotionally disturbed children. *NIMHANS Journal, 17*, 99–111.

Shenoy, J. (1992). A study of psychological disturbance in 5 to 8 year old school going children. Doctoral Thesis. Bangalore University, NIMHANS, Bangalore.

Shenoy, J., Kapur, M., & Kaliaperumal, V.G. (1996). Prevalence and pattern of psychological disturbance among five to eight year old school going children: Preliminary findings. *NIMHANS Journal, 14*, 37–43.

Shepherd, M., Oppenheim, B. & Mitchell, S. (1971). *Childhood behaviour and mental health.* London: University of London Press.

Shetty, G. (1975). Childhood hysteria—A study of phenomenology, personality and family interaction. M.D. Thesis. Bangalore University, NIMHANS, Bangalore.

Sidana, A., & Nijhawan, M. (1999, January). Prevalence of psychiatric morbidity in school going adolescent children and factors related to it. Paper Presented at the 51st Annual National Conference of the Indian Psychiatric Society, Bhubaneshwar, India.

Simmons, R. (1978). Psychophysiological disorders in childhood and adolescence. In D.D. Stienhauer & Q. Rae-Grant, Q. & Steinhauer, P.D. (Eds.), *Psychological problems of the child and his family.* London : Macmillan.

Simonds, J.D. (1977). Enuresis: A brief survey of current thinking with respect to pathogenesis and management. *Clinical Paediatrics, 16*, 79–82.

Singh, S.B., Nigam, A., & Srivastava, J.R. (1979). Personality characteristics of mothers and their problem children with overt and covert manifestation of the symptoms. *Indian Journal of Clinical Psychology, 6(2)*, 111–14.

Somasundaram, O., Veeraraghavan, G. & Krishnan, G. (1974). Hysteria in children and adolescents. *Indian Journal of Psychiatry, 16*, 274–82.

Spitz, R.A. (1946). Anaclitic depression: Psychoanalytic study of the child. Vol.2. New York: International Universities Press.

Spreen, O. (1989). The relationship between learning disability, emotion disorders and neuropsychology: Some results and observations. *Journal of Experimental and Clinical Neuropsychology, 11*, 117–140.

Srinath, S., & Bavle, A. (1987). Manic depressive psychosis in children. In S.M. Channabasavanna & S.A. Shah (Eds.) *Affective disorders.* Bangalore: NIMHANS Publications.

Srinath, S., Bhide, A., & Kaliaperumal, V.G. (1986). Child psychiatric disorders and abnormal psychosocial situations. Paper presented at the World Psychiatric Association Regional Symposium, Jaipur.

Srinath. S., Girimaji, S.G., Gururaj, P., Seshadri, S., Subbakrishna, D.K., Bhola, P., & Kumar, N. (2005). Epidemiological study of child and adolescent psychiatric disorders in urban and rural areas of Bangalore. *Indian Journal of Medical Research, 122*, 67–79.

Srinath, S., Bharat, S., Girimaji, S., & Seshadri, S. (1991). *Childhood hysteria: A report from India.* Report. Bangalore: NIMHANS.

Srinath, S., Vinutha, M.S. & Indiramma, V. (1992). *Breath holding spells—A study of 20 children.* Report. Bangalore: NIMHANS.

Sroufe, A.L., & Rutter, M. (1984). The domain of developmental psychopathology. *Child Development, 55*, 17–29.

Sultana, M., Siddiqui, A.O., & Siddiqui, M.A. (1982). A psychodemographic study of hysteria. *Indian Journal of Clinical Psychology, 9*, 69–74.

Sundberg, N.G., & Tyler, L.E. (1962). *Clinical psychology.* New York: Appleton.

Surya, N.C., Datta, S.P., Gopalakrishnan, R., Sundaram, D., & Kutty, J. (1966). Mental morbidity in Pondicherry (1962–63). *Transactions of All India Institute of Mental Health, 4*, 50–61.

Symonds, J.F. (1973). Conversion—Hypochondriacal dissociative symptoms in children. *Journal of Operational Psychiatry, 5*, 38–41.

Talge, N.M., Neal, C., Glover, V. & the Early Stress, Translational Research and Prevention Science Network: Fetal and Neonatal Experience on Child and Adolescent Mental Health (2007).Antenatal maternal stress and long-term effects on child neuro-development: How and why? *The Journal of Child Psychology and Psychiatry, 48*, 245–261.

Taylor, D.C. (1986). Hysteria—Play acting and coverage. *British Journal of Psychiatry, 149*, 37–47.

Taylor, E., Everitt, B., Thorley, G., Schachar, R., Rutter, M., & Weiselberg, M. (1986). Conduct disorder and hyperactivity: A cluster analysis approach to the identification of a behavioural syndrome. *British Journal of Psychiatry, 149*, 768–77.

Taylor, G.H. (1988). Psychological testing: Relevance for assessing children's learning disabilities. *Journal of Consulting and Clinical Psychology, 56(6)*, 795–800.

Teja, J.S., Khanna, B.S., & Subramanyam, T.S. (1970). Possession states in Indian patients. *Indian Journal of Psychiatry, 12*, 71–87.

Terman, L.M., & Merril, M.A. (1937). *Direction for administering forms L and M: Revision of the Stanford Binet tests of intelligence.* Boston, MA: Houghton Mifflin.

Thacore, V.R., Gupta, S.C., & Suraya, M. (1975). Psychiatric morbidity in a North Indian community. *British Journal of Psychiatry, 126*, 364–369.

Thomas, A., & Chess, S. (1977). *Temperament and development.* New York: Brunner/Mazel.

Treiber, F.A., & Lahey, B.B. (1983). Toward a behavioural model of academic remediation with learning disabled children. *Journal of Learning Disabilities, 16*, 111–16.

Tsiantis, J., Macri, I., & Maratos, O. (1986), Schizophrenia in children: A review of European research. *Schizophrenia Bulletin, 121*, 101–119.

Uma, H. (1988). Study of hysteria in children. Doctoral Thesis. Bangalore University, NIMHANS, Bangalore.

Uma, H., & Kapur, M. (1987). A retrospective study of hysteria in a child guidance clinic. *Indian Journal of Psychiatry, 29(3)*, 283–86.

Uma, H., & Kapur, M. (1990). *Project report on early childhood stimulation and optimal mental development.* Bangalore: NIMHANS.

Uma, H., Oommen, A., & Kapur, M. (2002). *Psychological assessment of children in the clinical setting.* Bangalore: NIMHANS.

Varma, I.P., Srivastava, D.K., & Sahay, R.N. (1970). *Possession syndrome. Indian Journal of Psychiatry, 12*, 58–70.

Venables, P.H., Fletcher, R.P., Dalais, J.C., Mitchell, D.A., Schulsinger, F. & Mednick, S.A. (1983). Factor structure of the Rutter children's behaviour questionnaire in a primary school population in a developing country. *Journal of Child Psychology and Psychiatry, 24*, 213–22.

Venter, A., Lord, C., Schopler, E. (1992). A follow up study of high functioning autistic children. *Journal of Child Psychology and Psychiatry, 33(3)*, 489–508.

Venugopal, M., & Raju, P. (1988). A study on the learning disabilities among IV and V standard students. *Indian Journal of Psychological Medicine, 11*, 119–123.

Verghese, A., & Beig, A. (1974). Psychiatric disturbances in children: An epidemiological study. *Indian Journal of Medical Research, 62*, 1538–1542.

Verhulst, F., & Akkerhuis, G.W. (1986). Mental health in Dutch children: III. Behavioural-emotional problems reported by teachers of children aged 4 to 12. *Acta Psychiatrica Scandinavica, 74, Supplementum No.330*, 1–74.

Vythilingam, M. (1991). Pervasive developmental disorder: An exploratory study. M.D. Thesis. Bangalore University, NIMHANS, Bangalore.

Wang, Y.G., Shen, Y.C., Gu, B.M., Jia, M.X., & Zhan, A.L. (1989). An epidemiological study of behaviour problems in school children in urban areas of Beijing. *Journal of Child Psychology and Psychiatry, 30*, 907–12.

Warren, W. (1965). A study of adolescent psychiatric in-patients and the outcome six or more years later: The follow up study. *Journal of Child Psychology and Psychiatry, 6*, 141–60.

Watson, J.B., & Rayner, R. (1920). Conditioned emotional reactions. *Journal of Experimental Psychology, 3*, 1, 1–14.

Wechsler, D. (1949). *Wechsler intelligence scale for children (Manual)*. New York: Psychological Corporation.

Weissman, M.M., Gershon, E.S, Kidd, K.K., Prusoff, B.A., Leckman, J.F., Dibble, E., Mamovit., J., Thompson, W.D., Pauls, D.L., & Guroff, J.J. Psychiatric disorders in the relatives of probands with affective disorders: The Yale–NIMH collaborative family study. *Archives of General Psychiatry, 1984, 41*, 13–21.

Werner, E.E. (1989). High risk children in adulthood: A longitudinal study from birth to 32 years. *American Journal of Orthopsychiatry, 59(1)*, 72–81.

Werner, E.E., & Smith, R.S. (1992). *Overcoming odds: High risk children from birth to adulthood.* Ithaca, NY: Cornell University Press.

Werry, J.S. & Quay, C. (1971). The prevalence of behaviour symptoms in younger elementary school children. *American Journal of Orthopsychiatry, 41*, 136–43.

Whitehead, L. (1979). Sex differences in children's response to family stress: A revaluation. *Journal of Child Psychology and Psychiatry, 20*, 247–54.

Wiederholt, J.L., Hammill, D.D., & Brown, V.L. (1983). *The resource teacher: A guide to effective practices* (2nd Ed.). Austin, TX: Pro-Ed.

Wig, N.N., & Nagpal, R.N. (1972). Why students fail: A psychological study of low achievers. *Indian Journal of Psychiatry, 14*, 381–88.

Wolff, S. (1985). Non-delinquent disturbances of conduct. In M. Rutter & L. Hersov (Eds.), *Child and adolescent psychiatry: Modern approaches.* London: Blackwell Scientific Foundations.

Wong, B.Y.L. (1986). Problems and issues in the definition of learning diabilities. In J.K. Torgeson & B.Y.L. Wong (Eds.), *Psychological and educational perspectives on learning disabilities.* Orlando, FL: Academic Press.

Yates, A., & Steward, M. (1976). Conversion hysteria in childhood: A case report and a reminder. *Clinical Paediatrics, 15*, 379–82.

Young, P., & Tyre, C. (1983). *Dyslexia or illiteracy? Realizing the right to read.* Milton Keyes: Open University Press.

Index

* Page numbers followed by *f* indicate figures.